Dissertation and Scholarly Research
Recipes for Success

Second Edition

A PRACTICAL GUIDE TO START AND COMPLETE YOUR DISSERTATION, THESIS, OR FORMAL RESEARCH PROJECT

Marilyn K. Simon, Ph.D.

Dissertation Success, LLC
www.dissertationrecipes.com

Dissertation and Scholarly Research: Recipes for Success, Second Edition

Copyright © 2010 by Marilyn K. Simon, Ph.D.

ISBN 1-4515-1730-0

EAN-13 9781451517309

Printed in the United States of America

Foreword

A Dissertation Guide for Professional Learners
By Jim Goes, Ph.D.

Doctoral education and learning has changed dramatically over the last two decades. Traditionally, the pursuit of a doctoral credential involved study at a large, traditional research university, and was reserved for those seeking careers in academia or research. The process of completing a doctorate usually required a commitment to full time study, varied tremendously between institutions, and was often somewhat mysterious. As a result of time and place demands, few professionals pursued doctoral degrees.

Today all of this has changed. The emergence and growth of online education and the competitive moves of large online universities from undergraduate and master's level programs into the doctoral ranks has led to a proliferation of doctoral learning possibilities for busy professionals. Along with greater access to doctoral training for nontraditional learners has come growing value in the doctoral credential within professional ranks. More and more professionally accomplished individuals in industry, the nonprofit sector, education, and other professional arenas pursue doctoral study as a means to advance their careers, their marketability, and their professional stature.

If this sounds like you, then *Recipes for Success* is the right book to launch you on a successful quest for the doctoral degree. The research-based dissertation is the hallmark of most doctoral programs, and sets doctoral-level study apart from other levels of learning. Yet few busy professionals have much of a sense of how to begin the process of dissertation development, how to do original research of credible academic quality, and how to craft research results into a dissertation. This book fills that gap. From the very beginning of your doctoral journey to the penultimate achievement of degree completion, this book is your guide to the process and content of dissertation and research creation.

Choosing a research topic and developing a conceptual and methodological framework around this topic challenges most learners. Unlike other levels of study, dissertation writing is a profound act of original scholarship, involving deep original thought, critical thinking, and creation of new knowledge. As a result, there is no shortage of books about how to write a dissertation. But most of them are not written for most of us. In *Recipes for Success*, Marilyn Simon has crafted a process by which anyone can build the pieces of a successful dissertation. Using a workbook approach rich in tools, frameworks, and examples, *Recipes* provides an easy to navigate process for crafting issues and ideas into research and results.

Dissertations are very personal, and originate with problems and issues that are meaningful and important to the individual. Most professionals are very grounded in their understanding of the issues and needs of their profession. *Recipes* begins with this understanding, helping learners to discover and frame issues they are passionate about, and to build a study around this passion. While most dissertation guides focus exclusively on the mechanics of writing and organization, this book approaches dissertation development as a process of thinking and self reflection that leads learners to discover what matters most to them and to their professions, to frame this meaning into a research problem and purpose, and to organize and execute a study design to fit this problem and purpose. Once this basis of meaning for the dissertation is established, the entire process and organization of dissertation writing becomes more natural and understandable, and has a much higher likelihood of success and importance.

As you embark on your research and dissertation journey, you may encounter barriers, roadblocks, and the occasional dead end. *Recipes* is your guide and companion to navigate around these bumps on the road to completion. Based on 30 years of experience in the online setting mentoring over 200 professional learners to success in completing their doctorates, including numerous award winners, Simon identifies the most important factors for success and the traps to avoid.

Whether you are just considering doctoral study, already in a doctoral program, or working to develop and complete your dissertation, you will find *Recipes for Success* a key ingredient in your success as a doctoral learner. Good luck on your doctoral journey!

Introduction

Congratulations! By procuring your copy of *Recipes for Success*, and by reading the information that you are now reading, you have taken an important first step toward securing the successful realization of your goal—you have shown an interest. Your next step is to turn your interest into result-getting actions. Putting together an excellent dissertation is like planning and preparing a *gourmet feast* for a gathering of distinguished guests who are connoisseurs of *fine cooking*. You, the researcher, can think of yourself as the *chef* and *chief meal engineer* for this eloquent *repast*. Careful preparation is needed each step of the way, along with a formal means to reach your desired goal.

Recipes for Success is presented in three phases. In **PHASE 1** you will start your initial preparation, gather *ingredients,* and prepare the *menu* for your feast. This includes your mental, physical, and psychological preparation along with the selection of the type of *meal* (topic and research method) you will serve. In **PHASE 2** you will gather your *accoutrements* and *utensils* to collect and analyze data to help you solve the problem you pose, answer your research questions, and obtain your purpose. In **PHASE 3** you will learn how to put your *meal* (dissertation) together to ensure a *delicious* high-quality study to *serve* at your *feast*. Included are several presentations and hyperlinks to serve as your *maître d'* for your *banquet.*

TABLE OF CONTENTS

PHASE 1

PLANNING YOUR FEAST—GETTING STARTED

PROCEED
[7 Easy Steps to a Great Start]
PICK YOUR REPAST
[Choose Your Topic]
CLASSIFY YOUR REPAST—"WHAT'S COOKING?"
[Identify Your Study]
BE AWARE OF HEALTH HAZARDS
[Ethics of Research]
CHOOSE YOUR ATTIRE
[Form and Style]

The following *ingredients* are part of your *Recipes for Success* secrets to an excellent beginning to an excellent *feast* (dissertation). An acronym, decree, and seven-step *recipe* that will ensure your initial and ultimate success is

P R O C E E D!

Research is to see what everybody has seen and to think what nobody else had thought. —Albert Szent-Gyorgyi

1 cup	P ossess a Positive Attitude
1 cup	R ead Efficiently
1 cup	O rganize Your Time
1 cup	C reate a Space to Work
1 cup	E xtend Your Note-Taking and Writing Skills
1 cup	E nter Information onto a Computer and Journal
1 cup	D esign a Survival Kit

1 cup "P"ossess a Positive Attitude

For a positive attitude, mix with a dash of each: visualization, physical exercise, determination, and sound nutrition.

Remember: Your attitudes shape your future!

It is important that you work on a research project that you, as well as your advisors, mentors, and committee members, are enthusiastic about. Arnold Schwarzenegger, five-time Mr. Universe, four-time Mr. Olympic, and governor of California, told reporters, "As long as your mind can envision that you can do something, then you can do it." Winston Churchill said, "Attitude is a little thing that makes a big difference."

The following activities will enable you to use visualization techniques to assist you in creating and maintaining a positive attitude through the successful completion of your dissertation or research project.

1. Visualize yourself successfully producing an excellent dissertation.
2. Imagine enjoying each aspect of creating your dissertation.
3. Conjure up an image of yourself working in a pleasant environment accomplishing the goals that you will recognize and see to fruition.
4. Picture yourself obtaining the degree and the recognition you are seeking.
5. Acknowledge and celebrate all the milestones along the way.
6. Think of your setbacks as a lesson on what NOT to do. ☺
7. Repeat these steps each time you begin work on your dissertation.

Fill out the information on the Cutting Board to assist you further in visualizing your preparation of an outstanding *feast*.

 Cutting Board

1. Take a few minutes to reflect on the benefits you will receive upon the successful completion of your goal. What are some of those benefits?

2. Visit ProQuest http://www.proquest.com/en-US/products/dissertations/ and find a current dissertation in your field and a current dissertation from your university. If you cannot gain entry into this URL, check with your university. Take time to *digest* this

information. Check the style and form, the table of contents, and the number of pages in each chapter. Imagine what your dissertation will look like. Can you see it bound with your name and degree on the cover? ____ Will you have it hardbound, soft bound, or both? ____ How many copies do you think you will make of your final dissertation text? _____ Who will appear in your acknowledgment section?

3. Most dissertations are between 100 and 200 pages. Approximately how many pages do you envision your dissertation to be?

4. Do you envision having graphs and charts? __ How many references do you think you will have consulted? __

5. What will change once you get your degree?

6. Who will you tell about your successes?

7. What do you see as their reaction?

8. What type of support system do you have or need to obtain?

9. The next time you call directory assistance, introduce yourself as Dr. (surname), and see how that title feels to you.

Your body and mind are closely related. Your mental efficiency is affected by the state of your body. Check to see that your diet is healthful. Many studies suggest that protein helps keep the brain alert and that the brain's performance is also affected by choline (a B-complex vitamin that is found in egg yolks, beef liver, fish, raisins, walnuts, and legumes). Other B vitamins, such as niacin and folic acid, as well as Vitamin C and iron are also essential in maintaining a healthy brain. To keep your memory sharp, eat lots of folic acid, found in leafy green vegetables, lean meat, fish, legumes, dairy products, grains, citrus fruits, and dried beans and nuts.

Stay away from alcohol during your research days. See to it that your exercise is efficient and enjoyable. At the very minimum, you should be doing 20 minutes of cardiovascular exercise three times a week. Thirty minutes a day of a fitness program that combines flexibility, endurance, and strength is better. The mental effects of regular exercise are profound and extensive, affecting your intellect, memory, and emotions.

We cannot always avoid stress; in fact, sometimes we don't want to. Often it is controlled stress, or eustress, that gives us our competitive edge in performance-related activities such as athletics, giving a speech, acting, or doing outstanding research. It is eustress that provides us with focus and gives us our competitive edge. It helps us think quickly and clearly and enables us to express our thoughts as we write our research paper.

Some stressors can cause both good and bad stress. Radiation, left uncontrolled, may cause cancer, and yet, if the radiation is controlled and pinpointed, it can cure some cancers. Exercise is most often a good stressor. But overtraining can cause injury and illness. To continue to exercise when your body is fatigued or weak can result in a variety of overuse injuries and predispose you to illness. In all cases, common sense should prevail to differentiate between distress and eustress.

 Cutting Board

1. What in your diet needs to be improved to see that you have the best possible nutrition?

   _____

2. What type of exercise do you enjoy doing that could help you become more fit?

   _____

3. What other measures can you take to support yourself in the successful obtainment of your goal?

   _____

4. Sleep is important for the renewed health of the brain. When you drift off into dreamland—a procedure that happens in stages—your brain goes through a series of psychological processes that restores both mind and body. At certain stages, memories are consolidated and at other stages your brain is working out resolutions to unconscious conflicts. Certain factors such as the use of alcohol or drugs, a noisy bedroom, an uncomfortable bed, "dis"stress carried over from the day, or other disruptions may upset this pattern. What can you do to improve your sleep?

   _____

   Too much sleep can be as detrimental as can too little sleep. Most adults need 7–10 hours of sleep. It is important to know what is ideal for you. How much sleep do you really need to feel great? _____ See that you get that amount during your research working days and try to eliminate any conditions that disrupt your sleep.

5. What are the good and bad stresses in your life?

6. What can you do to decrease the bad stresses?

7. What can you do to celebrate your successes?

---

1 cup "R"ead Efficiently—Understand Scholarly Language

The book exists for us perchance which will explain our miracles and reveal new ones —
Walden, Henry David Thoreau

All research projects, and thus dissertations, require a voluminous amount of reading from texts, journals, periodicals, newspapers, Web pages, archived documents, and so on. Successful researchers have employed the following tasks to help make their readings more productive. Put an asterisk (*) next to the activities that you already cultivate and an exclamation point (!) next to the ones that you could employ to make your reading more constructive.

__1. Take time to reflect on what it is you are hoping to find before you begin to read.

__2. Survey the table of contents and note major headings.

__3. If there are chapter summaries in a text, or an abstract for a paper, read them before exploring the chapter or paper.

__4. As you read, try to relate the information to something you are already familiar with.

__5. Take notes or highlight important ideas. If you can do this at the keyboard, you can save yourself quite a bit of time.

__6. Check for patterns that the author might be applying such as:

Cause and effect: The author explains a situation or theory and then delves into the consequences of its application.

Compare/contrast: The author examines two or more different theories or situations and their relationship to each other.

Process-description: A certain concept, program, or project is delineated and then examples are provided.

Sequential: A case is built in a linear or historical manner.

__7. Be an active reader. Always ask yourself questions about what you are reading: What is the author's purpose? Why am I reading this? What conclusions does the author come to? Is this reasonable? Who else supports this view? How does this document relate to my study?

__8. Imagine that the author is personally speaking with you (just like your *Recipes for Success* does).

> Note: When you check out http://www.umi.com/umi/dissertations/ to find dissertations in your field, you will notice there is a great deal of variety with regard to quality and style between dissertations. However, checking out recent dissertations from your university in areas that you wish to investigate can be extremely helpful. Your university will likely grant you free access to this URL or have a place where you can visit recent dissertations approved by the university.

Academic/Scholarly/Doctoral Writing

The ink of the scholar is more sacred than the blood of the martyr. —Mohammed

In academic writing, a specialized form of discourse often develops. At times this rarefied language is necessary to capture the complexity and distinctiveness of processes not easily described in colloquial terms. At other times, however, writers use terms that are understood only by an *in* group of ideologically sympathetic theorists. The purpose of scholarly writing is to demonstrate comprehensive knowledge of a subject; to assert the validity of all claims made; and to convey the value of the author's ideas through evidence, authoritative style, and scholarly voice to consumers of the research. Academic writing needs to be specific and objective. It is very important to present a variety of opinions on controversial issues to achieve the highest level of scholarship. It is also important to check for possible biases and use primary sources whenever possible.

Choosing only the evidence that supports an argument detracts from the writer's credibility. If there is evidence that appears to refute the researcher's claim, that evidence must be addressed and effectively challenged. The writing needs to be clear, precise, and devoid of redundancy and hyperbole. Use no more words than are necessary to convey your meaning. Your meal should be prepared *al dente* (only to the point of doneness). ☺

Both over- and understatement should be avoided. Statements should be specific and topical sentences established for all paragraphs. The flow of words should be smooth and comprehensible, and bridges should be established between ideas. According to Gilovich (1991), to truly appreciate the complexities of the world and the intricacies of human experience, it is essential that we understand how we can be misled by the apparent evidence of our experiences. If an author agrees with our thinking, we are less apt to question his or her research and the evidence provided. Thus, we need to think clearly about our experiences, question our assumptions, and challenge what we think we know, even when the data *agree* with what we believe is true.

> Note: APA formatting requires *data* to be treated as the plural of *datum* (APA 5th ed., Section 3.10, p. 89, and APA 6th ed., 3.19, p. 79). If you have any doubt on how to use the term data in a sentence, substitute the word toys—just like toys ARE us, data ARE us. ☺

Words are weapons that have great power invested in them. They create, as well as mirror, reality. They serve to advance certain ideals, images, stereotypes, paradigms, and sets of assumptions. They play an important role in creating the conditions for scholarly discourse. They frame what is considered to be the limits of acceptable practices, philosophies, and purposes. To be effective, they need to be governed by logic at the most abstract level of critical analysis.

For example, the following statement found at http://www.connected.org/learn/bangemann.html does not adhere to good scholarship. The author claims:

> *New information and communication technologies are key contributors to the evolution of teaching and learning methods, and must therefore be fully integrated in the education system.*

Critique: It does not necessarily follow that because technologies could change teaching and learning methods that they therefore *must* be used. This apparently logical statement is misleading in its attempt to convince the reader that the use of technology in teaching and learning is inevitable and beneficial. To evaluate the efficacy of this argument, it is prudent to ask some basic and underlying questions. What exactly needs changing, if anything? Why should it be changed? How can communication technologies help achieve these desired changes, if at all? Also, what is meant by the term "fully integrated."

When you write in an academic manner, you are identified as a member of the *club* of scholars. Those who *consume* what you write can substantiate it. Academic writing enables academicians to express ideas more forcefully and intelligently and helps eliminate ambiguity. A negative effect is that academic writing can also be used (intentionally or unintentionally) to intimidate those not in the club. Scholarly literacy is a moving target, and it is crucial that you keep up with the professional literature to be aware of the terminology and guidelines in current use. A problem delineated in 1995 could have been solved by the date you begin your research. When you frame the problem for your dissertation, be certain to *baste* your study with the most current research.

To cope with the demands of a discipline, you must be able to grasp the implications of important concepts that permeate the literature. For example, in reading scholarly work you frequently come across terms such as paradigm, theory, validity, and bias. It is important to understand the meaning of these terms in the context in which they are found. Many of these important terms are in various sections of your *Recipes for Success.*

Scholars are expected to analyze and synthesize rather than merely summarize information. A scholar studying the causes of the Civil Rights movement of the 1960s does more than summarize the movement; rather, the scholar would examine closely the reasons—practical, moral, psychological, social, economic, and dramatic—that led to the Civil Rights movement. Analysis and synthesis reveal the essence of the subject and lead to a greater understanding of truth.

Doctoral writing is the highest level of academic writing. The purpose of doctoral writing is to demonstrate comprehensive knowledge of a subject; to assert the validity of all claims made; and to convey the value of the author's ideas through evidence, authoritative style, and scholarly voice. Doctoral writing needs to be both objective and credible. All statements and claims must be supported with sufficient evidence to ensure their veracity. Additionally, scholars must address statements that seemingly counter or refute their claims to present a well-rounded overview of the topic. Primary sources and recent peer-reviewed and refereed journals make up the overwhelming majority of references. Germinal (classical) works in the field of study also need to be included in doctoral writing to present a historical overview of the topic and its prior research.

Note: The rationale for peer review is that it is rare for an individual author or research team to spot every mistake or flaw in a complicated piece of work. An opportunity for improvement may be apparent only to someone with special expertise or experience. Therefore, showing work to others in your field increases the probability that weaknesses will be identified and advice for improvement will be obtained.

In academic/scholarly/doctoral writing, it is important to *show* the truth rather than *tell* the truth. That is, merely stating something as fact affords a reader the ability to refute the claim as being only a representation of the author's opinion. Important points must be developed, rather than merely asserted. In the following example, it is difficult to ascertain the validity of the claim, as it is stated without any form of support. The revision provides effective evidence and is written in a much more authoritative tone. The revised statement demonstrates greater validity, as the truth is being shown and not just told to the reader.

Example: Students in private schools outperform those in public schools.

Revision: A comparison of scores among high school students enrolled in a cross-section of 25 middle schools in Chicago's public and private schools indicated that private school students performed 17% better on standardized tests in reading and 23% better in mathematics than their peers in public schools (Author, 2009).

It is important that work is edited to remove unnecessary words. Lanham (1987) called the use of excess verbiage the *lard* factor. Lantham gave a formula to see how much *lard*, or unnecessary verbiage, is in a paragraph.

To compute the *lard* factor:

(Word Count of Original – Word Count of Revision)/ Word Count of Original

Example: In the event of the case occurring where a social services worker is unable to find the location of the domicile of the applicant who has been involved in the initiation of the request for exemption request (RER) form, he/she shall make a note of the incident of the Unsuccessfully Attempted (UA) files. [53 words]

Revision: Social workers who cannot find where an RER applicant lives should write a note in the UA file. [18 words]

$$Lard \text{ Factor} = (53-18)/53 = 66\%$$

Active voice is preferable in academic writing. In sentences written in active voice, the subject in the sentence performs the action expressed in the verb—the subject acts. In sentences written in passive voice, the subject receives the action expressed in the verb—the subject is acted upon. The agent performing the action may appear in a "by the . . ." phrase or may be omitted. Additionally, sentences in active voice are more concise than those in passive voice because fewer words are required to express action.

Passive: Action on the bill is being considered by members of Congress.

Active: Members of Congress are considering action on the bill.

> Note: "George chopped down the cherry tree" sounds a lot better than "The cherry tree was chopped down by George." The former is simple and straightforward; the latter is wordy and clumsy. Occasionally you will have no choice but to use passive—for instance, when the subject of the sentence is unknown—but in most cases use the active voice .

Right or wrong, most significant research contributions are hidden in education and/or discipline-specific journals and use scholarly *jargon* that could limit the practical application of the findings. The following sections will help you become familiar with the language of the scholar, help you sound more like a scholar when you use these terms appropriately, and assist you in *devouring* and *digesting* the scholarly literature.

Writing in the Past Tense

When referring to a published study, you need to use the past tense, except when referencing a theory that is still in use. It is possible that the author's views regarding this event has changed with the passage of time—especially if he or she is deceased.

For example, Goldstein (1919) *concluded,* Smith (2001) *wrote,* Brown (1999) *found,* Schwartz (2009) *posited,* etc., but Herzberg's theory (1954) of hygiene and motivation *indicates…*

Noun clauses (clauses using *that*) immediately follow many verbs that refer to what someone else has written. Some of the most common of these verbs are posited, implied, confirmed, suggested, indicated, inferred, stated, decried, maintained, suggested, presumed, revealed, concluded, argued, denied, …

What Scholarly Writers Need to DO and NOT DO – A Baker's Dozen List

1. Avoid vague pronouns like *we, me, you, your, I, our, us, they,* etc. when it is not clear who these terms apply to. If you must use a pronoun, abide by the following rules:

    a. Pronouns must agree in number.

    b. Pronouns must agree in gender.

    c. Pronouns can be subjects or objects.

    d. Use *who* as the subject of a verb and *whom* as the object of a verb or a preposition.

    e. If you use a pronoun like "their" or "they," make certain it is clear to whom the pronoun is referring.

    f. NEVER use a pronoun to start a paragraph.

2. Use proper in text citations. The way to cite sources in text using APA style is to cite only the author's last name and year of publication (Smith, 2009) the first time a source is cited in each paragraph.

    a. If you start a paragraph with a quote or paraphrase, use the author's name and then the date in parentheses. For example: According to Simon (2009), APA formatting is challenging to master.

    b. Do not use first names or initials unless the work includes another reference by an author with the same last name. The period comes after the citation if it appears at the end of a sentence.

    c. If you are quoting directly, add the page number.

    d. If you use the same reference in the same paragraph, you do not include the year of publication after the first time the document is cited in that paragraph if the first citation is not in parentheses (i.e., Smith (2009) not (Smith, 2009)); the author's last name will suffice, unless the first citation is in parentheses.

    e. If two or more authors are cited, the & (ampersand) is ONLY used when the citations are in parentheses, otherwise use "and."

f. Do not use the title of the book or the journal article unless no author is provided. In text citations, never use URLs. The reference section contains information to locate the source.

g. Be careful to not overcite any source.

3. Make certain every statement is supported with sufficient evidence. Any assertions made without adequate substantiation appear to be rhetoric. Your extensive research of the topic might convince you that your statements are supportable, but you need to convince readers that they are indeed supported by providing validation.

4. Make certain every paragraph has one, and only one, topic sentence (main idea) and is properly developed. Development in a paragraph is any word, phrase, or sentence that answers one or more of the critical questions—who? what? where? when? why? or how?—about the main idea of the paragraph. Paragraphs should flow from one to the other with transition statements. Most paragraphs contain 3-5 sentences.

5. Review the document to ensure that all references used in the document appear in the reference section and all references in the reference section appear in the document.

6. Work to reduce or eliminate personalization and use of the phrase 'the researcher' or 'the author' in reference to yourself throughout the manuscript (shift focus more appropriately from the researcher to the research). It is understood that you will conduct the study. Occasional use of passive voice is acceptable to avoid both anthropomorphism and first-person expression. An exception is when the biases of the researcher are explained.

7. Make certain your writing is appropriately and consistently scientific in tone and avoid the use of colloquial language, slang, jargon, and trite expressions, (APA 5th ed., p. 38 and 6th ed., p. 68), redundancy, and hyperbole.

8. Make certain that your writing is accurate, balanced, objective, tentative, without conclusive or definitive statements, and a reflection on your opinions (i.e., your proposal and dissertation should reflect doctoral-level scholarly tone and presentation).

9. Avoid vague references to time such as *today, recent, the past few decades*, or *currently*. Replace with specific dates or time frames. Many times eliminating these words as

qualifiers is acceptable. If you are writing in 2011 and something happened "a decade ago," then it started in 2001. When you discuss a problem or situation, it is assumed that you are speaking about current times unless otherwise stated.

10. Avoid anthropomorphic or personification in your writing, that is, instances in which inanimate objects are granted conditions normally reserved for animate (living) objects. Wrong: The data demonstrated the effect clearly. Research stated that writing is a necessary skill. (Data can't demonstrate anything; they're inanimate. Research can't state anything; it's not alive.) Right: The effect is apparent from the data. One can conclude from research (provide references) that writing is a necessary skill (see APA 5th ed., p. 38, and APA 6th ed., p. 69).

11. Try to convey an *open-mindedness* to ideas, even when ideas of others may conflict or contrast with your own. You want to convey a sense of tolerance and fair play, in a word—objectivity. This can be accomplished by avoiding intensely emotional language, seemingly biased or slanted references, innuendo, sarcasm, hostility, and arrogance. In fact, scholarly writing exhibits a certain degree of *humility* in its appreciation for the complexities of a topic and a *respect* for collegial opinions and ideas.

12. Seek to reduce the number of quotations. Wherever possible, paraphrase the work of other authors instead of quoting them directly. Limit quotes to instances where the author uses a particularly striking turn of phrase, and where his or her precise meaning would be lost in a paraphrase. An unofficial rule is that you should keep the number of direct quotes to about 3 per 10 pages.

13. Bold, underlined type, and bullets are not permitted in a document formatted according to APA 5th ed. Times New Roman 12-point type and double-spacing are used throughout the document. In a document formatted according to APA 6th ed., bold type is used in some headings (p. 62) and bulleted lists are also allowed (p. 64).

The Language of the Scholar—Some Scholarly Jargon

Bias: This is an unknown or unacknowledged error created during the design, measurement, sampling, procedure, or choice of problem studied. The term is often used in a more specific sense to denote a source of systematic error derived from a conscious or unconscious tendency on the part of a researcher to produce or to interpret data in a way that could lead to erroneous conclusions that are in line with his or her commitments and beliefs. There are many different types of biases described in the research literature. The most common categories of bias that can affect the validity of research include the following:

1. Selection biases, which may result in the participants in the sample being unrepresentative of the population of interest.

2. Measurement biases, which include issues related to how the outcome of interest was measured.

3. Intervention (exposure) biases, which involve differences in how the treatment or intervention was carried out or how participants were exposed to the factor of interest.

Conceptual framework: Many scholars use the term conceptual framework and theoretical framework interchangeably; however, Eisenhart (2001) pointed out that "a conceptual framework is more of a justification, and assures that anticipated relationships will be appropriate and useful, given the research problem under investigation" (p. 209). While the theoretical framework is the theory on which the study is based, the conceptual framework is the operationalization of the theory.

The conceptual framework is linked closely to a critical review of the literature with the clustering of arguments by schools of thought allowing for the acceptance or rejection of positions and beliefs. A conceptual framework provides a structure for the logic of a study, and a path to help guide the study. A conceptual framework enables the researcher to operationalize concepts in order to collect the required evidence and data to test hypotheses and answer research questions, while ensuring that there is a viable plan to complete the study. For more please see: http://tinyurl.com/233ktv8

Constructivism: Constructivism is a theoretical framework that has its roots in medieval philosophy and has been applied to sociology and anthropology, as well as cognitive psychology and education. The constructivist philosopher Giambatista Vico commented in a treatise in 1710 that "one only knows something if one can explain it" (Yager, 1991). Immanual Kant further elaborated this idea by asserting that human beings are not passive recipients of information. People actively take knowledge, connect it to previously assimilated knowledge, and make it their own through their interpretation (Tower, Brown, & Cheek, 1992). In a constructivist setting, knowledge is not objective and meaning is intimately connected with experience.

Deconstruction: Deconstruction emphasizes how words, stories, and events have multiple meanings. Deconstructionists note that the interpretations derived by any particular community, for example a group of managers, are an arbitrary limit imposed upon the writing of management principles. Stories have hegemonic (dominant) constructions within particular times and places. French philosopher Jacques Derrida coined the term "deconstruction" in the 1960s. In general, deconstruction is a philosophy of meaning that deals with the ways that meaning is constructed by writers, philosophers, texts, and consumers. Deconstruction is considered by many to be a method of literary criticism that contends multiple conflicting interpretations of a text and that bases such interpretations on the philosophical, political, or social implications of the use of language in the text rather than on the author's intention.

Empiricism: Empiricism is the reliance on experience and observation as the source of ideas and knowledge. More specifically, empiricism is the epistemological theory that genuine information about the world must be acquired by a posteriori means, so that nothing can be thought without first being sensed. Prominent modern empiricists include Bacon, Locke, Berkeley, Hume, and Mill.

Epistemology: Epistemology is the branch of philosophy that studies knowledge and examines the nature of understanding how knowledge is derived, justified, verified, validated, and tested. It attempts to answer the basic question: What distinguishes true (adequate) knowledge from false (inadequate) knowledge? Knowledge can be acquired, a priori (innate, before experience, generally deductive, and analytic) or a posteriori (through the sense experiences, generally inductive in nature, and synthetic). Methodological debates in the social and behavioral sciences generally stem from different epistemological questions http://tinyurl.com/pj7qp. The first theories of knowledge stressed its absolute, permanent character. Later theories put the emphasis on its relativity or situation-dependence, its continuous development or evolution, and its active interference with the world and its subjects and objects. This trend moves from a static, passive view of knowledge toward a more adaptive and active one.

Existentialism: This is a term that designates a concern in philosophy, literature, and art with the irreducibly personal and subjective aspects of human existence. Existentialists attempt to make rational decisions despite living in an irrational universe. Some existentialists believe that life is without inherent meaning (existential atheists) while others believe life is without a meaning we can understand (existential theists). Existentialists argue that we are forced to define our own meanings, knowing that this definition might be temporary. Soren Kierkegaard and Friedrich Nietzsche are often considered the fathers of existentialism. Other prominent names associated with existentialism are Fyodor Dostoevsky, Martin Heidegger, Jean-Paul Sartre, Franz Kafka, Albert Camus, and Simone de Beauvoir (who might be called the mother of feminist existentialism and of feminism at large). Contemporary expressions of existentialism are in the novels of Milan Kundera (e.g., *The Unbearable Lightness of Being*), some films by Woody Allen (e.g., *Crimes and Misdemeanors*), and Peter Shaffer's play *Equus*. Some themes found in existentialism include an emphasis upon the individual, a critique of current society, a goal of a comfortable existence, objectivity, and an emphasis upon the dynamic and incomplete versus the static and complete.

Methodological: How should the researcher go about finding out knowledge? A broad, complex array of ideas, concepts, frameworks, and theories surrounds the use of various methods or techniques employed to generate data on the social world. Questions about the collection of either quantitative data via surveys or questionnaires or qualitative data via participation and involvement are methodological questions. Research methods are the particular strategies researchers use to collect the evidence necessary for testing or creating theories.

Note: The differences between qualitative and quantitative research approaches or paradigms are like fraternal twins. They both have similar origins, yet do not necessarily have similar appearances. Of the *fraternal twins*, the quantitative approach is the *left-brained* sibling that is more analytical and numbers focused, answering questions about relationships among measured variables with the purpose of explaining, predicting, and controlling a phenomenon. The qualitative approach is the *right-brained sibling*, or a more global form of research, being more interpretative in nature and seeking to describe phenomena from the point of view of the participant. The qualitative twin is usually more verbose and explained in narrative form instead of numbers. The *left-brained sibling* is more taciturn and to the point.

There have been many lengthy and complex discussions and arguments surrounding the topic of *which twin* is better. Different methodologies become popular at different social, political, historical, and cultural times. Every methodology has its specific strengths and weaknesses. What you will find, in selecting your methodology, is that your instincts probably lean toward one of the *twins*. Listen to these instincts as you will find it more productive to conduct the type of research with which you will feel comfortable, especially if you're to keep your motivation levels high. However, be aware that the problem you pose might lend itself better to one type of research paradigm and method over another. If this is the case, you might have a harder time justifying your chosen methodology if it goes against finding the solution to the problem you pose and the purpose of your study.

Ontological: What is the nature of the "knowable" or what is the nature of "reality?" How is the social world perceived and understood (Hitchcock & Hughes, 1995)? Ontology attempts to answer such questions as, "What is real?" It studies being or existence as well as the basic categories thereof—trying to find out what entities and what types of entities exist. Ontology has strong implications for the conceptions of how one views reality.

Paradigms: These are commonly held beliefs about the way things are done among a group of people, such as scientists, members of a profession, or members of an organization. The two major paradigms of research are the empirical (quantitative) and the constructivist (qualitative) paradigms. According to Kuhn (1962), a paradigm is a "constellation of concepts, values, perceptions and practices shared by a community which forms a particular vision of reality that is the basis of the way a community organizes itself" (p. 5).

Postmodernism: The postmodern movement dismantles the procedures and assumptions used to establish universal truths or principles. It is fundamentally a revolutionary political movement argued in intellectual terms. Perhaps the most characteristic tenet of postmodern critical work is that what European philosophy and science has held to be fundamentally true at an abstract level (ontology, epistemology, metaphysics, and logic) is not. Rather, it is a contingent, historically specific cultural construction that has often served the function of empowering members of a dominant social class at the expense of others. For more information check out

http://www.cs.cmu.edu/afs/cs.cmu.edu/user/phoebe/mosaic/postmodernism.html

Research: Research is a careful study of a given subject, field, or problem in a scholarly and often scientific manner. A researcher, like a master chef, finds that planning is the essence of his or her art. Structure, conceptualization, practical methodology, and up-front planning are basic requirements to secure an excellent outcome in both fields. According to Kerlinger (1986), "Scientific research is systematic, controlled, empirical, and critical investigation of hypothetical propositions about the presumed relations among natural phenomena. It is a more in depth and critical analyses and exploration than the mere gathering of information" (p. 11). According to Albert Szent-Gyorgyi (1893-1986), "Research is to see what everybody has seen and to think what nobody else had thought." Zora Neale Hurston noted, "Research is formalized curiosity. It is poking and prying with a purpose."

Theoretical framework: A framework is simply the structure of the idea or concept and how it is put together. A theoretical framework interrelates the theories involved in solving the problem posed and answering the research questions generated. A theoretical framework helps to place a study in perspective among other studies and to justify asking participants to take part in the study. It is used to support studies looking for relationships between variables. For example, a relationship might exist between prenatal nutrition of mothers and intellectual performance of their offspring. "If no framework is provided, there is no indication of where the study might fit in the universe of research and thus the value of the study is questionable" (Wood & Brink, 1989, pp. 108-109). The diffusion of innovation framework states that adopting innovation is a process that includes the following steps: knowledge, attitude, decision implementation, and confirmation. This framework also characterizes individuals in five categories: innovators, early adopters, early majority, late majority, and laggards. How the investigator views the world and establishes a theoretical framework affects the entire process—from conceptualizing a problem, to collecting and analyzing data, to interpreting the findings.

Theory: The purpose of theory is to describe, explain, predict, or understand human phenomena in a variety of contexts. Theories help us make sense of patterns and provide a systematic means to explain what we observe. We act upon the basis of theories about people, society, and the world we inhabit (i.e., ideas that explain what people, society, and the world are all about). A theory guides us in thinking about the world and suggests what is and is not important to look at. It also suggests how things go together and how one thing influences another (sometimes called a cause).

Although theory is usually distinguished from practice, Kurt Lewin (1952) remarked, "There is nothing as practical as a good theory." Theories structure our beliefs and enable others to confirm or disconfirm them through scientific inquiry. Good theories help explain findings and usually build upon other good theories. Theories also set limits or boundaries for which the theorist is responsible. Another function of theory formulation is to generate new ideas for research by suggesting specific relationships that need further study. Theory creates the shared understanding and terminology that is a necessary prerequisite for discussion and debate of practice, research, and research on practice. The extent to which observations can be accounted for by a theory is the extent to which a theory is credible. Social theory is a theory about how society, and its constituents, work. Bandura's social learning theory helps explain aggressive behavior. Bandura argued that individuals, especially children, learn aggressiveness from observing others, either personally or through the media and environment. He stated that many individuals believe that aggression will produce reinforcements. These reinforcements can formulate into the reduction of tension, gaining financial rewards, gaining the praise of others, or building self-esteem (Siegel, 1992, p. 171).

Variable: A variable is an observable factor, phenomenon, or characteristic that has more than one value or category. In research studies, variables typically are measured by either instrumentation, observation, or administration of surveys or tests. The value of the research depends on the quality of the data collected and the accuracy of the measurement of variables. The four levels of data measurement can be remembered by the French word for black, NOIR (Nominal and Ordinal – considered low levels of measurement, and Interval and Ratio – considered high levels of measurement). If only one value is possible, the term or construct is a constant and not a variable (Sproull, 1995). A study at an all girls school, for example, would not have gender as a variable unless compared to an all boys school. A dependent variable (y value) depends on some other variable that has usually preceded it in time. An independent variable (x value) can be manipulated, measured, or selected prior to measuring the outcome or dependent variable. Research could be considered the study of the relationship between variables.

There is some confusion between a concept and a variable. Concepts cannot be observed directly. Some examples include attention, emotion, learning, prejudice, biases, leadership, and commitment. They are abstractions that exist only as mental images of things we want to discuss. To conduct research, we convert concepts to things we can observe. We do this by defining concepts in terms of measurable *variables*.

Variables represent concepts. Like concepts, variables are defined in words, but, as used in social research, variables have a special characteristic – they have two or more observable forms or values. In short, they vary. Any condition or aspect of social behavior or social life that has at least two conditions or amounts of something is a variable.

Variables that can be assigned numbers are *quantitative* variables. A few examples of quantitative variables include your age, your height, your intelligence, your family's income, your GPA, or the number of students at your university. Other variables exist in terms of qualities or categories rather than in terms of numbers. Gender is a variable with only two (the minimum) categories - male and female. Other examples of *categorical* or *qualitative* variables are social class, which can be described as high, middle, or low; occupation, which can be expressed in various categories as baker, merchant, educator, and so on; or marital status, commonly described as single, married, divorced, separated, or widowed.

Worldview: A worldview provides a model of the world that guides its adherents. Sire (1997) asserted, "A world view is a set of presuppositions (or assumptions) which we hold (consciously or subconsciously) about the basic makeup of our world" (p. 5). Philips and Brown (1989) claimed, "A worldview is, first of all, an explanation and interpretation of the world and second, an application of this view to life" (p. 21). A worldview should pass certain tests. First, it should be rational. It should not ask us to believe contradictory things. Second, it should be supported by evidence and consistent with what we observe. Third, it should give a satisfying comprehensive explanation of reality. Fourth, it should provide a basis for living. Some educators take a behaviorist worldview of education and support a rewards/punishment system in which students will be motivated to learn if they are rewarded for their efforts. Behaviorists are in favor of standardized tests to improve and assess learning, whereas educators that hold a constructivist worldview believe that learning takes place when learners can create meaning from their own life. The constructivist is in favor of projects and portfolios to enhance and assess learning.

The following adages illustrate both the beauty and the bafflement one encounters in scholarly discourse. These two "simple statements" epitomize how brevity can belie the complexity inherent in the language of the scholar. Determine which camp you are in, or under which conditions you favor one philosophical view over the other. Try saying and sharing these expressions with a friend or colleague. This will make you sound like a true scholar and a *master chef*!

Camp 1: Epistemology presupposes ontology

This is the realist view, which contends that in order to know (episteme) there must be something real (ontos) to know. It is a belief favored by those who employ quantitative methodologies. Members of this camp contend there is a solution to a problem that can be found using the scientific method of deduction. Researchers who prefer the quantitative paradigm support this view.

Camp 2: Ontology presupposes epistemology

This is the constructivist view, which contends that our knowing (episteme) gives reality its realness (ontos). It is a belief held by postmodernists and constructivists who believe that there is no single reality and that context is everything. Qualitative methodologists support this notion with the belief that reality is socially constructed through individual or collective definitions of the situation. This philosophy is more concerned with understanding and consistency than in trying to explain a phenomenon. Members of the constructivist camp contend that conclusions are based on induction and context sensitivity and that universal context-free generalizations are nonexistent.

 *Cutting Board*

1. Which of the active reading strategies above do you already employ?
   _____

2. Which of these suggestions do you need to practice?
   _____

3. Which of the two camps are you a member of? _____
   Why? _____

1 cup "O" rganize Your Time

By planning your future, you can live in the present....Time is one of your most valuable resources, and it is important that you spend it wisely. —Lee Berglund, founder of Personal Resource Systems

The key point in time management is recognizing the finite nature of time as a resource. This is both good news and bad news. The bad news, of course, is that time is limited. It moves at the same rate and there is no way to manipulate the passage of time. The good news is that time is a constant. It is known and, hence, its stability provides a basis for predicting future outcomes.

Time management includes good program planning whereby resources (people, time) can be used effectively. Daily work is easier when a model provides a continuing guide for action and various levels of accountability and responsibility and when essential tasks and sequences of tasks are specified along with a timeline for completion.

Managing time is a decision process. It is a set of choices that parse time as a finite resource among tasks that are competing for this resource. The effectiveness of such decisions is an outcome of task achievement skills as well as the priority to which each task was assigned. The quality and quantity of any outcome are dependent on the skill with which the task was addressed and the amount of time that was devoted to the task.

An excellent first step in effective time and activity management is to write down your goals. On the Cutting Board below, write down the day that you plan to complete your dissertation (DCD). (You might want to revisit this after you have completed PHASE 1 of your *Recipes for Success.*)

 *Cutting Board*

My DCD will be _____ (date). At that time I will have successfully completed the written part of my dissertation/research project and sent it to the proper authorities.

Next, it is important that you recognize other things that you have to do and want to do between now and DCD.

On the Cutting Board below, write down the things in your life that you have to do and then the things that are not on the list that you want to do between now and DCD.

 Cutting Board

1. I have to do the following activities between now and DCD:

   _____

2. In addition, I want to do the following activities:

   _____

Good Job! Now let us break this down into smaller *bites* and make a plan for next week. First, fill in the following calendar with all the time that you will be attending to your "have to's." Next, fill in quality time that you can dedicate to your research. Choose something that you want to do that is not on the schedule and plan for that as well.

Monday	Tuesday	Wednesday	Thursday	Friday	Saturday	Sunday

 Cutting Board

1. Make an affirmation for the next 7 days. Share this with a colleague.

By _____, I will have achieved the following goals in my research:

_____

_____

2. Make an affirmation for the next month.

_____

By _____, I will have achieved the following goals in my research:

3. Share this with a colleague.

4. Begin each new week with a similar affirmation until DCD.

5. Remember, to achieve a goal it must be

   o Conceivable—capable of being put into words

   o Believable—to you

   o Achievable—so you have the strength, energy, and time to accomplish it

There are many activities that you can do to support yourself in the preparation and serving of your feast. You might want to learn how to learn a new software program such as Excel, SPSS, or NVivo; familiarize yourself with American Psychological Association (APA) formatting (http://www.perrla.com); learn how to do online searches on the Internet (http://www.kryltech.com); or purchase a new computer. Software companies such as Guildford (http://www.guilford.com) provide programs to assist you with some helpful research tasks. You also might need to obtain office supplies, research a variety of preliminary topics, take a refresher course in statistics at a local college, arrange for child care, join a Listserv or professional organization, consult with advisors in your field or in other fields, relieve yourself from a prior responsibility, and so on. Consider keeping a daily dissertation journal where you will record your successes and the challenges you face.

On the Cutting Board below, make a list of five things that will support you in completing your research by DCD (dissertation completion date) and the times that you will be able to attend to these things.

 *Cutting Board*

By _____ (date) I will: _____

By _____ (date) I will: _____

By _____ (date) I will: _____

By _____ (date) I will: _____

By _____ (date) I will: _____

Some additional time management tips:

Learn to Prioritize: Prioritizing your responsibilities and engagements is very important. One method is the DWM list. The items placed in the D section are those needed to be done that day. The items placed in the W section need completing within the week. The M section items are those things that need to be done within the month.

Be aware of the 24-gallon barrel syndrome. This is a syndrome where we feel that we have been given a 24-gallon barrel to fill each day and we are already at capacity. To help us do quality research, we might need to take something out of the barrel so that we can add our research to the barrel. Think about what you are doing now that you could give up, at least temporarily, so you can dedicate more time to your scholarly research.

Combine several activities: Multi-task. While commuting to work, listen to taped notes or books on tape. This allows an hour or two of good study review each day. While showering, make a mental list of the things that need to be done for that day. When watching a sit-com, laugh as you pay your bills. These are just suggestions of what you can do to combine your time, but there are many others. Above all, be creative and flexible, and make it work for you.

After scheduling becomes a habit, then you can make adjustments as needed. It's better to be precise at first. It is easier to find something to do with extra time than to find extra time to do something. Most important, make it work for you. A time schedule that is not personalized and honest is not a time schedule at all. Be flexible. Life happens!

Don't be a perfectionist. Trying to be a perfect person sets you up for defeat. Nobody can be perfect. Difficult tasks usually result in avoidance and procrastination. You need to set achievable goals, but they should also be challenging. There will always be people both weaker and stronger than you.

Learn to say no. For example, an acquaintance of yours would like you to see a movie with him or her tonight. You made social plans for tomorrow with your friends and tonight you were going to read a journal article that you just received related to your research. You really are not interested in this movie. You want to say no, but you hate turning people down. Politely saying no should become a habit. Saying no frees up time for the things that are most important.

Understand when you are most efficient. During the times when you feel the most alert you should be doing the most creative and original aspects of your research. When you are less alert you can still work on some of the more mundane tasks like formatting or doing searches.

1 cup "C"reating a Working Environment

Your own space—a little time with your own thoughts in (your) own space...where there is no one else but (you) to meet inside. [A place which is relatively serene and conducive for productive work. A place where you have the freedom to think and work on your research]. — "My Own Space" (The Act). A play by Fred Ebb

Your special space or your *kitchen* where you will be preparing your *feast* should have the following luxuries:

1. Proper lighting. Poor lighting increases eye fatigue. Ideal lighting is indirect and free from glare.
2. Proper ventilation. The brain needs fresh oxygen to function at its optimum.
3. Reasonable quietness. Try experimenting with soft classical or jazz music in the background, and see if that increases your concentration and productivity.
4. Proper supplies and support systems. (See Designing a Survival Kit.)

5. A "DO NOT DISTURB" sign. When you display this sign, it needs to be respected by those with whom you cohabitate.

6. Optional: There is a subtle but intimate connection between our olfactory environment and our mental and emotional well-being. The fragrance of vanilla can be very soothing, and peppermint can help improve task performance. Give them a try.

1 cup "E"xtend Your Note-Taking and Writing Skills: Record Keeping, Mind Mapping, PIE Writing

You need to keep a record of references (titles of books or periodicals) that pertain to your research. You will want to be sure that you denote the author's name, the reference—book, journal, magazine article—publisher, relevant page numbers, any excerpts you might want to cite, and the exact page numbers of potential quotations or paraphrases. Two commercially available products, EndNote and ProCite, might be useful tools to assist you with keeping track of your references. Both create databases that store the references; both can be sorted and exported. Electronic sources need to be entered manually but EndNote stores the URL as a link that can be clicked-upon to immediately bring up that site in your browser. Both are available as 30-day trial versions and are sold by the same company (ISI ResearchSoft).

EndNote: www.endnote.com

ProCite: www.procite.com

Also check this free web page: http://www.bibme.org/

You might wish to consider using different colors to indicate different types of references; for example, pink (or highlighting) could be used for texts, green for periodicals, yellow for research reports, etc. This system will be extremely helpful to you when preparing the research/literature chapter of your dissertation (see **PHASE 3**) or research project and when compiling your bibliography or reference list. You might also wish to create real and virtual folders to store articles and references that you obtain related to your topic.

You can use your laptop computer or PDA to take notes; you'll find excellent note-taking capabilities in the simple text editors that come bundled with most machines, and strong organizing capabilities in the database software that is easily available.

Note Taking

A form of note taking that is rapidly replacing the traditional outline form of note taking is mind mapping. Some characteristics of a mind map are that it

1. stimulates the way that most people think
2. is a means of brainstorming that allows your thoughts to flow freely
3. helps you to categorize information and determine how this information relates to other information
4. gives you an overview of your project

Figure 1 is a mind map of a mind map. Carefully study the mind map for its structure, purpose, and usefulness. Notice a mind map requires only one page (preferably a blank page held horizontally) where related ideas are linked together. The Roman numerals that are used in traditional outlining appear as branches on a mind map.

Note: Researchers claim that people who have switched from traditional outlining to mind mapping significantly increase their retention and heighten their organizational skills. In addition, mind mapping is fun, easy, and creative. Try using colored pens or pencils when creating mind maps. Experiment with each branch construed in a different color. You might want different shades of a particular color to signify supporting ideas. Electronic mind mapping software can be found at http://tinyurl.com/348x5g4.

Mind Mapping

Tony Buzan of the Learning Methods Group in England originated mind mapping. This technique is based on research findings that show that the brain works primarily with key concepts in an interrelated and integrated manner.

Traditional thinking opts for columns and rows as illustrated by traditional outlining techniques. Buzan felt that *working out* from a core idea would suit the brain's thinking patterns better. The brain also needs a way to *slot in* ideas that are relevant to the core idea. To achieve those ends, Buzan developed mind mapping.

Mind mapping is an individual brainstorming process. In brainstorming, you are interested in generating as many ideas as possible, even wild and crazy ones. Just write or otherwise record whatever comes into your head, as it occurs. Quantity, not quality, is what you are after. No criticism is allowed during the brainstorming itself. Later you can go back and critique your work. You can also generate new ideas by looking at what you have already written—piggybacking on the work you've done before.

To begin a mind-mapping session, write the name or a brief description of the object or problem in the center of a piece of paper and draw a circle around it. Then brainstorm each major facet of that object or problem, drawing lines outward from the circle like roads leaving a city. You can draw branches from those roads as you brainstorm them in more detail.

You can brainstorm all the main lines at once and then the branches for each. Or you can brainstorm a line and its branches before moving on to the next line. Or you can jump from place to place as thoughts occur. To make the mind map more useful, you might draw each major branch extending from your central thought in a different color. As you branch out, you may notice related topics appearing on different branches. You can emphasize those relationships by circling the items in question or by drawing lines under or between them.

Finally, study your mind map and look for interrelationships and terms that appear more than once. Mind mapping is an excellent technique, not only for generating new ideas, but also for developing your intuitive capacity. It is especially useful for identifying all the issues and subissues related to a problem, as well as possible solutions to a problem. To do that, use the main branches on your mind map for solutions. The subbranches from each of them become the perceived benefits and obstacles related to these solutions. Mind mapping also works well for outlining presentations, papers, and book chapters. In fact, it is useful in a wide variety of situations. For more information on mind mapping see http://www.edrawsoft.com/freemind.php

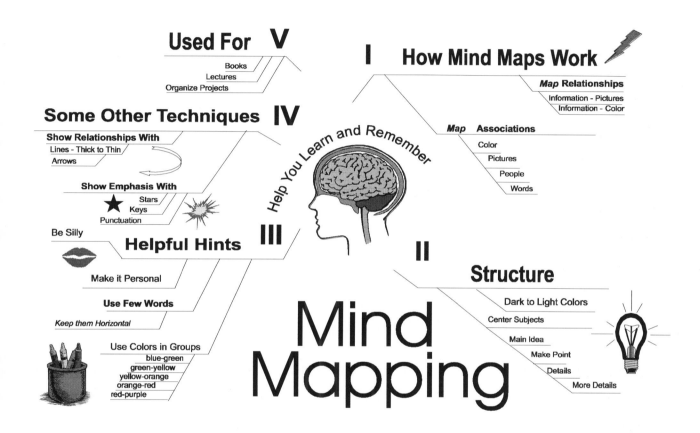

Figure 1 A mind map of mind mapping

A helpful tool closely related to mind mapping is concept mapping. Concept mapping was developed by Prof. J. D. Novak at Cornell University in the 1960s and is based on the theories of David Ausubel, stressing the importance of prior knowledge in being able to learn about new concepts. Novak posited, "Meaningful learning involves the assimilation of new concepts and propositions into existing cognitive structures." For more on concept mapping, check out http://tinyurl.com/cehwfz.

 Cutting Board

Use a blank sheet of paper to create a mind map of a topic that you might want to research. Put the name of the topic in the middle of the paper. Use branches to indicate main ideas (beliefs, attitudes, and opinions) related to this topic. Several excellent computer programs are available for mind mapping, including Verio by Microsoft and Inspiration.

PIE Writing

To transform your notes into written passages, you might want to try a formula developed by Hanau (1975). Hanau advanced the idea that written materials contain statements that are the declaration of beliefs, attitudes, or opinions. These statements are the keys that allow the reader to understand what you, the writer, are trying to convey. Each paragraph should contain a statement or statements in conjunction with supporting evidence that have the function of elucidating the statement. These supporting elements can be classified into one of the three categories, which can be remembered by the acronym *PIE*: Proof, Information, or Examples.

1. **Proof** - any kind of supporting documentation that a statement is true and/or important. In a dissertation or research paper, proof usually comes from a review of related research, a quote from a well-known person, current statistical data, a statement by an authority figure, or information from archival data.
2. **Information** - any clarifying material, such as a definition, that limits the scope of your statements and seeks to clarify what your statements mean within a certain context. This clarification brings your supporting material to bear in an effective manner.
3. **Example** – a concrete illustration that serves to elucidate any statement that you make while attesting to a statement's truth or importance.

It is not necessary to have all three supporting elements in every paragraph of your paper, but you will probably wish to include at least two *pieces of PIE* per paragraph. You also need not adhere to any particular order of presenting a statement with its accompanying pieces of *PIE*, so long as your paragraphs are clear, sufficiently detailed, and coherent. You want to make sure that there is sufficient evidence for you to make a strong point and that the evidence is relevant, reliable, and representative.

Evidence can come from either primary or secondary sources. A primary source is an original source of data that puts as few intermediaries as possible between the production and the study of data. For example, if one was studying the way Shakespeare used metaphors, books written by Shakespeare would be primary sources and books written about Shakespeare would be secondary sources. A primary source is an original document containing firsthand information about a topic.

Secondary sources are opinions or interpretation of others on the topic (your published research will become a secondary source when someone wishes to quote it).

A secondary source contains commentary on, or discussion about, a primary source. The most important feature of secondary sources is that they offer an interpretation of information gathered from primary sources. In most dissertations and formal research projects, the overwhelming sources of evidence should come from peer-reviewed current primary sources. An individual document might be a primary source in one context and a secondary source in another. Time is a defining element. For example, a newspaper article reporting on a murder is not a primary source unless the author was at the scene of the crime, but a newspaper article from the 1860s might be a primary source for Civil War research. When in doubt, check with your committee members.

If your paragraphs are only statements without any *pieces of PIE*, the predominant impression that comes across is assertion without foundation. Similarly, having *pieces of PIE* without a statement makes it difficult for the reader to comprehend the point of what is written. Once your paragraph has a statement with a satisfactory *helping of PIE*, you are ready to move to the next paragraph.

Note: Every statement of fact must be supported with sufficient evidence. Any assertions made without adequate substantiation could be perceived as rhetoric. Your extensive research of the topic might convince you that your statements are supportable, but you need to convince readers that they are indeed supported by providing that validation. An exception would be information considered common knowledge. Common knowledge is information or facts that most educated people know or can find out easily in an encyclopedia or dictionary. For example, Albany is the capital of New York State; in the United States there are private, public, and parochial schools. When it is unclear if information is common knowledge, the general rule is "if in doubt, cite it."

 Cutting Board

Look at the main branches of the mind map that you created on a topic that you might wish to research. See if you can support these ideas (main branches) with the PIE elements described in this section.

---

1 cup "E"nter Information Into a Computer, Journal, or Tape Deck

Alfieri, the great Italian dramatist, allegedly had his servants tie him to his writing table so that he would be forced to write.

Hopefully, you will not need to go to the extremes that Alfieri did to discipline yourself into putting your thoughts and notes into the formation of your *feast*.

Much of what makes writing challenging is trying to write and edit at the same time. Get your ideas on paper, or in a Word document, first; critique, rework, and polish them later. Critiquing ideas as you are trying to express them often represses them. If you reach a stumbling block, try to write past it—often the best ideas lie right beyond the hurdle, tempting you to give up. If you are still stuck, take a break and think over the problem in a relaxed setting. By the time you return, you will probably have the answer.

Be prepared to write at any time, in any place. Keep pen and paper in your car, purse, gym bag, pocket, etc., or keep your PDA handy or your laptop in standby mode. The best ideas often come when you are not trying for them. You can save yourself a significant amount of time by transposing your written notes, on a regular basis, onto your computer. It would be good to have a computer nearby as you read articles and books for your dissertation research.

If you are fortunate enough to have a dedicated secretary who can transcribe your dictation onto a word processor, that might be your ideal method for formulating your dissertation. This method of transcription offers you the liberty of creating your *feast* while in the midst of traffic. You can experiment with tape recording your ideas and using voice dictation software like Dragon Naturally Speaking http://www.nuance.com/naturallyspeaking/ to transcribe your notes. Voice-activated word processing programs are getting better each day.

If computers are not your thing, and you do not have a dedicated secretary to transcribe your notes on a regular basis, perhaps you and your *feast* would be best *served* by obtaining a wonderful pen and an ingratiating journal or notepad and proceeding to WRITE. When your document is near completion, you should probably hire someone to enter your document onto a word processor so that you can make corrections and deletions and obtain an exquisite *feast* shortly thereafter. Be aware, however, that mastering the computer yields many benefits now (faster completion of work) and later (most organizations require a high degree of computer literacy). Most doctoral students in the 21st century could not imagine attempting a dissertation without owning at least one computer and several storage devices for back-up.

 Cutting Board

1. What will you use to create your *feast*?

    _____

2. When will be your first (next) time to utilize this method?

    _____

The following is a rubric that can be used to help develop better writing skills. You might want to write a few pages and then ask someone whose opinion and editing skills you value to critique what you have written based on this rubric. (See Scoring Key below.)

Rubric for Writing	0	1	2	3
General organization: coherency/integration				
Each paragraph is fully developed and related to the intent of the paper.				
Each paragraph begins with a topic sentence that introduces and summarizes the point to be made. Every sentence in a paragraph supports the main idea expressed in the topic sentence.				
There is clarity of thought and expression. The author's meaning is always clear. There are no unnecessary words.				
The reader can follow the author's thoughts easily throughout the essay.				
Words are well chosen; statements are free from contradiction; the essay as a whole is free of jargon and clichés.				
The writing is free from grammatical, punctuation, and spelling errors.				
There is a clear statement of thesis in the writing; in it the author defines the boundaries of the document.				
Wholeness: The author presents the topics to be addressed in an integrated way and summarizes the major points.				
The writing has cadence and flows easily and logically; the reader can sense the person behind the words.				

0 = Blank, off topic. Incoherent

1 = Below average, weak. Does not respond to most parts of the question, weak subject knowledge.

2 = Satisfactory, average. Demonstrates a basic understanding of the information.

3 = Above average, outstanding. Demonstrates a thorough understanding of the question. Provides a strong explanation and understanding of the concepts and information relevant to the question.

Creating a Journal

Journals and diaries have a long history as forms of self-expression. By keeping a dissertation journal, you can write away stress, anxiety, indecision, problems, unfinished business, confusion, writer's block, and procrastination.

There are many benefits to be gained by keeping a journal: Some benefits include the following:

1. Writing can flow without self-consciousness or inhibition.
2. Your thought processes and mental habits can be revealed.
3. You can improve your memory.
4. You can provide tangible evidence of mental processes.
5. You can obtain mental growth through critical reflection.
6. You can help make meaning out of what is experienced or read as it relates to your research.
7. You can articulate connections between new information and what you know.

One type of journal you might wish to keep is known as a reader response journal or literature log. Here you can record the response to your readings. It enables you to enter the literature in your own voice. If you would like to keep your personal diary or journal online, Cam Development at http://www.camdevelopment.com/mpd.htm has software to assist you.

1 cup "D"esign a Survival Kit

The following is a list of supplies and tools that you might find helpful to have in your *kitchen* while designing your *feast*: Remember to back up your work frequently and use a variety of back-up devices.

Computer	Modem/Wi-Fi	Printer and ink cartridges
Pencils Pencil sharpener	Erasers	Post-it notes
Ruler	Graph paper	Waste basket
Dictionary	Thesaurus	
Scissors	Three-hole punch	Tape
Book case	Writing table	Printer paper
Highlighters	Colored pens	Paper clips
Calculator	Index cards	Writing paper

Clock	Comfortable chair	Surge protector
Backup drives	Folders	Filing cabinet
Thumb drives	Blackberry	Kindle (electronic reader)

 Cutting Board

1. Put an asterisk (*) near the objects that you now own.

2. Put an exclamation point (!) next to the ones that you feel you should own.

3. Write down any other objects you will be needing or wanting to have in your dissertation kitchen/workspace:

_____

PICK YOUR REPAST

[Choose Your Topic]

½ cup   P ossess Knowledge of What a Dissertation Is and Is Not
1 cup   I dentify Your Cooking (Researching) Style
½ cup   C lassify Yourself Professionally
1 cup   K (c)onduct the ROC Bottom Test

½ cup "P" ossess Knowledge of What a Dissertation Is and Is Not

Before you go through the process of selecting a dissertation project and topic, keep in mind that a dissertation is *not* necessarily

1. a Nobel Prize project

2. the final answer to a pressing problem

3. the last research paper that you will write

4. about the hottest topic in your field

5. going to excite all your friends.

What then is a dissertation (I hear you cry)? A dissertation is the written report of a formal research project required to complete a doctoral degree, designed around solving an important problem in your profession that you

1. could "put your arms around"; in a couple of minutes you could tell someone in your profession, as well as in another profession, what it is about
2. already know a great deal about where it will fit into a larger picture
3. are truly concerned and curious about
4. could conceivably present at a professional meeting
5. are willing to dedicate a great deal of time to complete
6. can call your own
7. can proclaim is researchable, original, and contributory to your profession and to society [see (K)conduct a ROC bottom test]
8. will know when you have completed, i.e., ascertained enough information to answer your research questions and accept or not accept your hypotheses

According to Van Slyke et al. (2003), because the dissertation serves as the starting point for producing publications, ideally the topic should be the foundation for a substantial research stream. Make sure you choose a topic that is of great interest to you. For most people, the dissertation is the largest research project they will ever do. It is important that the topic matches your long-term interests and abilities. Your interest is even more important when considering how long you are likely to be working on the topic. It will likely take longer than you think to complete. With some finesse, you will be crafting articles based on the dissertation for some time.

As stated earlier, doctoral writing is the highest level of academic writing. The Council of Graduate Schools (2005) described the purpose for doctoral-level research *as being able to apply generally accepted theory to a current problem in order to find a viable solution*. Thus, you need to identify a research problem, design an empirical study to address the problem in an appropriate manner, and then carry out the research while abiding by ethical principles. When the research is conducted, you will write up the study and, in so doing, make an original contribution to your profession that provides evidence of originality in thinking.

1 cup "I" dentifying Your Style

Choosing Your Research Project/Topic
What type of cook (researcher) are you?

Most of us have our own unique style of inquiry. Some styles embody the traditional norms of science while others exemplify nontraditional norms. There is no one right or wrong way to investigate a problem per se, but if you have a very strong research style, you might find it frustrating to work on a project that is designed for a different type of researcher. A dissertation topic should be an original contribution to scholarly research that fills a void in the literature and extends prior knowledge. A dissertation or thesis can replicate a study in a different environment or time or develop a new theory. Regardless of its intent, you should find a project that you are passionate (or extremely interested) about working diligently on.

> Note: It is important to keep in mind that in doing research there is room for the daring, speculative, inventive spirit who creates new theories or tries bold, imaginative experiments, as well as for the cautious, critical spirit who examines theories searchingly or for those who will patiently design experiments requiring complete attention to detail. There are researchers who prefer the precision of mathematics and those who prefer the color of words; those who prefer to deal with human beings and human problems and others who prefer to work with computers or microscopes. However, according to Goldstein and Goldstein in their book *How We Know* (1985), "for all there should be the same goal—the joy and excitement of discovery and the same outcome—knowledge."

On the Cutting Board that follows you will find a typology of major ways in which people make inquiries, adapted from Mitroff and Kilmann's *Methodological Approaches to Social Science* (1978).

Answer each question and record your answers in the spaces provided. This will give you an opportunity to discover what method(s) of doing research would work well for you.

FOR YOUR INFORMATION AND EDUCATION

Although there are many different ways to classify types of scientific thinking, C. G. Jung's classification has been chosen because it takes into account both affect (feeling) and cognition (thinking).

 Cutting Board

Read each statement below and indicate on the accompanying Likert-type scale how strongly you agree with each declaration.

Note: This activity is **not** designed to serve as a model for survey design. It is instead intended to help give you get a *taste* of a variety of research methodologies that fit your research style and enable you to solve the problem you pose. This survey is based on Mitroff and Kilman's (1978, 1983) typologies of research and uses a 4-point Likert-type scale. The questions are intentionally complex and force a commitment to one view rather than allowing for a neutral view or a no opinion option.

T: To truly understand the AIDS epidemic, one must ascertain the truth about AIDS. A researcher must look at the data, make recommendations for further study based on these findings, and not base conclusions on information obtained through subjective means or anecdotal stories that rely too heavily on his or her personal feelings.

    disagree totally   agree totally

         1   2   3   4   T = _____

F: To truly understand the AIDS epidemic, one must look at the individuals afflicted with the disease and note the similarities and differences that exist between those tormented with AIDS. Recommendations for further study should be based on the immediate needs of those individuals as well as how the researcher feels he or she could best be personally involved.

    disagree totally   agree totally

         1   2   3   4   F = _____

S: To deal with environmental problems, one should look at the methods available and determine the most practical way to solve these problems now and not spend the time on some vague plan in the unspecified future.

disagree totally   agree totally

     1   2   3   4   S = ____

I: To deal with environmental problems, one should look at all the possibilities that exist now and, more important, could exist and take a broad, long-range view of the situation. A quick fix to the problem should be avoided.

disagree totally   agree totally

     1   2   3   4   I = ____

To discover your research typology:

1. Enter your T, F, I, and S numbers in the spaces provided.

2. Fill in the table by computing the sums of T + I in cell I,

   T + S in cell II, S + F in cell III, and I + F in cell IV.

3. Your research style(s) is (are) the cell(s) with the largest

   sum.

4. Underline the style(s) with the largest sum.

	T-value: ____	**F-value:** ___
I-value: ___	I.	IV.
S-value: ___	II.	III.

I. Conceptual Theorist   II. Analytical Scientist
III. Particular Humanist   IV. Conceptual Humanist

What follows is a description of the archetype associated with each of the research styles above. See if the research style (s) you have underlined suits your style of inquiry.

I. Conceptual Theorist. This type of researcher believes in TOE, i.e., the Theory of Everything. A conceptual theorist is holistic and imaginative. He or she believes in multiple causations and the development of a coherent testable framework through large-scale correlation. Science holds a definite privilege in this type of thinking but it is not the only way that a conceptual theorist views a problem. Motto: Intellectual conflict is an important characteristic of research and should not be dismissed. Such conflict is vital to the development of both methods and theories. The following methodologies would likely appeal to a conceptual theorist: correlational studies, factor analyses, descriptive research, repertory grid analysis, Q-methodology, and Delphi study.

II. Analytical Scientist. This type of researcher prefers exactness, precision, and unambiguous situations. Science is also paramount and exact in this type of thinking. The analytical scientist sees science as ruled by nature. The ideal experiment is one where all the variables are controlled. Motto: In order to label something a scientific theory, it must be cast into a logical form so that, given the proper antecedent conditions (X,A), one can make the valid deduction (Y). Otherwise (according to the analytical science view) it is nonscientific. The following methodologies would likely appeal to an analytical scientist: experimental design, quasi-experimental design, semiotics, trend analysis, design-based research, regression-discontinuity design, and retrospective record review.

III. Particular Humanist. This type of researcher prefers personal knowledge to rational knowledge. Science is not privileged in this type of thinking and is subordinate to other disciplines such as poetry and literature. The particular humanist believes that humans are too complex to study as a whole. Motto: It is absurd to think that science has remained immune to outside influences. The challenge is to develop a methodology that does justice not only to the humanity of the participants studied but to the researcher as well. Only a person who is passionately involved in his or her research can make a difference. The following methodologies would likely appeal to a particular humanist: case study, appreciative inquiry, action research, semiology, phenomenology, grounded theory, critical incident technique, and hermeneutics.

IV.   Conceptual Humanist. This type of researcher prefers holistic knowledge. Science has no special privilege in this type of thinking. Knowledge exists only to better humanity. To further understand humanity, a conceptual humanist believes that one must study human behavior from many points of view and constantly develop new approaches to improve human life based on these observations. Motto: The question is not, "Is storytelling science?" but "Can science be used for the betterment of humanity?" The following methodologies would likely appeal to a conceptual humanist: grounded theory, phenomenology, evaluative case study, causal-comparative research, historical research, appreciative inquiry, content analysis, Delphi method.

Note: If you found this test effective and have the luxury of selecting your own faculty advisor(s), you might want to determine what type of researcher(s) they are. Offer to conduct this test with potential advisors to see if you have compatible research styles.

Below are research topics that would likely appeal to the people with archetypes described above who wish to conduct an investigation of the relationship between smoking and health. Note: Smoking is the leading cause of statistics☺ . Read each research topic and see if the research topic described for your archetype appeals to you.

If asked to choose a research topic on smoking and health, where funding is not a concern, the following topics would be of interest to:

I.   Conceptual Theorist: Determine the correlation between smoking and diseases, smoking and personality types, why people smoke, and as many multiple correlations as one can ascertain between smoking and other factors.

II.   Analytical Scientist: Determine definitively if cigarette smoking causes cancer. Simulate smoking in laboratory animals and determine if cancer is caused.

III.   Particular Humanist: Study a smoker and determine why this person started smoking and any ill effects attributed to smoking. Have cancer patients who have smoked keep a diary and study their feelings and concerns.

IV. Conceptual Humanist. Survey ex-smokers and determine the most effective ways each person was able to stop smoking. Use this information to develop a program to help people stop smoking.

Choosing Your Research Method: A Glossary

There are many types of research methods and designs. The list below can be helpful in choosing a research method that can help you solve the problem you are investigating and answer your research questions. This list is by no means exhaustive, but it can be helpful to understand and appreciate the variety of research methods available. Further elaboration on some of these methods will come later in this text. If you have any questions about, or need further information about, any of these very basic descriptions of research, you should do a Web search and learn more about the method. Once you select a methodology, you need to obtain a germinal text on the method. Such texts provide a *cookbook* that a dissertation *chef* will consult frequently during each stage of the *meal* preparation.

Look over this list and put a check (✓) next to methods that seem appealing, an × next to ones that seem unappealing, and a dash (-) next to ones that you have no opinion about. You need to make a decision about the methodology that would work best for your study. Finding a methodology that works for you is a major milestone in the research process. You may also want to check out http://tinyurl.com/3xf6ljx for further guidance.

- **Action research**: This methodology is based on a grass-roots problem negotiated between the researcher and the researched. It is known by many other names, including participatory research, collaborative inquiry, emancipatory research, action learning, and contextural action research, but all are variations on a theme. Usually a members of a group identify a problem, do something to resolve it, see how successful their efforts were, and, if not completely satisfied, try again. Thus, there is a dual commitment in action research to study a system and concurrently to collaborate with members of the system in changing it in what is together regarded as a desirable direction. Accomplishing this twin goal requires the active collaboration of researcher and client, and thus it stresses the importance of colearning as a primary aspect of the research process (Zuber-Skerritt, 1996).

- **Appreciative inquiry**: This is a form of action research that attempts to help groups, organizations, and communities create new, generative images for themselves based on an affirmative understanding of their past. Working from a socio-rationalist theory of change (Barrett, Thomas, & Hocevar, 1995; Bushe, 1995; Cooperrider, 1990; Gergen, 1990), these new images are expected to lead to developmental changes in the systems in which they are created.

- **Case study research**: Here the background, programs, current conditions, and environmental interactions of one or more classrooms, communities, schools, or institutions are observed, recorded, and analyzed in an attempt to find patterns of internal and external influences. Case study research generally answers one or more questions that begin with "how" or "why." The questions are targeted to a limited number of events or conditions and their interrelationships. Because case study research generates a large amount of data from multiple sources, systematic organization of the data is important to prevent the researcher from becoming overwhelmed by the amount of data and to prevent the researcher from losing sight of the original research purpose and questions. The case study method can be used to build upon theory, to produce new theory, to dispute or challenge theory, to explain a situation, to provide a basis to apply solutions to situations, or to explore or describe an object or phenomenon. The advantages of the case study method are its applicability to real-life, contemporary, human situations and its public accessibility through written reports. Case study results relate directly to the common reader's everyday experience and can facilitate an understanding of complex real-life situations.

- **Causal-comparative research**: Here the objective is to identify causal relationships among variables that cannot be manipulated. Variables that cannot be changed normally are variables such as sex, origin of birth, and ethnicity. Causal research is used to determine whether variables cause or affect one or more outcome variables. This study involves no direct manipulation. However, controversy exists as to whether the name causal is appropriate and if a relationship is found it could likely be the result of the operation of a third variable. To learn more check out:

http://it.coe.uga.edu/itforum/paper43/paper43.html

- **Content analysis**: Here the researcher quantifies and analyzes the presence, meanings, and relationships of words and concepts and then makes inferences about the messages within the texts, the writer(s), the audience, and even the culture and time of which these are a part. Klaus Krippendorff (1980) defined content analysis as "a research technique for making replicable and valid inferences from texts (or data) to a context of their use." That is, it refers to methods for inferring meaning from the text. Content analysis involves computer programs used to help analyze textual materials, such as presidential speeches, government documents, party platforms, newspaper editorials, professional publications, and so on. By analyzing words and texts rather than numbers, content analysis fits in the qualitative paradigm. Texts can be defined broadly as books, book chapters, essays, interviews, discussions, newspaper headlines and articles, historical documents, speeches, conversations, advertising, theater, informal conversation, or really any occurrence of communicative language (Weber, 1990). Babbie (1998) described the method as unobtrusive. Researchers often attempt to uncover the validity of commonly held views by looking at the artifacts that report on those views. Babbie discussed a feminist researcher that looked at a group of classic children's stories for the role stereotyping of girls looking for a Prince Charming character. The researcher compared the characters in a variety of stories and noted similarities and differences in the portrayal of young women in the stories. Content analysis lends itself to the genre of political or social change research intent on promoting a particular point of view. Therein lay its strengths and weaknesses. For more information check out http://tinyurl.com/33p274k.
- **Correlational research**: Here the researcher collects data to determine whether, and to what degree, a relationship exists between two or more quantifiable variables. When

there is a particular situation and an outcome is consistently occurring in that situation, causation might be suspected. Correlation is more of a descriptive aspect of the events that appear to be taking place concurrently. Causation must be proved beyond a reasonable doubt. According to Davis (see http://tinyurl.com/2gpkv8),

> The designs for this kind of a research are founded on the assumption that reality is best described as a network of interacting and mutually causal relationships. Everything affects—and is affected by—everything else. This web of relationships in not necessarily linear, as assumed in experimental research.

- **Critical incident technique** (CIT): CIT had its origins in the 1950s when researchers started to focus studies on human behavior and quantifying it. Founded by John C. Flanagan in 1954, CIT supports the theory that there must be a clearly demarcated event for it to be considered a critical incident. If a detailed account of an event cannot be obtained, the incident is thrown out because the incident itself is the basic unit of analysis.

- **Delphi research**: Here the focus is future oriented. The Delphi technique was originally used to target future problems and foresee solutions. The method involves utilizing the knowledge of experts, combining it, and redistributing it. The study opens up doors and forces new thought processes to emerge. It also allows for respondents to see how closely they responded to other experts in their field and to justify their train of thought (McPhillip, 1997; Lindstone & Turoff, 1975).

- **Descriptive research**: This does not fit neatly into the definition of either quantitative or qualitative research methodologies, but instead can utilize elements of both, often within the same study. Descriptive research is the study of phenomenon "as it is" without making any "changes or modifications" (Leedy & Ormrod, 2001, p. 191). Unlike experimental research, there is no treatment that is manipulated or controlled by the researcher. This research method is not used to determine "cause and effect" relationships (Leedy & Ormrod, 2001, p. 191). Types of descriptive research include correlational studies, developmental studies, and observation studies. Descriptive research involves gathering data that describe events and then organizing, tabulating, depicting, and describing the data collected. Here the researcher will describe systematically the facts and characteristics of a given population or area of interest accurately and within a contextual framework. A descriptive study tries to discover answers to the questions who, what, when, where, and sometimes how. The researcher attempts to describe or define a topic, often by creating a profile of a group of problems, people, or events. The descriptive study is popular in business research because of its versatility across disciplines (Cooper & Schindler, 2002).

- **Design-based research or decision analysis**: Here the practitioner and researcher models merge to produce meaningful change in the context of practices. It is a way to link process to outcomes in a particular setting. Researchers in the decision analysis field have often encountered difficulties in transforming theoretical ideas into practical decision support tools.

- **Ethnographic**: Here the researcher looks at an entire group—more specifically, a group that shares a common culture—in depth. The researcher studies the group in its natural setting for a lengthy period of time, often several months or even several years. The focus of investigation is on the everyday behaviors (e.g., interactions, language, rituals) of the people in the group, with intent to identify cultural norms, beliefs, social structures, and other cultural patterns. Ethnography has it roots in the fields of anthropology and sociology. Present-day practitioners conduct ethnographies in organizations and communities of all kinds. According to Agar (1996), ethnographers can study schooling, public health, rural and urban development, consumers and consumer goods, and any human arena. While particularly suited to exploratory research, ethnography draws on a wide range of both qualitative and quantitative methodologies, moving from *learning* to *testing* while research problems, perspectives, and theories emerge and shift.

- **Evaluation research**: Here research is undertaken to determine the effectiveness or impact of a social program or intervention and whether a program or curriculum followed the prescribed procedures and achieved the stated outcomes, sometimes referred to as summative evaluation research. Five main areas to evaluate are outcomes, process, costs, comparisons, and generalizability: http://tinyurl.com/2k7n25.

- **Experimental research**: Here one or more variables are manipulated and the results analyzed in a scientific manner. A major strength of this methodology, gained from random assignment of participants, is its internal validity: One can be more *certain* about attributing a cause to the independent variables. A major weakness is external threats to validity: It is inappropriate to generalize beyond the results of the experiment.

- **Factor analyses**: Here the researcher uses a statistical approach to analyze interrelationships among a large number of variables and explain these variables in terms of their common underlying dimensions (factors). The information contained in the number of original variables is condensed to a smaller set of dimensions (factors) with a minimum loss of information

- **Grounded theory**: Here the researcher seeks to generate a theory that explains a process or action. The researcher would use this design for developing theories through primary interviewing, developing patterns or themes, and composing a visual that describe this theory. Creswell (2002) says in this way the theory is *grounded* in the data from the participants. The researcher can then develop hypothesis and predictions about the experiences of individuals. Creswell (2002) warned that the researcher must be careful about making a premature commitment to a set of analytical categories. There are three general designs in grounded theory: systematic, emerging, and constructivist (Creswell, 2005). The systematic design by Strauss and Corbin (1998) represents the most rigorous type of grounded theory because it uses specific data analysis steps. The emerging design by Glaser (1992) stresses letting a theory emerge from the data rather than forcing data into a systematic model. The constructivist design by Charmaz (2000) focuses on using "views, values, beliefs, feelings, assumptions, and ideologies" (Creswell, 2005, p. 402) rather than facts and observable acts. In their classic text *Discovery of Grounded Theory*, Glaser and Strauss (1967) described what they believe to be the primary goal of qualitative research: the generation of theory, rather than theory testing or mere description. According to this view, theory is not a "perfected product" but an "ever-developing entity" or process (p. 32). Glaser and Strauss claimed that one of the requisite properties of grounded theory is that it be "sufficiently general to be applicable to a multitude of diverse situations within the substantive area" (p. 237). What differentiates grounded theory from most other research methods is that it is explicitly emergent. The grounded theory researcher sets out to discover what theory accounts for the research situation as it is, grounded in the data. In this respect it is like action research: the aim is to understand the research situation. The aim, as Glaser in particular states it, is to discover the theory implicit in the data.

- **Hermeneutic research**: Here activities and things are seen as a text, and studied for what they mean, what they mean to those involved in them, and what they mean to others. Historically, hermeneutics has been associated with the interpretation of biblical texts and encompasses the attempt to explore and identify the process of understanding (Babbie, 1998). Hermeneutics emphasizes the sociocultural and historic influences on inquiry. According to Thompson (1990), hermeneutics was "derived from the Greek verb, hermeneueuein, 'to interpret,' and from the noun, hermeneia, or 'interpretation'" (p. 230). In the social sciences, this looks like research into the metacognitve realm—a participant interprets his or her life by some process that a hermeneuticist attempts to discover. A researcher might be interested in teachers' adoption of technology in the classroom. A teacher might say there is no time to learn the computer, and probing and observation might uncover that fear of failure is actually the root cause limiting the teacher's use of the technology. The researcher reconsiders time as the obstacle and begins to look at how the teacher reconciles the interaction with the computer and the lessening of the fear of the unknown with time to spend learning the skills. The hermeneutic researcher attempts to discover the processes needed to move beyond denial.

- **Historical research**: Here the life activities of an organization or person are related, with insights about their significance and meanings being explicated. Both quantitative and qualitative variables can be used in the collection of historical information. For more on historical research check out http://tinyurl.com/38uvj94

- **Meta-analysis research**: Here data are collected from several studies on a similar area to find patterns and formulate principles whose goal is to guide future organizational decisions and actions. http://tinyurl.com/35js764

- **Narrative research**: Here the researcher focuses on the study of a single person, gathering data through the collection of stories and reporting individual experiences. The researcher retells stories reported by individuals and focuses on events or activities so they can be analyzed for categories or themes. Creswell (2002) identified the following for strengths and weakness.
    - Strengths – Establish a close bond with the participants. Can bring a participant's voice to the forefront.
    - Weakness – Might tell the researcher's story and not the participant's. The gain the researcher might get could be at the expense of the participant.

- **Needs assessment**: A needs assessment is the first step for any institution or organization considering the development of a new program, product, or treatment. Institutions and organizations must establish the existence of a market demand for their program, product, or treatment. If one exists, they must determine the market demography and the potential audience's specific needs.

- **Phenomenography**: This is an empirical research tradition designed to answer questions about thinking and learning, especially in the context of educational research. It is concerned with the relationships that people have with the world around them. The word *phenomenography* has Greek etymological roots. It is derived from the words *phainonmenon* (appearance) and *graphein* (description). Thus, *phenomenography* is a "description of appearances" (Hasselgren & Beach, 1997).

- **Phenomenology**: Here the meaning of an experience is narrated using story and description. Phenomenology is an attempt by qualitative researchers to "discover participants' lived experiences and how they make sense of them" (Babbie, 1998, p. 281). Phenomenologists focus on persons who have shared the same experiences and on eliciting commonalities and shared meanings. For example, a researcher might want to know how the voters of Palm Beach County, Florida, viewed the controversy surrounding the presidential election of 2000. The election was a specific event and the voters might have a variety of responses that can be analyzed for common threads. The research is very personal, and the results are written more as stories than as principles, yet the researcher stays somewhat detached. In heuristic research, the researcher is more intimately connected to the study.

Note: Qualitative researchers tend to use the term transferability rather than generalizability (Rubin, 2007). Rubin posited that findings from qualitative studies can be transferable to a particular group (small or large) versus generalizing the finding to a population. Hence, a good qualitative study provides a large quantity of information that helps the reader decide the applicability of the finding to their specific need or practice.

- **Quasi-experimental**: When a true experimental design is not available to a researcher for various reasons, e.g., where intact groups are already formed, when treatment cannot be withheld from a group, or when no appropriate control or comparison groups are available, the researcher can use a quasi-experimental design. As in the case of the true experimental design, quasi-experiments involve the manipulation of one or more independent variables and the measurement of a dependent variable. There are three major categories of quasi-experimental design: the nonequivalent-groups designs, cohort designs, and time-series designs (Cook & Campbell, 1979).

- **Q-Method**: This method was first developed in the 1930s by British physicist-psychologist William Stephenson. It is the systematic study of subjectivity. According to Stephenson (1953), the goal of Q-method is to uncover different patterns of thought. Studies using Q-method typically use small sample sizes. The results of these studies are less influenced by low response rates compared with the results of survey studies. The qualitative methods of Q-method allow participants to express their subjective opinions and the quantitative methods of Q-method use factor analytic data reduction and induction to provide insights into opinion formation as well as to generate testable hypotheses. Q-method research emphasizes the qualitative how and why people think the way they do. http://www.qmethod.org/about.php.

- **Regression-discontinuity design** (RD): Here the researcher determines whether a program or treatment is effective. In RD designs, participants are assigned to a program or comparison groups solely on the basis of a cutoff score on a preprogram measure. Thus the RD design is distinguished from randomized experiments (or randomized clinical trials) and from other quasi-experimental strategies by its unique method of assignment. RD is most appropriate when a researcher wishes to target a program or treatment to those who most need or deserve it. http://tinyurl.com/293nm6v

- **Retrospective record review**: Here the researcher analyzes a treatment from data that have already been collected. A data source must be identified that contains information on those who were exposed to an intervention or condition and those who were not. The data source must contain information on the outcomes of interest in both groups. Comparisons can then be made on the association of particular outcomes with exposure to the intervention of interest. It is important that the two groups share similar demographic or risk factors that could influence the occurrence of a targeted outcome.

- **Semiology**: Here the researcher studies the meaning of symbols. Taken in its broadest sense, it deals with the systems of meaning through which a culture is manifested. The language may be verbal visual, etc., and transmitted through symbols, colors, graphic styles, etc. Supporters believe that semiology has great promise to model several aspects of human thought and action. http://tinyurl.com/27evesx

- **Trend analysis research**: Here the researcher attempts to predict or forecast the future direction of organizational activities. It is a form of regression analysis used to discover linear and nonlinear relationships. The trend analysis module allows the researcher to plot aggregated response data over time. This is especially valuable when conducting a long-running survey and the researcher would like to measure differences in perception and responses over time. http://www.questionpro.com/trend/

- **True Experimental research:** Here the researcher structures the research situation by creating a true experiment that isolates the variable of interest and controls for other confounding examples. Experimental design is the "gold standard" approach for testing a particular treatment or procedure, and is often used in psychological or medical research. http://tinyurl.com/3x8utm4.

Check out http://socialresearchmethods.net/ for more information on choosing a research method.

 Cutting Board

1. Which of these studies appealed the most to you?
   _____

2. Which appealed the least to you?
   _____

3. Did you approve of the study defined for your archetype? ____ Explain:
   _____

4. Which three methodologies appeal to you the most?
   _____
   Why?_____

5. Which three methodologies appeal the least to you? _____
   Why? _____

Keep this knowledge in mind when you select your dissertation topic. Check out http://tinyurl.com/2vkamsn for more suggestions on choosing a topic to research.

½ cup "C" lassify Yourself Professionally

Now that you have an idea about your research style, it is important that you take this opportunity to objectively classify yourself within your profession. Choosing a project that will sustain your enthusiasm, help you remain dedicated, and enable you to complete it in a reasonable amount of time requires an *ample serving* of knowing who you are professionally, what attracted you to your discipline, and what *nourishes* your interest in your profession.

By using a process in which you will be going from a broad to a narrow perspective, you will be able to discern a researchable project that you are capable of pursuing with vigor. Be aware, however, that once you are immersed in your research, you might decide to change or modify your focus. Be assured that each time you modify your study you are more knowledgeable and have fewer obstacles to overcome. One excellent way to find a topic is to network with other researchers around the globe. With the Internet this can be easily accomplished by joining Listservs. A review of the literature often reveals a topic worthy of researching. Also, most dissertations have a section called Recommendations for Future Research. This could be another excellent way to find the problem you wish to work on.

The Cutting Board that follows can also assist you in formulating a dissertation topic. Dr. M. will share with you how she obtained her dissertation topic. You will be referred to as Dr. I during this exploratory activity. (Remember to keep in mind what a dissertation is and is not and what your research typology told you about how you like to investigate a problem.)

 Cutting Board

1. What is (are) your professional role(s) or the role that you are seeking (e.g., are you an educator, physician, nurse, administrator, actress, lawyer, political scientist, manager, accountant, salesperson, media person, anthropologist, engineer, computer scientist)?

    Dr. M. is an educator.

    Dr. I. is

2. What is (are) your principal area(s) of interest (PI) or your subspecialty within your profession?

Dr. M. is a mathematics educator and consultant.

Dr. I. is _____

3. What area(s) of your PI are you most enthusiastic about or involved with? (What made you decide to go into this profession? What keeps you in the profession?)

Dr. M. is interested and involved with helping people overcome mathematics anxiety, technology in the classroom, teacher training, statistics, and the future of mathematics education. She enjoys mathematics and believes that every person can be successful in mathematics if they are given the opportunity to do math their way.

Dr. I. is interested and involved with:

The reasons Dr. I chose this profession are:

---

4. What are some problems that you are interested in that you believe need some new light or need to be looked at critically for the first time?

Dr. M. believes that calculators are not being used in the elementary school classroom because of the anxiety of elementary school teachers.

Dr. I. believes that:

_____

5. Restate the most pressing problem you have described using a preferred style of inquiry and/or method:

Dr. M. (a conceptual theorist who favors correlational research): What is the relationship between mathematics anxiety and lack of calculator use in the classroom?

Dr. I.: _____

6. Select a title (topic) based on this problem:

Dr. M.: *The Wasted Resource: Attitudinal Problems in Calculator Use among Elementary School Teachers.*

Dr. I.:

> Note: Your title is limited to 15 words. The title needs to be very clear, and provide readers with information about what to expect from the research paper. The problem and the type of investigation should be discernable from the title.

Fantastic! You have yourself a research topic, Dr. I. Now, before you start your celebration, you will need to (K)conduct the ROC bottom test to see if the topic you have selected has the attributes of researchability and originality and if it is contributory.

1 cup "K" (c)onduct the ROC bottom test

1/3 cup	**R** esearchability
1/3 cup	**O** riginality
1/3 cup	**C** ontributory

1/3 cup "R" esearchability

Use the Cutting Board that follows to test whether your topic is researchable. You should be able to answer "yes" to the majority of questions below.

If this is not the case, then you might want to go *FISH*, **F**ind **I**nterest **S**omewhere **H**enceforth. (You would probably not want to plan a *dinner* of an exotic *Asian fish* that you could not obtain to a group of *vegetarians* who would not *eat* this *fish* even if you somehow managed to obtain it), would you?

 Cutting Board

1. How do you know that the research problem is important?
   _____

2. What are the journals, texts, and periodicals that deal with this topic?
   _____

3. What Web sites you can visit to obtain information?
   _____

4. How can you obtain access to files and documents you will need?

    _____

5. How will you access a sample of your population or the population itself?

    _____

6. How will you know when you have obtained the information you are seeking?

    _____

7. How will you obtain authorization to do your research?

    _____

8. How do you know that the research is free of any ethical problems?

    _____

9. What knowledge and skills do you have to conduct the research?

    _____

10. What are your qualifications to undertake this research?

    _____

11. How will you obtain the support of people that are essential to your project?

    _____

12. Do you have the financial resources you need to conduct the study?

    _____

13. How will you overcome the limitations and obstacles needed to conduct the study?

    _____

1/3 cup "O" riginality

According the Council of Graduate Schools (2005)
(http://www.socialresearchmethods.net/kb/index.htm), in its most general sense, *original*
describes research that has not been done previously or a project that creates new knowledge; it
implies that there is some novel twist, fresh perspective, new hypothesis, or innovative method
that makes the research project a distinctive and unique contribution. An original project,
although built on existing research, should not duplicate someone else's work.

A "yes" to one or more question on the Cutting Board below will satisfy the "O" requirement and indicate that your topic has originality. If all the answers are no's, you might want to go *FISH*.

Cutting Board

1. Will this study provide some new way to look at an existing problem? ___

2. Will this be a missing piece to an existing problem? ___

3. Is this a new contradiction to an accepted point of view? ___

4. Is this a new way to look at a historical work? ___

5. Is this a recommendation from a published study? ___

6. Is this a repetitive study using a different population or another look at a population studied after the passage of time? ___

7. Is this a new approach to an old problem? ___

8. Will this be the first time a program or treatment is being evaluated in this manner? ___

1/3 cup "C" ontributory

That which is not worth doing is not worth doing well. —A. Maslow, 1970

Simple curiosity is not a good enough reason to perform doctoral research, i.e., carry out research for research's sake. A "yes" to at least one question on the Cutting Board below will satisfy the "C" requirement and indicate that your research will be contributory. If all the answers are no's, you might want to go *FISH*.

 *Cutting Board*

1. Is there a need in your profession, community, or society to know the results of this study? ____

2. Will there be people in your profession or people who plan to enter this profession who will be need the information that this study will ascertain? ____

3. Will people outside of your profession gain new insight into something in your profession after this study is complete? ____

4. Will some members of society, or society at large, suffer if this study is NOT done? ____

5. Will the results of the study likely change the perception of people in your field or profession? ____

Once you have passed the ROC bottom test, you will have made a major step toward obtaining your goal. Congratulations! You should feel proud and happy.

> Note: A doctoral dissertation or formal research project must have a very high level of quality and integrity. The entire research project and paper must be clear, lucid, and logical; have an appropriate theoretical base; contain appropriate statistical analysis (if needed); and have proper citations.

Now that you have nailed down your topic, you will need to develop a solid problem statement. When this major task is accomplished, put this statement in your working environment and carry a copy of it with you whenever you are working on your dissertation. It is important to never lose sight of what you are researching and why you are conducting this research.

Cutting Board

In bold print write out your research topic again in the space below:

_____

The Problem Statement

The greatest challenge to any thinker is stating the problem in a way that will allow a solution.
—Bertrand Russell (1872 - 1970)

The heart of a doctoral dissertation, and most formal research projects, IS the PROBLEM STATEMENT. This is the place where most assessors go first to understand and appraise the merits of your proposal or your research. After reading the problem statement, the reader will know why you are doing (did) this study and be convinced of its importance. In 250 words or less (about 1–3 paragraphs) you need to convince the reader that this study must be (had to be) done!

The reason you write a doctoral dissertation or formal research study is because society, or one of its institutions, has some pressing problem that needs closer attention. The problem statement delineates this problem while hinting at the nature of the study—correlation, evaluative, historical, experimental, etc.—that is, how you will (did) solve the problem. A problem is appropriate for doctoral research if the problem leads to a "study [that] will contribute to knowledge and practice" (Creswell, 2005, p. 64). To paraphrase Maslow (1970), a problem not worth solving is not worth solving well.

Once a clear and lucid problem statement is formed, all the research you put into your dissertation should be focused on obtaining a solution. You will be judged by the degree to which you find the answer to the problem you pose and thus achieve your purpose.

Warning: Do not solve a problem in research as a ruse for achieving self-enlightenment.

Note: A problem (or research question) that results in a "yes" or "no" response is not suitable for formal research. For example, a problem such as determining how many hours of homework is appropriate for elementary school students is not a research problem, but the researcher can form a suitable problem statement around this topic with a bit of finesse. If you can present evidence that elementary school students and parents do not understand why students are given several hours of homework a day, then a study can be designed to determine what benefits, if any, homework has for elementary school students. Determining if stock options are beneficial for employee morale is not a problem (actually it is a proposed solution) and is not appropriate for research, because this statement leads to a binary conclusion (either it is beneficial or not). However, if a problem exists retaining quality employees, then a study can be conducted to determine what types of benefits can increase job commitment.

A problem statement that is too narrowly focused might direct the researcher only toward trivia. A statement that is too broad might not adequately delineate the relationships or concepts involved in the study. Development of a well-constructed problem statement leads to the logical outgrowth of well-constructed research questions or hypotheses and supports all aspects of a research project. Many researchers have difficulty formulating a succinct problem statement. The following activity can assist you in preparing a *delectable* problem statement. Further suggestions are offered in **PHASE 3**.

 Cutting Board

By answering the following questions, you will be able to develop *mouth-watering* problem statement. Fill in the blanks as best you can, and from these *ingredients* try to *cook up a delicious* problem statement.

1. What is the problem? _____

2. Where is this problem found (what profession(s), subspecialty)? [This will help in your literature review]

   _____

3. What are some of the ill effects of this problem on society at large and/or some subset of society? [This will help with your background section]

   _____

4. Why are you interested in this problem? [This will help in your significance statement] Why would someone else be interested in this problem?

   _____

5. Who is affected? (What group would care about this problem?) [This will help define the sample and population and help justify significance] What part of this problem can this study help solve? _____

6. How can this study help (assist in making wiser choices, debunk a myth)? [This will help define your purpose and significance]

   _____

7. What professional value will the research have? (Clarify an ambiguous point or theory, look at a new aspect of a problem, aid in an important decision-making process, etc.)

[This helps establish the purpose and significance] What journal would be interested in publishing this study?_____ _____

8. What needs to be done (analyze, describe, evaluate, test, understand, determine). [This will help decide the method(s) and instruments to be used]

   _____

9. What topics, subjects, or issues are involved (stock market, drugs, violence, language development, glass ceiling, assessment, euthanasia, etc.) [This will help in the literature review] _____

10. How does the study relate to the development or the refinement of theory? [This will help with your theoretical framework]

    _____

11. What could result from this study (clarify, debunk, relieve, assist, create, recommend)? [This will help in interpreting the results] _____

12. What harm would (could) be done if this study was NOT done? [This will help with the significance of the study].

    _____

13. (optional) What has already been done about it? What hasn't been done? Who is requesting such a study? [This will help with your literature review].

    _____

FOR YOUR INFORMATION AND EDUCATION

The problem statement gives us the "why" a study is needed. The purpose statement explains "what" your study will accomplish. The purpose statement succinctly creates direction, scope, and the means of data collection. The objectives are formulated in a way that assures the reader that they can be obtained, and once these are accomplished, the problem will be solved.

Note: Sometimes there is confusion in constructing the following components of a dissertation: problem statement, research question, purpose statement, significance, theoretical framework, and hypothesis. The following example might help differentiate these sections.

Problem: A family is *hungry*.

Research Question: What can be done to resolve a *hunger* problem?

Purpose: Gather *flour, cheese, sauce, pepperoni, and tomatoes* to make a *pizza* to relieve this family's *hunger* pains.

Significance: The family will be happier once they are *satiated*.

Theoretical Framework: Drive reduction theory -- internal physiological needs create motivational states known as drives. This theory explains *hunger* in terms of a deficit within the body.

Hypothesis: *Eating* a *pizza* will relieve *hunger* pains.

Null Hypothesis: *Eating* a *pizza* will not relieve *hunger* pains.

According to Merriam (1988), there are three basic types of research problems: Conceptual, Action, and Value (CAVe).

A *conceptual problem* is two juxtaposed elements that are conceptually or theoretically inconsistent. This is the way it should be—this is the way it is. For example, short-term economic and political interests can limit the vision of a corporation and inhibit the achievement of long-term improvement, or we would like the top undergraduate students to be teachers but the entry salary is not commensurate with the salaries these students could earn.

Sample Conceptual Problem Statement:

The Iowa State Park system's first mission is to protect and preserve the State Parks for their natural beauty and delicate ecosystems. The second mission is to provide an outdoor recreational resource for the general public. Foot traffic, vehicle traffic, tents, fires, boats, and facilities for the public contribute to the degradation of the protected natural elements of the State Parks. This degradation costs Federal and State governments hundreds of millions of dollars. Both missions are necessary but a balance based on science and public interest demands is sometimes hard to negotiate. A study using a modified Delphi technique to target future problems and foresee solutions utilizing the knowledge of environmental experts, combining it and redistributing it, could be used to offer viable solutions to this problem. [See Dalkey (1984)]

An *action problem* arises when a conflict offers no clear choice of an alternative course of action. An undesirable outcome results from an apparent lack of choices. For example, hazardous material responders at UPS are required to wear personal protective equipment when responding to a spill, but the gear is not always available at the places where the spills are located, or students are required to use the Internet for their homework assignments but do not have access to computers.

Sample: Action Problem Statement:

Bullying is one of the most critical issues facing school-age children. Beane (1999) found that 1 in 7 children is subjected to bullying behavior and that it affects about 5 million elementary and junior high students. Bullies who once cornered their victims on the playground are now tormenting them online (Blair, 2003). E-mail messages and Web sites have increasingly become vehicles to threaten, tease, and humiliate other students. Incidents of online bullying can be just as hurtful as face-to-face bullying, yet are less likely to be detected or prevented by adults. Program PCBN (Prevent Cyber Bullying Now) was designed to help families understand how to prevent, address, and report cyberbullying, cyberharassment, and cyberabuses. It is important that an evaluative case study be conducted to determine the efficacy of PCBN and determine if this program reduces online bullying.

The value problem arises when there is a conflict about what people consider ethical, moral, worthwhile, or desirable. The following are examples of value problems: employees who believe their dress is a matter of freedom of choice and companies requiring a dress code or the desire to have a multicultural student body and the removal of affirmative action programs.

Sample: Value Problem Statement:

Although Latinos represent 12.7% of the workforce, there exists a significant lack of Hispanics in leadership positions in the United States (Charles, 2007; U.S. Department of Labor Bureau of Labor Statistics [USDLBLS], 2003). This is particularly true in the field of public school education, in which 16.3% (National Council of La Raza, 2004) of the student body is Hispanic but only 4.1% of secondary school principals are Hispanic. A phenomenological study of successful Hispanic educational leaders and the intrinsic and extrinsic values that have supported their efforts toward the achievement of leadership roles, while overcoming prevalent challenges, is important and can add meaningfully to the leadership literature.

Cutting Board

1. To help you develop your problem statement, fill in the blanks:

   There is a problem in _____ (societal organization). Despite _____ (something that should be happening), _____ is occurring. This problem has negatively impacted _____ (victims of problem) because _____.
   A possible cause of this problem is _____. Perhaps a study that investigates _____ by _____ (method) could remedy the situation.

2. Use the following checklist to make certain the problem statement meets doctoral level requirements.

PROBLEM STATEMENT page 200-250 words	Average of ½ - ¾
1. General Problem/Observation identifying the need for the study, with sufficient current evidence and data to support the extent of the problem.	
2. Specific "Problem" proposed for research; the problem statement is clear, concise, and reflective of the purpose statement. Evidence is provided that this is a current problem. However the words *current* or *today* should not be in the problem statement.	
3. Introductory words describing method and research design are given and are appropriate to the "problem."	
4. **General** population group of proposed study is identified.	
5. Sufficient evidence is provided to convince the reader that the problem is current and solvable.	
6. The gap in the literature is explained.	
7. The problem statement is written in a scholarly voice with APA formatting and no grammatical errors.	
8. The problems statement does not exceed 250 words	
9. There are no unnecessary words.	
10. The problem is in accord with the university or program mission.	

3. Rework the problem so that it includes all the components of a good problem statement.

4. In big and bold letters, write your problem statement in the space below. Be aware that this will likely be modified as you proceed to put the other components of your study together.

Keep this with you whenever you are conducting your research!

To check the feasibility of your research project, check out http://tinyurl.com/3xx8bfb

CLASSIFY YOUR REPAST: HOW WILL YOU COOK UP YOUR STUDY?

The value of research is defined by how the work underway fits into the overall context of the theory or paradigm being researched. Thus, researchers must be fully cognizant of why they are doing what they are doing and what they expect the return on their efforts to be. —T. Gilovitch, 1991.

Quantitative and Qualitative Research

There are two major paradigms for doing research: quantitative and qualitative. Deciding if you should go with a predominantly qualitative or quantitative design is like making a choice regarding what type of food you would like for dinner while dining out: American food or ethnic food? Once you decide the general type of food, you need to choose the restaurant (the particular type of methodology). Then you can select your meal (use the method to solve the problem you pose).

Quantitative research is "a formal, objective, systematic process, in which numerical data are utilized to obtain information about the world" (N. Burns & Grove, as cited in Cormack, 1991, p. 140). Therefore, objectivity, generalizability, and numbers are features often associated with quantitative research. When an approach is selected to investigate a problem, it should be the most suitable approach available. However, it is also reasonable to expect that it reflects the bias of the researcher. The majority of medical research is quantitative (and considered to produce hard, generalizable results). The majority of research in the social sciences is qualitative (and considered to produce soft results). Most quantitative studies test a theory using statistics and hypothesis testing.

Qualitative methodologies favor the view that the world is holistic and that there is not a single reality. These methodologies support the view that reality, which is based on perceptions, is different for each person, changes over time, and derives meaning primarily from context. Qualitative research is conducted in a natural setting and usually involves multiple methods of data collection, collecting data that emerges with the process, is essentially interpretive and holistic, and involves personal reflection. Many qualitative studies develop hypotheses.

We will examine some of the differences between qualitative and quantitative studies.

Scientific discipline or rigor is valued because it is associated with the worth of research outcomes and studies are critiqued as a means of judging rigor. Qualitative research methods have been criticized for lack of rigor. However, the criticisms have occurred because of attempts to judge the rigor of qualitative studies using rules developed to judge quantitative studies. Rigor is defined differently for qualitative research because the desired outcome is different (J. M. Burns, 1989; Dzurec, 1989; Morse, 1989; Sandelowski, 1986).

In quantitative research, rigor is reflected in narrowness, conciseness, and objectivity and leads to rigid adherence to research designs and precise statistical analyses. Rigor in qualitative research is associated with openness, scrupulous adherence to a philosophical perspective, and thoroughness in collecting data, as well as consideration of all the data in the development of a theory. In order to be rigorous in conducting qualitative research, the researcher must be willing to let go of certain long-held beliefs that have become unshakeable, although they might be mistaken, such as that standardized tests are reliable and valid. This process is often referred to as deconstructing knowledge. The qualitative researcher will often seek to form new ideas (reconstructing) while continuing to recognize that the present paradigms exist.

Both paradigms, quantitative and qualitative, are said to be systematic. In fact, having a system or following a process is a defining principle of research. Broadly speaking, quantitative research is thought to be objective whereas qualitative research is considered subjective. This is in accord with the belief that in gaining, analyzing, and interpreting quantitative data, the researcher can remain detached and objective. Often this is not possible with qualitative research, where the researcher may actually be involved in the situation of the research. However, techniques such as bracketing can be performed to make qualitative research more objective.

If the Department of Motor Vehicles (DMV) wished to conduct a study on waiting times, a quantitative approach could be used to measure how long people wait and could be purely objective. However, if the researchers wanted to discover how the customers felt about their waiting time, they would need to come into contact with the customers and make judgments about the way they answered their questions. If a researcher asked: "How are you feeling after waiting an hour to get your license processed?" the researcher would be able to register the customer's nonverbal behavior as well as document the response. In this way the researcher is adding a subjective element to the study.

Quantitative research is inclined to be deductive. In other words it tests theory. However, since statistical analyses, often used in quantitative studies, involve investigating a sample to generalize to a population, it is also considered inductive. This is in contrast to most qualitative research, which tends to be more inductive. In other words, the main goal is to generate theories. Quantitative designs of research tend to produce results that can be generalized, whereas qualitative studies tend to produce results that are less likely to be generalized. This has to do with the problem of the sample used at the time. Let's go back to the DMV example. We all know that our feelings about waiting can change depending on our particular set of circumstances. Even if the researchers encountered the same group of customers on another day, they may find different results. Generally, it is difficult to generalize with qualitative results.

Another major difference between quantitative research and qualitative research is that quantitative research uses data that are structured in the form of numbers or that can be immediately transported into numbers. If the data cannot be structured in the form of numbers, they are considered qualitative.

Note: Qualitative data can sometimes produce quantitative data; e.g., a researcher exploring feelings of customers can analyze the responses in clusters that are negative or positive to produce a figure or percentage of negative patient and positive patient feelings and data can be analyzed using programs such as NVivo.

QUALITATIVE	QUANTITATIVE
Theory development	Theory testing
Naturalistic or organic settings	Synthetic settings
Subjective	Objective
Observations, interviews	Tests, surveys
Descriptive statistics	Descriptive and inferential statistics
Generates hypothetical propositions	Generates predictive relationships
Philosophical roots: Phenomenology	Philosophical roots: Positivism,
Goal: Understanding, description, generate hypotheses	Goal: Prediction, control, confirmation, test hypotheses

Some questions to answer in designing a qualitative study:

- Are the basic characteristics or assumptions of a qualitative study clearly stated?

- Will the reader have an understanding on how this qualitative study differs from a quantitative study?

- Is there information provided so that a reader will understand the origins of the qualitative design for this research study?

- Will the reader gain an understanding on how the experiences of the researcher shape his or her values and bias to the research?

- Is information provided on how the researcher will gain entry to research sites (if needed) and how approval will be obtained to collect data?

- Are the procedures for collecting data thoroughly and clearly discussed? Are reasons provided for the particular method of data collection?

- Are methods to code information set forth?

- Are the specific data analysis procedures identified in relation to specific research designs, such as for ethnographic approaches, grounded theory, case studies, and phenomenology?

- Is it clear how information validity and reliability will be conducted (see verification of information in qualitative study)?

- Are definitions, delimitations (boundaries), and limitations (weaknesses) stated?

- Are the research outcomes presented in view of existing theory and the literature? Is there a contribution to the existing theory base? Are you developing altogether new theory?

FOR YOUR INFORMATION AND EDUCATION

- Internal validity is the extent to which one can draw valid conclusions about the causal effects of one variable on another. It depends on the extent to which extraneous variables have been controlled by the researcher.

- Internal reliability is the extent to which items in an instrument are correlated with one another and measure the same construct. Cronbach's alpha is usually used to measure this.

- External validity is the generalizability or the extent to which the findings in the study are relevant to participants and settings beyond those in the study.

- External reliability is consistency or stability of a measure when repeated measurement gives the same result.

- Trochim (2004) http://www.socialresearchmethods.net/kb/rel&val.htm points out the relationship between reliability and validity through an interesting metaphor. He presents a set of concentric circles, where the center is the target or the true value of the variable that the researcher is trying to measure. Imagine that the instrument is a means of shooting at the target and each "shot" is a measure of the variable. If you measure the concept perfectly you hit the target at the bull's eye, if you don't, you are missing the bull's eye. If you find most of your shot points are clustered in one small place, but away from the center, the instrument is reliable, but not valid. If the points are scattered all over the target such that the mean value would be the center, the instrument is valid but not reliable. If most of your points are scattered in one half of the target, but not near the center, the instrument is neither valid nor reliable. If most of the points are near the center then your instrument is both valid and reliable.

- Other types of validity and reliability exist. For example, concurrent validity is a method of determining validity by correlating results with known objective measures. An example would be to validate a measure of political conservatism by correlating it with reported voting behavior. Construct validity hypothesizes a relationship between scores obtained for one variable with scores obtained from another variable that is known to be associated with it. For example, depression is a construct regarding a personality trait manifested by behaviors such as lethargy, loss of appetite, difficulty in concentrating on tasks, and so forth.

Verification in a Qualitative Study

Validity and reliability must be addressed in a qualitative study. The accuracy, dependability, and credibility of the information depend on it. There are various ways to address validity and reliability, including triangulation of information among different sources, receiving feedback from informants, and forming the unique interpretation of events. Creswell (1997) provides an excellent example of a qualitative procedure. The opening descriptions of the qualitative research paradigm, which has been taken from several authors (as cited in Creswell, p. 161), are as follows:

The intent of qualitative research is to understand a particular social situation, event, role, group, or interaction. It is largely an investigative process where the researcher gradually makes sense of a social phenomenon by contrasting, comparing, replicating, cataloguing and classifying the object of study. . . . This entails immersion in the everyday life of the setting chosen for the study; the researcher enters the informant's world and through ongoing interaction, seeks informants' perspectives and meanings.

According to Guba and Lincoln (1989), criteria that are meaningful within an evaluative process include the following: credibility criterion, persistent observation, member checks, and expert review.

The credibility criterion is similar to internal validity, with the focus of establishing a match between the responses of the experts (e.g., teachers, administrators, and parents in an educational study) and those realities represented by the evaluator and designer of the instrument (the researcher and the research in this study).

Persistent observation (Guba & Lincoln, 1986, pp. 303-304) requires sufficient observation to enable the evaluator to identify those characteristics and elements in the situation that are most relevant to the issue pursued and to focus on the details.

Member checking is the process of verifying information with the targeted group. It allows the stakeholder the chance to correct errors of fact or errors of interpretation. Member checks add to the validity of the observer's interpretation of qualitative observations. In your research report, make certain that you describe how the results of the check elaborated or restricted conclusions. Expert review is one of the primary evaluation strategies used in both formative (How can this program be improved?) and summative (What is the effectiveness and worth of program?) evaluation. It is often a good idea to provide experts with some sort of instrument or guide to ensure that they critique all of the important aspects of the program to be reviewed.

It is important that the number of participants in a qualitative study reach a point of sufficiency. This is achieved when a representative number of participants that are typical of demographics such as age, race, experience, and gender are selected (Seidman, 2006). In qualitative studies, there is an ongoing process of categorizing during the data analysis process. The researcher should document how initial codes lead to more elaborate codes and linkages and finally to formal data analysis. The analysis continues until theoretical saturation is achieved, that is, when no new themes or issues arise regarding a category of data and when the categories are well established and validated.

Below you will find a sampling of different types of research methodologies through the perspective of time. An "L" has been placed next to the methods that are predominantly quaLitative and an "N" for those that are predominantly quaNtitative. However, since most studies will be triangulated, it is likely that both qualitative and quantitative data will be employed to help the researcher make conclusions. We will examine clusters of methodologies based on past, present, and future perspectives and see how a research problem could be defined with each of these methodologies.

A
Past
Historical (L)
Content Analysis   (N)
Phenomenological (L)

B
Present
Developmental (L)
Descriptive (N)
Pure/Basic/Experimental   (N)
Quasi-Experimental (N)
Causal-Comparative (N)
Correlational (N)
Case Study (L)
Q-method (N but also L)

C
Future
Action (L)
Applied (L)
Evaluative (N)
Delphi (L, then N)

D
Nouveau Cuisine
Heuristic (L)
Holistic (L)
Grounded Theory (L)
Ethnographic (L)

Now that you have selected your topic, you are in an excellent position to determine what you will use to *cook up* your research. You need to commit to a method. Research methodology refers to the broad perspective from which you will view the problem, make the investigation, and draw inferences. Most methods are subsets of qualitative and quantitative paradigms. A brief discussion of several research methods was presented earlier. We will now take a closer look at some of these methods through the perspective of time. This will give you an opportunity to validate that you are using the proper *recipe* to successfully prepare your *feast*.

Although no single research method is likely to describe each aspect of the problem you are planning to investigate, there are most likely general categories into which your study will fall. There is no universal standard for categorizing research designs and different authors might use different names of designs in their discussions of them. Thus what is shown here is intended more to be informative than exhaustive. This lack of universalism also causes problems when critiquing research as many published studies do not identify the design used. Selecting an appropriate design for a study involves following a logical thought process. A calculating mind is required to explore all possible consequences of using a particular design in a study. It is highly recommended that you find an excellent primer on the methodology you choose and cite this in your study at appropriate times.

Choose Your Method Wisely

Don't be too quick in running away from using a quantitative method because you fear statistics. A qualitative approach to research can yield new and exciting understandings, but it should not be undertaken because of a fear of quantitative research. A well-designed quantitative research study can often be accomplished in very clear and direct ways. A similar study of a qualitative nature usually requires considerably more time and a burden to create new paths for analysis where previously no path had existed. Choose your method wisely!

After reading the descriptions below, find the classification that best describes the nature of your study. We will primarily use problems associated with low socioeconomic class and its relation to education. An example will be provided to show how each of these methods could analyze a different aspect of the problem.

Past Perspective

If your primary interest is in past events or factors in the past that have contributed to the problem you are researching, then your method will likely be historical or causal-comparative.

Historical Research

The researcher looks back at significant events in the relatively distant past and seeks, by gathering and analyzing contemporary descriptions of the event, to provide a coherent and objective picture of what happened and arrive at conclusions about the causes, effects, or trends of past events that might be helpful in explaining the present or anticipating future events. The historical researcher deals with the meaning of events. There is usually a reconstruction of the past in relation to a particular theory or conceptual scheme. The heart of this research is the interpretation of facts and events to determine not just what happened, but why they happened. The data of historical research are subject to two types of evaluation: to determine if a document is authentic and, if indeed it is authentic, what the document means. The researcher is concerned with external or internal evidence and subjects the data to external or internal criticism. Historical research deals with the meaning of events. The heart of the historical method is not the accumulation of facts, but rather the interpretation of the facts (Leedy & Ormrod, 2001). The principle product of historical research is context—an understanding of the organizational, individual, social, political, and economic circumstances in which phenomena occur (Mason & McKenney, 1997).

Example: A study of 19th century teaching practices with children of low socioeconomic class using teacher diaries as primary sources.

Content Analysis

The researcher examines a class of social artifacts, typically written documents. Topics appropriate for content analysis include any form of communication answering who says what? to whom? why? how? and with what effect? This is an unobtrusive method of doing research, but it is limited to recorded information. Coding is used to transform raw data into standardized, quantitative form. Data are analyzed through the use of official or quasi-official statistics.

Content analysis examines words or phrases within a wide range of texts, including books, book chapters, essays, interviews, and speeches as well as informal conversation and headlines. By examining the presence or repetition of certain words and phrases in these texts, a researcher is able to make inferences about the philosophical assumptions of a writer, a written piece, the audience for which the piece is written, and even the culture and time in which the text is embedded. Due to its wide array of applications, researchers in literature and rhetoric, marketing, psychology, and cognitive science, as well as many other fields use content analysis.
http://writing.colostate.edu/guides/research/content/

Example: Documents from Title 1 programs are analyzed over a 10-year period to determine any patterns or trends in entitlements.

Present Perspective

If your study adopts a viewpoint that is in the present time, then you will likely be examining a phenomenon as it occurs with a view to understanding its nature, organization, and the way it changes.

Developmental Research

The researcher examines patterns and sequences of growth and change over time. This research can be done as a longitudinal study (the same group examined over a period of time) or as a cross-sectional study (different groups examined at the same time that might represent different ages or other classifications). Check out the following URL to learn more about developmental research techniques: http://tinyurl.com/2flrtms

Example: A group of freshman students from a high-risk school are studied to examine the factors that affect the ability to graduate in 4 years.

Descriptive Research

Descriptive research is the study of a phenomenon "as it is" without making any "changes or modifications" to it (Leedy & Ormrod, 2001, p. 191). Descriptive designs address the "what" and "how" rather than "why" questions. According to Babbie (1995), although descriptive approach to a study requires the researcher to observe and describe the phenomenon of interest, the process of description is more precise, accurate, and carefully done than is usual in causal descriptions. In descriptive studies, both survey and interviews can be used to collect data (Babbie, 1973). Surveys can result in large samples for the study while interviews can also provide detailed insights of the experiences of individuals. Unlike experimental research, no treatment is manipulated or controlled by the researcher. This research method is not used to determine "cause and effect" relationships (p. 191).

The descriptive researcher makes a systematic analysis and description of the facts and characteristics of a given population or event of interest. The purpose of this form of research is to provide a detailed and accurate picture of the phenomenon as a means of generating hypotheses and pinpointing areas of needed improvements. Descriptive studies are designed to gain more information about a particular characteristic within a particular field of study. A descriptive study may be used to develop theory, identify problems with current practice, justify current practice, make judgments, or identify what others in similar situations may be doing. Descriptive research can combine correlational, developmental, and observation methods. A descriptive study tries to discover answers to the questions who, what, when, where, and, sometimes, how. The researcher creates a profile of a group of problems, people, or events. The descriptive study is popular in business research because of its versatility across disciplines (Cooper & Schindler, 2002).

Example: A descriptive study of an urban ghetto is carried out to understand what programs are available to preschool children of low socioeconomic status and how effective these programs are in accomplishing their goals.

Correlational Research

The researcher investigates one or more characteristics of a group to discover the extent to which the characteristics vary together. Descriptive and correlational studies examine variables in their natural environments and do not include researcher-imposed treatments. Correlational studies display the relationships among variables by such techniques as cross-tabulation and correlations. Correlational studies are also known as ex post facto studies. This literally means *from after the fact*. The term is used to identify that the research has been conducted after the phenomenon of interest has occurred naturally. The main purpose of a correlational study is to determine relationships between variables, and if a relationship exists, to determine a regression equation that could be used make predictions to a population. In bivariate correlational studies, the relationship between two variables is measured. Through statistical analysis, the relationship will be given a degree and a direction. The degree of relationship determined how closely the variables are related. This is usually expressed as a number between -1 and +1, and is known as the correlation coefficient. A zero correlation indicates no relationship. As the correlation coefficient moves toward either -1 or +1, the relationship gets stronger until there a perfect correlation at the end points.

The significant difference between correlational research and experimental or quasi-experimental design is that causality cannot be established through manipulation of independent variables. This leads to the pithy truism: *Correlation does not imply causation*. For example, in studying the relationship between smoking and cancer, the researcher begins with a sample of those who have already developed the disease and a sample of those who have not. The researcher then looks for differences between the two groups in antecedents, behaviors, or conditions such as smoking habits. If it is found that there is a relationship between smoking and a type of cancer, the researcher cannot conclude that smoking *caused* the cancer. Further research would be needed to draw such a conclusion.

Example: The relationship between socioeconomic status and school achievement of a group of urban ghetto children is examined.

Causal-Comparative Research

The researcher looks at present characteristics of a problem, views them as the result of past causal factors, and tries, by examining those past factors, to discover the causes, critical relationships, and meanings suggested by the characteristics. Usually two or more groups are compared using these criteria.

Causal-comparative and correlational methods are similar in that both are nonexperimental methods because they do not involve manipulation of an independent variable, which is under the control of an experimenter, and random assignment of participants is not possible. This implies that variables need to be observed as they occur naturalistically. As a result, the key, and omnipresent problem, in nonexperimental research is that an observed relationship between an independent variable and a dependent variable might not be causal but instead the result of the operation of a third variable.

Causal-comparative research generally includes a categorical independent or dependent variable (hence the word "comparative," implying a group comparison) while correlational research only includes quantitative variables. Causal-comparative studies attempt to infer cause-and-effect relationships, whereas correlational studies do not. Correlational research attempts to determine whether, and to what degree, a relationship exists between two or more quantifiable variables. Causal-comparative is similar to experimental research since both usually involve a comparison of groups and an attempt is made to suggest a cause-and-effect relationship.

Example: Comparison of the socioeconomic status of a high-achieving group of children and a low-achieving group of children to ascertain whether and to what extent socioeconomic status influences school performance.

Pure/Basic/True Experimental Research

This type of research is typically oriented toward the development of theories by discovering broad generalization based on careful analysis of a sample of the population being studied. It usually follows a scientific type of inquiry emphasizing a rigorous, structured type of analysis in each of the research stages.

The paradigm for scientific method in research is the true experiment or randomized control trial. Experimental designs are set up to allow the greatest amount of control possible so that causality might be examined closely. The three essential elements of experimental design are as follows:

Manipulation: The researcher does something to at least some of the participants in the research.

Controls: The experimenter introduces one or more controls over the experimental situation. A control group is often compared to an experimental group in a test of a causal hypothesis. The control and experimental groups should be identical in all relevant ways except for the introduction of a suspected causal agent into the experimental group. If the suspected causal agent is actually a causal factor of some event, then logic dictates that that event should manifest itself more significantly in the experimental than in the control group. For example, if a reading program causes higher test scores, when we introduce the reading program into the experimental group but not into the control group, we should find higher test scores occurring in the experimental group at a significantly greater rate than in the control group. Significance is measured by relation to chance: if an event is not likely due to chance, then its occurrence is significant.

Randomization: The experimenter assigns participants to control and experimental groups on a random basis (see Polit & Hungler, 1991).

The classic example is the before–after design or pretest–posttest design. This is perhaps the most commonly used experimental design. Comparison of pretest scores allows the researcher to evaluate how effective the randomization of the sample is in providing equivalent groups. The treatment is under the control of the researcher. The dependent variable is measured twice during the study (before and after the manipulation of the independent variable).

There are many texts that specifically address experimental methods. If you are intending to conduct an experimental study, you should thoroughly familiarize yourself with the procedures.

The following checklist of questions was adapted from Creswell (1994).

Questions to consider when designing an experimental study:

- Who are the participants in the study, and to what population do they belong?
- How were the participants selected?
- Was a random selection procedure used?
- Will the participants be matched in some form?
- What will be the division of participants in the experimental and the control groups?
- What treatment will be given to the experimental group?
- How can I deal with threats to validity?

The goal is to ensure that each individual, event, observation, etc. has an equal chance of being selected from the population. A deliberate or convenience sample may be selected when circumstances warrant, that is, when access to an entire population is not possible. When volunteers participate in a study, this would be defined as a deliberate or convenience sample, since it might not be representative. Always be clear on how your sample is taken.

- What are the independent variables (predictors) in the study and how will they be measured?
- How many times will they be measured?
- What are the dependent variables (that are being predicted)? Be sure they are identified.

Remember that it is the IV or independent variables (x) that cause or influence an outcome on the DV or dependent variable (y). As Creswell (1991) noted, the dependent variable is the response or the criterion variable presumed to be caused or influenced by the independent treatment conditions. The independent variables are those variables that provide the treatment or those variables that act as factors in an experiment. The independent variables are under the control of the researcher and are manipulated by the researcher in conducting the experiment.

Creswell cited Rosnow (1991) in suggesting that there are three prototype outcomes measured in experiments. They include the general outcomes measures as (1) the direction of the observed changes; (2) the amount, volume, quantity, etc. of the change; and (3) the ease with which the change is effected. This may be an oversimplification, but it helps to provide a general orientation as to outcome measures. The researcher should further consider:

- What instruments will be used to measure the outcomes?
- Why was the particular instrument chosen?
- How was the instrument tested for validity and reliability?
- What procedural steps were taken regarding random assignments of participants to groups?
- What statistics were used to analyze the data?
- What assumptions were made before the statistical test was performed?

Consider seeking expert advice on statistical analyses if you have limited knowledge about the application and use of a particular statistical test that is needed. Keep in mind, however, that you ultimately must understand the nature, purpose, and intended use of the statistical tests in your study. Thus, the lengthy discussion of statistical analyses presented in your Recipes for Success should be studied and understood. Questions often arise in the oral presentation (or defense) of your research about the selection of statistical tests. You need to be aware of why a test was chosen, attest to its validity and reliability, and understand what assumptions are essential to utilize each test you choose.

If you would like to do your own stats:

An excellent e-book to assist you in using SPSS for your statistical analysis can be found at http://www.drjimmirabella.com/ebook/

The goal of experimental research is toward certainty that is precision, accuracy, and reliability. In its simplest form, the experimental method attempts to control the entire research situation. The matter of control is basic to this method. Any endeavor that cannot be subjected to this type of reasoning is often suppressed, devalued, or set aside.

In some studies the dependent variable cannot be measured before the treatment. For example, we cannot effectively measure the response to interventions designed to control nausea from chemotherapy prior to the beginning of treatment. Here we would use an approach known as the posttest only design. We may also wish to use this approach where pretest sensitization may occur. Participants' posttest response may be partly due to learning from, or as a reaction to, the pretest. In these instances the pretest phase can be eliminated, but doing so removes the possibility of applying some very powerful statistical analyses.

Example: Two groups of low socioeconomic children are randomly assigned to either an experimental enrichment program prior to entering school or a control group of traditional pre-school play. Comparison is made of their subsequent school performances to determine whether such enrichment influences achievement. For more information, check out http://www.fortunecity.com/greenfield/grizzly/432/rra2.htm

FOR YOUR INFORMATION AND EDUCATION

If you plan to do an experimental study, then you need to be aware of the following threats to validity that could taint your *feast*. Not paying attention can give you a great deal of *heartburn*, and even *food poisoning*.

The Halo effect: This is a tendency of judges to overrate a performance because the participant has done well in an earlier rating or when rated in a different area. For example, a student who has received high grades on earlier papers might receive a high grade on a substandard paper because the earlier work created a halo effect.

The Hawthorne effect: A tendency of participants to change their behavior simply because they are being studied. So called because the classic study in which this behavior was discovered was in the Hawthorne Western Electric Company Plant in Illinois. In this study, workers improved their output regardless of changes in their working condition.

Sensitization (from the pretest or posttest): Pretest sensitization (pretest sets the stage); A treatment might only work if a pretest is given. Because they have taken a pretest, the participants might be more sensitive to the treatment. Had they not taken a pretest, the treatment would not have worked. Posttest sensitization (posttest helps treatment fall into place); the posttest can become a learning experience. For example, the posttest might cause certain ideas presented during the treatment to fall into place. If the participants had not taken a posttest, the treatment would not have worked.

Treatment diffusion: Occurs when a comparison group learns about the program from program participants. The comparison group might then set up their own program by imitating the program group. This threat to internal validity will equalize the outcome between the groups. In this case it will be harder to tell if your program under study actually works.

The novelty effect: A tendency for performance to initially improve when a new treatment or technology is instituted, not because of any actual improvement, but in response to increased interest in the new treatment or technology.

John Henry Effect: A tendency of people in a control group to take the experimental situation as a challenge and exert more effort than they otherwise would; they try to beat the experimental group. This negates the whole purpose of a control group. So called because this was discovered at the John Henry Company where a new power tool was being tested to see if it could improve productivity. The workers using the old tool took it as a challenge to work harder to show they were just as good and should get the new tool.

Multiple treatment interference (catalyst effect): If a researcher were to apply several treatments, it is difficult to determine how well each of the treatments would work individually. It might be that only the combination of the treatments is effective. Also sometimes people participate in more than one study and it is difficult to measure the effect of one treatment versus another.

Rosenthal effect or Pygmalion effect: Changes in participants' behaviors brought about by researcher expectations; a self-fulfilling prophecy. The term originally comes from Greek mythology and was popularized by G.B. Shaw. Named from a controversial study by Rosenthal and Jackson in which teachers were told to expect some of their students' intelligence test scores to increase. They did increase based solely on the teachers' expectations and perceptions.

Note: A double-blind procedure is a means of reducing bias in an experiment by ensuring that both those who administer a treatment and those who receive it do not know (are blinded to) which study participants are in the control and experimental groups.

Quasi-experimental design

Quasi-experimental designs were developed to provide alternate means for examining causality in situations not conducive to experimental control. As in the case of the true experimental design, quasi-experiments involve the manipulation of one or more independent variables and the measurement of a dependent variable. The designs have been developed to control as many threats to validity as possible in situations where at least one of the three elements of true experimental research is lacking (i.e., manipulation, randomization, control group). There are many types of quasi-experimental design. Most are adaptations of experimental designs where one of the three elements is missing. The three major categories of quasi-experimental design are the nonequivalent-groups designs, cohort designs, and time-series designs (Cook & Campbell, 1979). The nonequivalent-groups design is the most frequently used quasi-experimental design (Heppner, Kivlighan, & Wampold, 1992; Huck & Cormier, 1996). This design is similar to the pretest-posttest control group experimental design. The difference is the nonrandom assignment of participants to their respective groups in the quasi-experimental design. Cohort designs are typically stronger than nonequivalent-groups design because cohorts are more likely to be closer to equal at the outset of the experiment (Heppner et al., 1992). An example of a cohort in this context would be students at middle school Alpha and students at middle school Beta during a similar time frame. The third class of quasi-experimental designs is the time-series design. These designs are characterized by multiple observations over time (e.g., Kivligham & Jauquet, 1990) and involve the same participant observations to record differences attributed to some treatment or similar but different participants. In the interrupted time-series design (the most basic of this class), a treatment is introduced at some point in the series of observations (Heppner et al., 1992).

Example: The researcher studies groups of prodigious young musicians from two inner-city schools to determine which group progressed more in a 6-month period. One group participated in a mentorship program, and the other did not. For more information, check out Burns and Grove (1993, pp. 305–316).

Case Study

Case study is a type of qualitative research that concentrates on a single unit or entity, with boundaries established by the researcher (Lichtman & Taylor, 1993). The case study method refers to descriptive research based on a real-life situation, problem, or incident and situations calling for analysis, planning, decision making, or action with boundaries established by the researcher. Case study research is often used when the questions are how and why, rather than what and how many, and when particularistic, descriptive, heuristic, and inductive phenomena are considered. Sudzina and Kilbane (1992) maintain that the method requires that every attempt be made to provide an unbiased, multidimensional perspective in presenting the case and arriving at solutions.

According to Goetz and LeCompte (1984), there are eight points in the case study process where important theoretical decisions need to be made: focus and purpose, research design, choice of participants, settings and context, the role of the researcher, data collection strategies, data analysis methods, and findings and interpretations. Case studies use inductive logic to discover the reality behind the data collected through the study.

Example: A high school in a low socioeconomic area is studied to gather data for an analysis of attitudes and practices as they relate to drug education.

Phenomenology

This type of research has its roots in existentialism. Phenomenology is a 20th-century philosophical movement dedicated to describing the structures of experience as they present themselves to consciousness, without recourse to theory, deduction, or assumptions from other disciplines such as the natural sciences. Phenomenology is both a philosophy and a research method. The purpose of phenomenological research is to describe experiences as they are lived in phenomenological terms (i.e., to capture the lived experience of study participants). The philosophers from which phenomenology emerged include Husserl, Kierkegaard, Heidegger, and Sartre.

Phenomenologists view the person as integral with the environment. The focus of phenomenological research is people's experience in regard to a phenomenon and how they interpret their experiences. Phenomenologists agree that there is not a single reality; each individual has his or her own reality. This is considered true even of the researcher's experience in collecting data and analyzing it. "Truth is an interpretation of some phenomenon; the more shared that interpretation is the more factual it seems to be, yet it remains temporal and cultural" (Munhall & Stetson, 1989).

There are four aspects of the human experience that are of interest to the phenomenological researcher:

1. Lived space (spatiality)
2. Lived body (corporeality)
3. Lived human relationships (relationality)
4. Lived time (temporality)

All of these aspects are taken into consideration with the understanding that people see different realities in different situations, in the company of different people, and at different times. The feelings expressed about one's life in an interview given at a certain time might be different from those given at another time.

The broad question that phenomenologists want answered is as follows: What is the meaning of one's lived experience? The only reliable source of information to answer this question is the person who has experienced this phenomenon. Understanding human behavior or experience requires that the person interprets the action or experience for the researcher, and the researcher must then interpret the explanation provided by each person.

The first step in conducting a phenomenological study is to identify the phenomenon to explore. Next, the researcher develops research questions. Two factors need to be considered in developing the research questions:

- What are the necessary constituents of this feeling or experience?
- What does the existence of this feeling or experience indicate concerning the nature of the human being?

After developing the research question, the researcher identifies the sources of the phenomenon being studied and from these sources seeks individuals who are willing to describe their experience(s) with the phenomenon in question. These individuals must understand and be willing to express their inner feelings and describe any physiological experiences that occur with the feelings.

Data are collected through a variety of means: observation, interactive interviews, videotapes, and written descriptions by participants. Typically, the majority of data are collected by in-depth conversations in which the researcher and the participant are fully interactive. Analysis begins when the first data are collected. This analysis will guide decisions related to further data collection. The meanings attached to the data are expressed within the phenomenological philosophy. The outcome of analysis is a theoretical statement responding to the research question. Statements are validated by examples of the data, often direct quotes from the participants. The researcher also depends heavily on his or her intuitive skills. It is usually wise for the researcher to frame his or her own feelings, attitudes, biases, and understandings of the phenomenon prior to conducting a phenomenological study and bracket this information prior to conducting the interviews.

Husserl conceived of phenomenology as a means of philosophical inquiry in which you exam and suspend all assumptions about the nature of any reality. Three terms emerged from Husserl's concept of phenomenological inquiry: epoché, reduction, and bracketing. Epoché, borrowed from the Greek skeptics, refers to the questioning of assumptions to examine a phenomenon fully.

Reduction is the consideration of only the basic elements of an inquiry without concern for what is accidental or trivial. Bracketing is the setting aside of some portion of an inquiry, so as to look at the whole. These three concepts are often used synonymously to explain the suspended judgment necessary for phenomenological inquiry. From the Husserlean philosophical stance, only from this point of suspended judgment can inquiry proceed unencumbered from masked assumptions about the nature of the phenomenon observed. More information on phenomenology is available at http://www.phenomenologycenter.org/phenom.htm

Example: A researcher spends several months at an inner-city high school to determine the perceptions of the teachers and students with respect to school policies.

Q-method

This methodology was invented in 1935 by British physicist-psychologist William Stephenson (1953) and is most often associated with quantitative analysis due to the statistical procedures involved. However, Stephenson was looking to reveal the subjectivity involved in any situation—e.g., in aesthetic judgment, choosing a particular profession, perceptions of organizational roles, political attitudes, appraisals of health care, experiences of bereavement— which is most often associated with qualitative methods. Proponents of Q-methodology claim that it "combines the strengths of both qualitative and quantitative research traditions" (Dennis & Goldberg, 1996, p. 104) and serves as a bridge between the two (Sell & Brown, 1984).

Some of the quantitative obstacles to the wider use of Q-method are reduced with the advent of the software package Q-Method (Atkinson, 1992).

Example: A researcher invites Head Start graduates to characterize the education rendered by sorting statements (each typed on a separate card) into a quasi-normal distribution ranging from "most like the education provided" (+5) to "most unlike the education provided" (-5), the result being a Q-sort table. The Q-sorting session is followed by focused interviews during which Head Start graduates are invited to expand on their experiences.

Future Perspective

If your prime interest is the future, in studying a current situation for the purpose of contributing to a decision about it, changing it, or establishing a policy about it, you will probably use one of the following research methodologies:

Applied or Evaluative Research

This type of research is concerned primarily with the application of new knowledge to the solution of day-to-day problems. The knowledge obtained is thus contextual. Its purpose is to improve a process by testing theoretical constructs in actual situations. This approach is based on the premise that the development and application of theories of explanation and new methods of analyses are essential to guide empirical research and to assist in the informed interpretation of evaluative findings. In medical research, a cardiologist might monitor a group of heart disease patients to see if the diet prescribed by the American Heart Association is truly effective. A great deal of social research fits into this category as it attempts to establish whether various organizations and institutions are fulfilling their purpose and if implemented policies are effective. The relationship between researcher and participant is one of expert and client.

Many social action programs have been researched in this manner. It highlights the symbols of measurement and scientific neutrality but attempts to minimize the influence of the behavioral science perspective.

Example: An income-enhanced program for raising the socioeconomic status of parents of preschool children is evaluated for its effects upon school performance of children.

Action Research

This is a type of applied research that is more concerned with immediate application, rather than the development of a theory. Slight variations on action research include participatory research, collaborative inquiry, emancipatory research, action learning, and contextual action research. Action research focuses on specific problems in a particular situation and usually involves those who can immediately create change. Bogdan and Biklen (1992) described action research as a systematic collection of information that is designed to bring about social change. This kind of research allows that there could be more than one right way to develop solutions to problems.

The beginnings of action research date back to Lewin (1946). In his study of group decision and social change, Lewin used his model to describe how to change people's relationship to food. His research consisted of analysis, fact-finding, conceptualization, planning, execution, more fact-finding, conceptualization, etc. Marrow (1969) saw the Lewin model as a means of studying participants through changing them and seeing the effect. This type of inquiry is based on the belief that in order to gain insight into a process, one must introduce a change and then observe its variable effects and new dynamics.

Action research is neither quantitative nor qualitative research. It has been argued that it is more of a tool for change than true research. Action research "is a way of doing research and working on solving a problem at the same time" (Cormack, 1991, p. 155). The research takes place in real-world situations and aims to solve real problems. The initiating researcher makes no attempt to remain objective, but openly acknowledges his or her bias to the other participants.

The method was developed to allow researchers and participants to work together to analyze social systems with a view to changing them. In other words, it was developed to achieve specific goals. It is seen as a community-based method and has frequently been employed in a wide range of settings from schools and health clinics to businesses and industry.

The approach might include doing some baseline measures using questionnaires, observation, or other research methods as an assessment of the problem. Objectives are then set and decisions made about how to bring about a change. When change plans are put into action, progress is monitored, changing the plans as necessary or appropriate. Once the change has been implemented, a final assessment is made and conclusions drawn, accompanied by the writing of a report on the project for those involved or for dissemination to others.

Therefore, action research "is a process containing both investigation and the use of its findings" (Smith, 1986, as cited in Cormack, 1991, p. 155). The role of the researcher is to assist practitioners to take control of and change their own work.

Action research, generally, has the following characteristics and components:

1. Includes an educational component

2. Deals with individuals as members of social groups

3. Is problem focused, context specific, and future oriented

4. Involves a change intervention

5. Aims at improvement and involvement

6. Involves a cyclic process in which research, action, and evaluation are interlinked

7. Creates an interrelationship where those involved are participants in the change process

Stringer (1996) used the phrase Look, Think, Act in his book *Action Research: A Handbook for Practitioners.* To conduct action research involves identifying the problem, discussing the problem with practitioners, conducting a thorough search of the literature, redefining the problem, selecting an evaluation model, implementing a change, collecting data, receiving feedback, making recommendations, and disseminating the results to a larger audience.

Example: A program in which teachers are given in-service workshops and new materials to use with low socioeconomic status children is implemented in two pilot schools, evaluated as it progresses, and continually modified to become more effective.

Delphi Method

In the Delphi method, a group of experts are asked, through a series of surveys, to make their forecasts, initially independently and subsequently by consensus, in order to discard any extreme views (Discenza, Howard, & Schenk, 2002). A traditional Delphi method brings together panelists in at least three rounds of surveys. This technique engages experts in issues around interests affecting the topic of research. You can obtain names and addresses of experts by using a snowball sample, where you ask experts in the field for lists of other experts in the field. During the first round, open-ended questions are sent to experts in the area of study. A second round of questions is developed based on the responses obtained in the first round of questioning. The respondents usually rate the responses on a Likert-type scale. The third round of questioning summarizes the questions of the second round, including the group's mean response to the questions from the Likert-type scale. The panel members are asked to reconsider previous answers in reference to the group's mean and revise their answers if desired. The participants are requested to provide a rationale for answers outside the mean. This justification provides the researcher with information why an expert's response differs from the majority of the group and adds richness to the data. In some circumstances, this wide array of expert opinion can generate a range of alternative solutions to issues and problems facing the researcher (Discenza et al., 2002). Delphi techniques are used when the problem does not lend itself to precise analytical techniques, but can benefit from subjective judgments on a collective basis.

Delphi is primarily used in two modes: exploratory (to find out what's out there) and refinement (using expert judgments anonymously elicited to fine-tune quantitatively oriented estimates). For the technique to work, the respondents' estimates need to be calibrated for over- or underestimation errors, the questions need to be neutrally phrased, and some technique or researcher oversight is necessary to control for the inclusion of mutually exclusive data components in the Delphi analysis. This technique is gaining more popularity as members of e-mail lists feed back information and perhaps try to come to a consensus on future directives. The Delphi method was originally developed at the RAND Corporation by Olaf Helmer and Norman Dalkey.

As it is difficult to make summaries of other than quantitative responses, the questions used in the Delphi process are usually quantitative, e.g., "What will the price of crude oil be in 20 years?" On the basis of this type of response, the researcher could calculate descriptive statistics such as the mean, standard deviation, and the ranges. One advantage of the method is that you can readily use the range as a measure of the reliability of the forecast. Of course, nothing prevents using qualitative or any other type of questioning if the nature of the object so requires. If the respondents are amenable to the extra effort, they may be asked to justify their opinion, especially if it differs from that of the majority. The Delphi procedure is normally repeated until the respondents are no longer willing to adjust their responses.

The modified Delphi technique, according to Custer, Scarcella, and Stewart (1999, p. 2), is similar to the full Delphi in terms of procedure (i.e., a series of rounds with selected experts) and intent (i.e., to predict the future events and to arrive at consensus). The major modification consists of beginning the process with a set of carefully selected items. These preselected items may be drawn from various sources including related competency profiles, synthesized reviews of literature, and interviews with selected content experts. The primary advantage of this modification to the Delphi is that it (a) typically improves the initial round response rate and (b) provides a solid grounding in previously developed work.

Example: A researcher directs identical questions to a group of experts, asking them to give their opinions on how the future of the Internet might affect the future of education. In the next step, the researcher makes a summary of all the replies she or he has received, sends this to the respondents, and asks if any expert wants to revise his or her original response.

Nouveau Cuisine

Below is a list of some nontraditional *meals* that have been successfully *served* at *modern day banquets*.

Heuristic Research

In action research, hypotheses are being created and tested whereas in heuristic research, the investigator encourages individuals to discover their own hypotheses in relation to a problem and decide on methods that would enable them to investigate further on their own. The heuristic approach to predict seeks to neither determine nor cause causal relationships. The heuristic methodology, by design, does not quantify the experience by tools of measurements, ratings, or scores. Heuristic researchers seeks to reveal more fully the essence or meaning of a phenomenon of human experience; discover the qualitative aspects, rather than the quantitative dimensions of the phenomenon; engage one's total self; and evoke a personal and passionate involvement and active participation in the process. The researcher illuminates thought through careful *descriptions, illustrations, metaphors, poetry, dialogue,* and other creative renderings.

In heuristic research, the emphasis is on personal commitment rather than linear methodologies. Its purpose is to describe a meaningful pattern as it exists in the universe without any redesigned plan, thus eliminating suggestive speculation. This type of research intrinsically tends to be more open-ended than most.

FOR YOUR INFORMATION AND EDUCATION

Clark Moustakas (1961) conducted a study on loneliness based on his own personal experiences and after its publication, several lonely people picked up on his work and furthered the study. He then published their studies so that others could gain more insight into this situation.

Moustakas felt this type of *heuristic research* recognized the significance of inner searching for deeper awareness. He saw this approach as an integration of searching and studying, and as an openness to new experiences, intuition, and process. Critics of heuristic research feel that it is just an elaboration of the problem stage of research and should not be construed as the research itself.

Example: An adult from a low socioeconomic background who obtained a Ph.D. seeks out other such people to ask them a series of questions to point out the similarities and differences in their responses.

Holistic Research

In holistic research, qualities of traditional research such as a systematic inquiry and rigorous search for the truth are given the same priority as relevancy, intuition, and human dignity.

Whereas traditional research relies almost exclusively on references to previously peer-reviewed studies, holistic research often gives details of political standpoints, current works, and relationships from a variety of sources. Generally, you would choose this type of research methodology if you feel a need to explore all methods of inquiry including the use of fictional literature, art, and music where applicable or if you are attempting to create a new theory or identify a new problem.

Holistic researchers feel that the tendency of traditional researchers to rely heavily on test results and to overspecialize is a serious shortcoming that trivializes people and shows little humility. Maslow (1970) has stated that "if you prod at people like things they won't let you know them."

FOR YOUR INFORMATION AND EDUCATION

If you choose one of the nontraditional research methodologies, you might wish to take a look at http://physicsed.buffalostate.edu/danowner/nontrad.html where you will find a discussion of the criticism of nontraditional research methods and some suggestions on how these denunciations might be overcome. The overall growth of nontraditional research might have been due, in part, to those who felt that the conventional methods (i.e., quantitative methods) of interpreting data were too limiting when investigating people and their situations (Eisner, 1997).

Example: Two preschool children, one from a low socioeconomic family and the other from a high socioeconomic family, are studied to determine the patterns of educational development in each. Their artwork, play activities, interaction with peers, etc. are used to help the researcher make inferences about their cognitive, conative, and affective domains of learning.

Grounded Theory

This type of inquiry, also known as *analytic induction*, is one of the most sophisticated and developed approaches to rigorous qualitative (nonnumerical) research. This type of research has its roots in symbolic interactionism and philosophy and is used in areas where there is little previous research or in familiar areas in which a new viewpoint would be greatly valued. Each piece of datum is compared to every other piece of datum as it is collected. Data are usually collected by participant observation and formal semistructured interviews. Data are simultaneously being collected, organized, analyzed, and interpreted to form new theories. What most differentiates grounded theory from other research methods is that it is explicitly emergent. Instead of testing hypotheses, it sets out to find what theory accounts for the research situation as it is. In this respect it is like action research: the aim is to understand the research situation. The aim, as Glaser (1998) noted, is to discover the theory implicit in the data.

Grounded theory emerged from the discipline of sociology. The term grounded means that the theory developed from the research has its roots in the data from which it is derived. Grounded theory is based on symbolic interaction theory. This theory holds many views in common with phenomenology. Durkheim (1951) wrote 'Suicide' to demonstrate the use of sociological grounded research methods to understand a critical social problem,

George Herbert Mead (1934), a social psychologist, was a leader in the development of this theory. Symbolic interactionism explores how people define reality and how their beliefs are related to their actions. Through attaching meaning to situations, people create reality. Meaning is expressed by symbols such as words, religious objects, and clothing. These symbolic meanings are the basis for actions and interactions. Grounded theory is used most often in studying areas where there has been little previous research and in gaining new insight into previously researched areas. Hence, it becomes an inductive method of gaining knowledge.

Interview, observation, records, or a combination of these methods may be used to collect data. Data collection usually results in large amounts of handwritten notes, typed interview transcripts, or video/audio-taped conversations that contain multiple pieces of data to be sorted and analyzed. Coding and categorizing the data initiate this process. The outcome is a theory explaining the phenomenon under study. The research report presents the theory supported by examples from the data. The report tends to be narrative discussions of the study process and findings. Clements (1990), carried out a grounded theory study that looked at how parents coped with difficult times when caring for a chronically ill child. They conducted audio-taped interviews of 30 families who used their clinic. The following is a brief statement of theory that came from their research.

> The family of a chronically ill child develops specific ways of coping in an attempt to meet the needs of all its members. If support is available, equilibrium is achieved. If needs increase dramatically or support changes there is a lack of equilibrium.

In grounded theory, the researcher decides what data to collect next on the basis of an emerging theory. Proponents of grounded theory (see Glaser & Strauss, 1967) believe that conjecture must be generated from data by a constant comparison method, that is, a series of double-back steps until a pattern finally emerges. Glaser (1998) further suggested criteria for judging the adequacy of the emerging theory. These include making certain that it fits the situation, that it works, and that it helps the people in the situation to make sense of their experience and to manage the situation better. For further information check out http://tinyurl.com/27ga3rf.

Note: After their germinal work in 1967 was published, Glaser and Strauss had a feud regarding what is considered grounded theory research, resulting in a split in the theory between Glaserian and Straussian paradigms. This divergence in the grounded theory methodology is a subject of much academic debate. Grounded theory according to Glaser emphasizes induction or emergence and the individual researcher's creativity within a clear frame of stages, while Strauss is more interested in validation criteria and a systematic approach. This methodical way of creating grounded theory (and still being acceptable to scientific standards) was explained by Strauss and Corbin (1990). In an interview conducted shortly before his death, Strauss named three basic elements every grounded theory approach should include (Legewie & Schervier-Legewie, 2004). The three elements are:

Theoretical sensitive coding, that is, generating theoretical strong concepts from the data to explain the phenomenon researched;

Theoretical sampling, that is, deciding whom to interview or what to observe next according to the state of theory generation, and that implies to start data analysis with the first interview, and write down memos and hypotheses early;

The need to *compare* between phenomena and contexts to make the theory strong.

Example: Parents of preschool children from a low socioeconomic class are interviewed to determine their concerns regarding their child's education. Once this information is collected, the researcher then explores the areas delineated with similar groups of parents to determine the extensiveness of these concerns and determine a theory to explain how parents in this population view education.

Ethnographic

An ethnographic study has its roots in anthropology and seeks to develop an understanding of the cultural meanings people use to organize and interpret their experiences. This can be done through an "emic" approach (studying behaviors from within a culture) or through an "etic" approach (studying behaviors from outside the culture and examining similarities and differences across cultures). Data are usually obtained through participant observation by the researcher or research assistant and then verified with the group living the phenomenon. Ethnography focuses on the culture of a group of people.

Ethnographic researchers can study broadly defined cultures (e.g., Californians, incarcerated teens, and indigenous people) in what is sometimes referred to as a macro-ethnography. Alternatively, they might focus on more narrowly defined cultures (e.g., the culture of the homeless in San Francisco, online mathematics teachers in traditional universities) referred to as micro-ethnography. An underlying assumption of the ethnographer is that every human group eventually evolves a culture that guides the members' view of the world and the way they structure their experiences.

The aim of the ethnographer is to learn from (rather than to study) members of a cultural group to understand their worldview as they define it. Ethnographic researchers sometimes refer to emic and etic perspectives. An emic perspective refers to the way the members of the culture envision their world—it is the insider's view. The etic perspective, by contrast, is the outsider's interpretation of the experiences of that culture.

Ethnographers strive to acquire an emic perspective of a culture under study. Moreover, they strive to reveal what has been referred to as tacit knowledge. Tacit knowledge is information about the culture that is so deeply embedded in cultural experiences that members do not talk about it or might not even be consciously aware of it.

Ethnographers almost invariably undertake extensive fieldwork to learn about the cultural group in which they are interested. Ethnographic research is typically a labor-intensive endeavor that requires long periods of time in the field; months and even years of fieldwork might be required. In most cases, the researcher strives to participate actively in cultural events and activities. The study of a culture requires a certain level of intimacy and trust with members of the cultural group, which can best be developed over time and by working directly with those members as an active participant. The concept of researcher as instrument is frequently used by anthropologists to describe the significant role the ethnographer plays in analyzing and interpreting a culture.

The steps of ethnographic research include identifying the culture to be studied, conducting a thorough literature review, identifying the significant variables within the culture, gaining entrance into the culture, immersing oneself in the culture, acquiring informants, gathering data, analyzing data, describing the culture, and developing theory.

Data collection involves primarily observation and interview. The researcher might become a participant/observer in the culture during the course of the study. Analysis involves identifying the meanings attributed to objects and events by members of the culture. Members of the culture often validate these meanings before finalizing the results.

Example: High school students from low socioeconomic families videotape different types of educational institutions that they have attended; determine, from their perspective, the most pressing problems within these institutions and make recommendations as to how these problems might best be remedied.

FOR YOUR INFORMATION AND EDUCATION

Mixed Methods versus Triangulation

There is a growing consensus among evaluation experts that both qualitative and quantitative methods have a place in the performance of effective evaluations. Both formative and summative evaluations are enriched by a mixed-method approach. Greene, Caracelli, and Graham (1989) claimed that underlying the notion of a mixed-method approach appears to be the pragmatic assumption that to judge the value of a social program or policy, an evaluator should employ whatever methods will best generate evidence of the warranted assertability of the program or policy. However, not all methodologies are compatible. Perhaps it is best to accept that different ways of framing and studying social phenomena yield different kinds of understandings, and a researcher might be better served using one method but then triangulating the findings.

It is important that you distinguish between mixed methods at the technical level (generating different data from different procedures) and at the philosophical and paradigmatic levels (using, for example, a quasi-experimental design along with an ethnographic one). If the latter is used, a clear explanation is needed to discern just what is being mixed when applying different philosophical frameworks. Creswell (2003) concluded that, in most cases, mixed methodology is not a realistic design, and it is better to conceptualize it as a method rather than a methodology (which covers all phases of research from the philosophical base to the actual data collection and writing - see http://tinyurl.com/2ak4eo6). If you feel the need to combine methods that normally do not fit together, you will need to *emulsify* these methods (slowly combine the methods while mixing rapidly). Most likely a researcher will be triangulating data rather than applying mixed methods at the philosophical or epistemological levels.

According to Crane (2004), there are five major types of triangulation:

1. Data triangulation - uses different data sources.
2. Investigator triangulation - uses multiple, rather than single observers.
3. Theory triangulation - uses more than one theoretical scheme in the interpretation of the phenomenon.
4. Methodological triangulation - uses more than one method and might consist of within-method or between-method strategies.
5. Multiple triangulations - combines in one investigation multiple observers, theoretical perspectives, sources of data, and methodologies.

Examples of triangulation in research can be found at http://tinyurl.com/2g2d4rg.

 *Cutting Board*

And the winner is . . .

1. Which research methodology best describes the way you plan to do your study?

2. Why is this the best methodology for the problem you want to study?

3. Which methodology was the runner up? Why?

4. If you plan to triangulate your findings, explain how you will do this.

Terrific! You have just taken another important step toward successfully completing your research project. Keep cooking! In the next Cutting Board, you can demonstrate your scholarly literacy by matching the research term with its description. Check your answers and make sure you master the nuances of the ones that you missed.

Cutting Board

A Test of Your Research Acumen

1. hermeneutics

2. postmodern

3. ontology

4. phenomenology

5. historical

6. epistemology

7. qualitative

8. deconstruction

9. case study

10. ethnographic

11. Delphi

12. theory

13. bias

14. instrument

15. quantitative

A) A theory in the field of criticism in which all texts and works of art have a multiplicity of meanings.

B) A philosophical movement founded by Edmund Husserl based on the relationship between a participant and the objects in his or her lived experiences.

C) The art and craft of interpretation that concerns itself with secret and hidden meanings in texts, music, and works of art.

D) Concerned with the nature of knowledge. In particular the methodology used to derive, elicit, and analyze data.

E) A test, survey, or questionnaire used for data collection.

F) A strong dislike of a person, a group, people, or things. An attitude that does not require action or elaborate rationale.

G) A philosophical view of seeking to understand what reality is or what reality consists of.

H) A study centered on culture. The purpose is to develop an understanding of the cultural meanings people use to organize and interpret their experiences.

I) A type of study based on feedback with the hope of coming to some type of consensus.

J) A movement that suggests multiple interpretations of events and that all knowledge is subjective.

K) A set of interrelated constructs, definitions, and propositions that presents a systematic view of phenomena.

L) Research focused on reliable and replicable data, mostly deductive in nature. Assumes that attributes can be expressed in measurable terms. Objective.

M) Research focused on inductive discovery, tends to be exploratory, descriptive, process oriented, and concerned with theory development.

N) A research method that aims to assess the meaning of events and to interpret what might otherwise be considered merely as the happenstance of blind fortune

O) An intensive description and analysis of a particular social unit that seeks to uncover the interplay of significant factors that is characteristic of a unit.

Answers: 1-C, 2-J, 3-G, 4-B, 5-N, 6-D, 7-M, 8-A, 9-O, 10-H. 11-I, 12- K, 13-F, 14-E, 15-L

BE AWARE OF HEALTH HAZARDS

[Ethics of Research]

1 cup   RESPONSIBILITY
1 cup   COMPETENCE
1 cup   MORAL AND LEGAL ISSUES
1 cup   PROPER REPRESENTATION

Now that you have selected a research topic and have placed it into a particular category, you are in an excellent position to *digest* research ethics.

The dictionary defines ethics as "moral principles or rules of conduct." Morals are defined as "that concerning right and wrong." Research ethics are, therefore, the rules of right and wrong concerning research. Since research almost always involves people, it is important that your research does not affect people in a negative way.

Research inherently contains many paradoxes. As a researcher you need freedom to investigate, that is, find out as much information as possible about the population you are studying, while adhering to an individual's right to privacy. Ethical principles have been established to balance these issues.

Note: In the 4th edition of the *APA manual* (a writing standard for social science research published by the American Psychological Association), it was suggested that researchers "write about the people in their study in a way that acknowledges their participation." Before this edition was published, researchers often described the individuals in their study as "subjects" (p. 49). However, most researchers now use less impersonal terms, such as participants, co-researchers, individuals, respondents, etc. In general, if a person signs a permission slip, he or she should be referred to as a participant.

---

1 cup RESPONSIBILITY

The researcher must have a fantastic love of truth. —Flaws and Fallacies in Statistical Thinking,
   Stephen Campbell

It is the responsibility of the researcher to have integrity, truthfulness, and honesty when carrying out the project. Deliberately changing or inventing research results to suit your own ideas is viewed as anathema in research and carries significant consequences if discovered.

In traditional scientific research, *objectivity* is the key word. Traditional research is based on facts and figures, not on personal opinions and biases. The researcher is not to affect or influence the participants' opinions.

It is important, regardless of the type of research that you are doing, that you respect the culture and customs of the people you are studying and be rid of any cultural biases when carrying out and reporting research. The American Educational Research Association's (AERA) code of ethics incorporates a set of standards designed specifically to guide the work of researchers in education http://tinyurl.com/2c7jcaa. Education, by its very nature, is aimed at the improvement of individual lives and societies. Much of the research in education is directed at children and other vulnerable populations. A main objective of this code is to remind educational researchers of the need to strive to protect these populations and to maintain the integrity of their research and the research community.

All ethical researchers should continually evaluate their research for its ethical and scientific adequacy and maintain the highest ethical standards. Ethical concern must focus on the rights of the human participants. Participants in a research study must have full knowledge of the purpose of the study and the nature of his or her involvement. In addition, participants must be assured of the principled behavior or conduct of the investigator(s) and the design procedures.

FOR YOUR INFORMATION AND EDUCATION

The following is a summary of the Code of Ethics of the American Sociological Association.

1. Researchers must maintain scientific objectivity.
2. Researchers must recognize the limitations of their competence and not attempt to engage in research beyond such competence.
3. Every person is entitled to the right of privacy and dignity of treatment.
4. All research should avoid causing personal harm to participants used in research.

5. Confidential information provided by research participants must be held in strict confidentiality by the researcher.

6. Research findings should be presented honestly, without distortion

7. The research must not use the prerogative of a researcher to obtain information for other than professional purposes.

8. The researcher must acknowledge all assistance, collaboration of others, or sources of information borrowed from others.

9. The researcher must acknowledge financial support in the research report or any personal relationship of the researcher with the sponsor that may conceivably affect the research findings.

10. The researcher must not accept any favors, grants, or other means of assistance that would violate any of the ethical principles set forth above.

Note: Prejudices are our preconceived notions of things, emanating from our past experience and socialization. Quantitative studies require that the researcher be objective and adhere to the words of the 12th-century scholar, philosopher, and physician Moses Maimonides: "Consider this, you who are engaged in investigation: If you choose to seek truth, cast aside: passion, prejudice, accepted thought, and the inclination toward what you used to esteem, and you shall not be led into error."

Some qualitative researchers see the way to eradicate prejudice from their research as maintaining objectivity by bracketing experiences or suspending and setting aside what is known about an experience being studied. However, theorists such as Heidegger believe this is impossible. These theorists embrace the notion that past experiences are essential to facilitate understanding. Rather than being an impediment to knowledge making, it is the researcher's values that provide contextual meaning to their research. An implication of this epistemological belief is to make the researcher's judgments explicit and explain how these judgments affect the research process. The researcher needs to decide how and in what way his or her personal experiences will be introduced into the study.

Statistical Truths and Fallacies

Statistics are like bikinis. What they reveal is suggestive, but what they conceal is vital.

—Aaron Levenstein

You have an obligation, as a researcher, to use statistics responsibly. An awareness of statistical fallacies and deceptions can serve as a guide for what not to do in reporting information and help you become a more critical consumer of the research you review. Some common statistical fallacies to be aware of are the following:

Spurious accuracy: The story is told about a man who, when asked the age of a certain river, replied that it was 3,000,006 years old. When asked how he arrived at this conclusion he claimed that when he first started coming to this river he was told it was 3,000,000 years old and that was exactly 6 years ago. This is an example of spurious accuracy. Many things can simply not be measured with as much accuracy as some purveyors wish to pretend.

Faulty comparisons: In 1960, commercials for Hollywood Bread claimed it had fewer calories per slice than any other bread. The Federal Trade Commission maintained that the only reason a slice of Hollywood bread contained fewer calories was that it was more thinly sliced. The comparison was based on unequal units. Whenever two or more things are being compared with respect to one characteristic, it is necessary that important characteristics (dependent variables) are kept as similar as possible. (It is unethical that while comparing apples and oranges, the reader is given the impression that what is being compared are two apples.)

Accommodating averages: There are many kinds of averages. From a formal statistical standpoint, some are more common than others. The average that most people relate to is the (arithmetic) mean, an average which is a measure of central tendency obtained by adding all entries and dividing by the number of entries.

The median average is the number in the middle when all the entries are listed in chronological order (if there are an even number of entries, then the median is the arithmetic mean of the middle two, the $n/2$ entry and the $n/2 +1$ entry). The median is easy to compute and takes into account all the data, but is not sensitive to the magnitude of the data. (For example, it doesn't care if the smallest number was 0 or -34.)

The mode average is the term that occurs the most often. Although it is usually the easiest figure to obtain, it is only sensitive to the most common occurrence and thus does not take into consideration all the numbers.

Less frequently used averages include the harmonic mean, which is used to average different rates. For example, if you traveled at 50 mph for 2 hours and 60 mph for 3 hours then you would have traveled a total of 280 miles in 5 hours at an average of 56 miles for the entire trip, the geometric mean.

A manager of a baseball team might find the median or mode average more advantageous than the mean average when negotiating salaries with players. The players, on the other hand, might prefer to use the arithmetic mean salary so that the salaries of the players who are making astronomical amounts would be considered and weighted into the determination of their wages.

The arithmetic mean average, although it is sensitive to all the data, does not, by itself, give us a picture of how the data are dispersed. To accomplish this, the standard deviation or the variance, which is the standard deviation squared, should be reported. The variance is found by taking the difference between each entry and the mean, squaring these differences, and obtaining the (arithmetic) mean of the squared differences. To obtain the standard deviation all you, or your calculator, need to do is take the square root of the variance.

If the standard deviation is relatively large compared to the mean, a wide dispersion of numbers is indicated. Conversely, a small standard deviation indicates that the numbers are clustered around the mean. Thus, it is generally expected that the researcher report the mean and standard deviation when presenting his or her findings.

The following is an empirical rule (68, 95, and 99) that applies to data having a distribution that is approximately bell shaped:

About 68% of all scores fall within one standard deviation of the mean and about 95% of all scores fall within two standard deviations of the mean. About 99% of all scores fall within three standard deviations of the mean.

That is, the mean IQ on the Stanford-Binet test is 100 and the standard deviation is 15. Thus, 68% of those who have taken the test have IQ's between 85 and 115. This is often referred to as normal. IQs between 115 and 130 are considered above average, those with IQs between 130 and 145 are considered genius, and those above 145 are classified as brilliant.

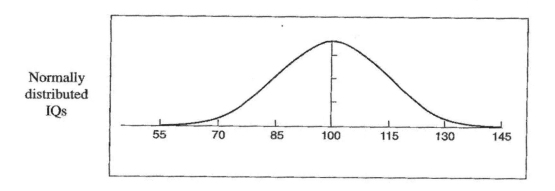

Normally distributed IQs

55   70   85   100   115   130   145

Ad hoc definitions: Whenever a term can be defined in more than one way, you must decide which of the possible definitions seems most sensible and which definition lends itself best to efficient data collection. It is also important that you clearly define all concepts in your study that might be unfamiliar to your reader.

A classic case of the need for a proper definition was found in 1955 when the population of London was reported in three different studies as

5,200   325,000   8,315,000,

whereas New York City was reported (in three different studies) to have a population of:

1,910,000   10,350,000   8,050,000.

What became clear from these accounts is how meaningless a comparison between the populations of these cities (or any city) is without clearly defining geographic boundaries.

Rubber graphs: The human eye has difficulty assimilating raw data or columns of numbers. Graphs often aid in making information more easily understood. A line graph is customarily used to note trends or compare amounts. The vertical axis generally has the measures (quantities) represented. The scales that are used will affect the appearance of the graph and should not be used to deceive people.

The murky notion of cause and effect: The story is told about a man who wrote a letter to an airline requesting that their pilots cease turning on the little light that says "FASTEN SEAT BELTS," because every time that light went on, the ride got bumpy. Be aware that in all correlational studies, effects may be wrongly attributed to factors that were merely causally associated rather than cause-and-effect related.

1 cup COMPETENCE

You should be qualified to carry out your research project. You should look at the problem you plan to study critically, and then as objectively as possible, and judge your own abilities to devise procedures appropriate for examining the problem.

A competent researcher possesses certain personal qualities such as creativity, flexibility, curiosity, determination, objectivity, tolerance of frustration, logical reasoning abilities, and the ability to make scholarly observations. (Having come this far in your *Recipes for Success*, you have already demonstrated many of these qualities.)

1 cup MORAL AND LEGAL ISSUES

The legal and social rules of the community you are investigating should be respected. If you think your work could break either the legal or the social rules of the community, your research efforts should be curtailed until these issues are resolved.

Researchers are expected to be proactive in designing and performing research to ensure that the dignity, welfare, and privacy of research participants are protected and that information about an individual remains confidential. Participants often need to be assured that all personal information given to the researcher will be seen only by those who are carrying out the research project. It is unethical to discuss a person or the information he or she gives you in confidence with your family or friends. There is one exception to the confidentiality rule—legal obligation. If someone tells you about a serious legal offense or crime, you may have to break the confidentiality rule and notify the proper authorities.

Most research reports on groups of people keep the identity of individuals anonymous. When reporting anecdotal cases, identities can be hidden by the use of a false name or initials.

When you interview or test people you should explain to them the following:

1. Who will see the information they give,
2. What will be done with the information, and
3. How their privacy will be protected.

It is important for you, the researcher, to be viewed as a person concerned about the people being studied. You should not leave confidential questionnaires, surveys, papers, or interview notes lying around so that anyone can read them. It is best to keep these items somewhere safe or, if possible, locked away so that they don't fall into the wrong hands.

Plagiarism

In conducting research, we are continually engaged with other people's ideas: we read them in texts, hear them in lectures we attend, share ideas on e-mail, discuss them with others, and incorporate them into our own writing. As a result, it is very important that we give credit where credit is due. Plagiarism is using someone else's ideas and words without clearly acknowledging the source of the information. As a general rule, if the idea is not totally yours, give credit to the source of the idea. If ever there is a question of "I don't remember the source," abandon the particular citation or conduct an Internet search to locate the reference. A student needs to always follow the specific guidelines issued by the university to avoid complications. If you find as you write that you're following one or two of your sources too closely, deliberately look back in your notes for other sources that take different or contrasting views; there is a set limit to how many words you can quote and paraphrase before you need to obtain permission from the copywrite holder. The overreliance on a few sources makes the authenticity of your research questionable.

It is important to remember that when you cite a source you are engaging in a conversation with other researchers and scholars and adding credibility to your own research. By responding reasonably to those who oppose your views, you are acknowledging that there are valid counterarguments. Thus, appropriate quoting and citing of sources shows respect to the creators of these ideas and arguments—honoring thinkers and their intellectual property—and adds integrity to your work. As a researcher, you have a vested interest in maintaining a respect for intellectual property and giving proper attribution to ideas and words. Other forms of plagiarism include having someone else write a paper for you, paying someone else to write a paper for you, and submitting as your own someone else's unpublished work, either with or without permission. There are also serious consequences to pay if you are found guilty of plagiarism.

Harris (2001) offers some helpful suggestions on how to avoid plagiarism.

To prevent plagiarism, you must give credit whenever you use:

- another person's idea, opinion, or theory;
- any facts, statistics, graphs, drawings—any pieces of information—that are not common knowledge;
- quotations of another person's actual spoken or written words; or
- paraphrases of another person's spoken or written words.

These guidelines are adapted from the Student Code of Rights, Responsibilities, and Conduct found at Indiana University's Web page: http://tinyurl.com/6hma3. With the advent of the World Wide Web and the proliferation of distance learning institutions, a limitless reservoir of digital documents can be downloaded, studied, and—in some cases, unfortunately—plagiarized. If plagiarism is suspected, the Web can also be used to search for the original source. Pasting key, specific phrases into a search engine like www.yahoo.com or www.google.com will often lead to the original source. In addition, there are Web sites, like http://www.plagiarismchecker.com and http://turnitin.com/static/index.html that can run a plagiarism check and find documents with contents that match or are similar to the contents in a research paper.

Note: To use the Turnitin service, you need to go to Turnitin.com, have a class account number, and a class password. You will then be able to set up your own student login account. Once you have an account, you will be guided on how to submit your papers electronically from your own computer. You will select the "Submit" icon for the appropriate assignment, navigate to the electronic version of your paper, and click the "Submit" button. The Turnitin.com service compares your paper to several types of sources: student papers, paper mills (services that sell term papers), online books and journals, and Internet sites. Any matches found will be highlighted in the originality report and linked to their original sources. Two views are available: side-by-side and print version. Compare both views to decide which works best for you. If the highlighted region is properly cited, then this is not plagiarism. It would be a good idea to view the videos that Turnitin provides at http://www.turnitin.com/static/support.html.

Another method to check for plagiarism is to look at the document in Word or Excel and check File -->Properties to see who originally drafted the document and when. Another site used to combat plagiarism is http://scout.cs.wisc.edu. Glatt Company at http://www.plagiarism.com/ provides software that helps "detect and deter" plagiarism. There is a student tutorial that provides computer-assisted instruction on what constitutes plagiarism and how to avoid it. This includes definitions of direct and indirect plagiarism, when and how to provide attribution, and a mastery test of concepts. This software is typically used in academic institutions or in the legal profession for cases of copyright infringement.

The research to be undertaken should be the researcher's and the researcher's alone; however, expert assistance may be sought. If APA editors or statisticians, for example, are consulted, it is still the responsibility of the researcher to understand, explain, defend, and synthesize this outsourced work and to be accountable for every aspect of the research and the research paper. A good consultant will teach you as well as assist you with improving your study. A good online source on how to avoid plagiarism can be found at http://www.utoronto.ca/writing/plagsep.html

Note: An excellent APA dissertation editor who has assisted hundreds of doctoral students make it to the finish line is Toni Williams: http://www.linkedin.com/pub/toni-williams/8/195/966

Internal Review Boards: Ethical Issues Related to Conducting Research Using Human Participants

There is a code of ethical standards to be adhered to in order to provide protection for all stakeholders involved in research. Even the best-intentioned research projects can provoke concerns about protecting the human participants involved. To address these issues, most institutions and organizations have created an Institutional Review Board (IRB). The IRB is a panel of people who review proposals and examine the ethical implications. The IRB decides whether additional action should be taken to protect the rights of participants and guarantee their safety.

Ethical protections for participants of research include several elements, but the major area of concern is the protection of human participants. Voluntary participation in research ensures that the participants have not been forced to participate or are not held captive to the study. Additionally, participants must give informed consent to be included in a study. These standards evolved from the previous use of humans in research without their consent and often without choice. People being held in prisons, universities, or hospitals were often used as participants without their knowledge or consent.

There have been recent ethical concerns surrounding a participant's right to service when the research conducted uses an experimental group and a control group. The control group does not receive the treatment being researched. If the treatment is perceived to be beneficial to those receiving it, those in the control group may claim that their rights to equal access to benefits may be violated. For more information on this and other important ethical issues, check out the following site: http://www.uncp.edu/home/marson/ethical_issues.html

Note: Subject versus Participant Controversy: In past studies, humans were universally referred to as subjects (with its implications of subservience). Today, any person that signs a permission slip (or has someone sign on his or her behalf) will likely be referred to as a participant. Many believe that the term *subject* was used to separate that human connection when *experimenting* with human beings and that one is more likely to disassociate him or herself from someone thought of as a subject rather than a participant. This is similar to the situation in prison when someone is identified by a number rather than a name. However, the conversion from using the term subject to participant has been met with some resistance.

1 cup PROPER REPRESENTATION

Misrepresentation should not occur. When you carry out research, you might find you have a powerful position and high status. You should not claim to have more qualifications than you actually have.

Researchers are responsible for protecting the welfare and dignity of the people they are researching. You must have informed consent from all participants taking part. If people do not want to continue, they must have the right to withdraw without any repercussions. In human research, it is unethical (and often impossible) to arrange for negative conditions such as poor teaching, abusive parenting, alcoholism, etc.; however, the consequences of such conditions can be studied.

WARNING: In this age of information, sponsored studies have become a powerful and popular tool of persuasion. Although the studies and surveys wear the guise of objective science, their findings almost invariably reflect their sponsors' intentions. Many sponsored studies are designed with a certain outcome in mind, and it is all but guaranteed to achieve that outcome. The result is a corruption of information—the information used every day by voters, consumers, and leaders. "Studies have become the vehicle for polishing corporate images, influencing juries, shaping debate on public policy, selling commercial products, and satisfying the media's—and the public's—voracious appetite for information." In *The Tainted Truth* (1995), Cynthia Crossen details popular studies that succinctly illustrate this grave situation.

What Can Be Done?

It is unrealistic to believe that academic institutions, researchers, pollsters, or the media will universally decide to stifle their self-interest and clean up the information industry. One of the unfortunate results of our obsession with numbers and information is that we allow them to supersede our eyes, our judgment, and our common sense. Many people are afraid to question statistics because they are "not good in math." What follows are things to think about while evaluating the veracity of other people's research:

1. A little skepticism goes a long way: Does this make sense? Does it seem right? Does it pass the "smell" test?

2. Unless and until a study has been replicated, it should be looked at with care.

3. Beware of "independent" researchers; this means they have many paying clients instead of one.

4. Beware of nonprofit researchers; they still count on a regular salary.

5. Beware of phrases like "as many as"; this indicates hyperbole.

6. What kind of reputation does the researcher enjoy as a supplier of the information or as an authority on the subject?

7. Does the investigator have an ax to grind?

8. What supportive evidence is offered?

9. Some basic questions:

    a. How many people were involved?

    b. Over what period of time?

    c. How was the study controlled for bias?

    d. What did earlier studies find?

    e. How were results presented?

    f. Was the research peer-reviewed?

    g. What kind of reputation does the source enjoy as a supplier of this type of information?

h. Is the source an authority on the subject?

i. What supportive evidence is offered?

j. Do estimates appear plausible?

k. Who is supporting or sponsoring the study?

Ultimately, the job of cleaning up the research business is everyone's responsibility.

CHOOSE YOUR ATTIRE
(Form and Style)

When you attend a formal *dinner*, you are often advised on what the dress code will be: white tie, black tie, casual attire, etc. The same can be said for the serving or presenting of your *feast* (research): a certain form and style should be adhered to.

The assembling of your final manuscript of your dissertation usually requires adherence to a certain form and style with respect to each of the following aspects: pagination, footnotes, abbreviations, tables, fonts, preliminary pages, illustrations, bibliography, references, quotations, citations, layouts, capitalization, italicizing, graphs, indenting, table of contents, acknowledgments, title page, chapter headings, parentheses, spacing, list of tables, hyphenation, using numerical information, etc.

Shortly after you start writing your preliminary draft of your research paper, it would be an excellent idea for you to determine the format of your paper. The most important rule to follow is consistency, so once you have determined that you will be using a certain style and form of writing, continue to use that exact style and form throughout your manuscript. Most universities require APA formatting.

You should obtain a manual that aids writers in your discipline with respect to form and style. Such manuals exist for the biological sciences, engineering, humanities, law, mathematics, physical science, social science, and psychology. If you are writing a dissertation, it would be helpful for you to scrutinize a recently approved dissertation from a colleague or classmate in your field with respect to the form and style. If you are planning to publish your study in a peer-reviewed journal, make sure you have a recent copy of that journal.

The APA manual is the most common style and form guide used by researchers in the social and behavioral sciences. An excellent resource can be found at http://www.apastyle.org/learn/faqs/index.aspx

Some rules to keep in mind:

Headings are used to organize the document and reflect the relative importance of sections. For example, many empirical research articles utilize Method, Results, Discussion, and References headings. In turn, the Method section often has subheadings of Participants, Instruments, and Procedure.

APA Style Headings: 6th Edition

Level	Format
1	**Centered, Boldface, Uppercase and Lowercase Heading** Then your paragraph begins below, indented like a regular paragraph.
2	**Flush Left, Boldface, Uppercase, and Lowercase Heading** Then your paragraph begins below, indented like a regular paragraph.
3	**Indented, boldface, lowercase paragraph heading ending with a period.** Your paragraph begins right here, in line with the heading.[a]
4	***Indented, boldface, italicized, lowercase paragraph heading ending with a period.*** Your paragraph begins right here, in line with the heading.
5	*Indented, italicized, lowercase paragraph heading ending with a period.* Your paragraph begins right here, in line with the heading.

[a] For headings at Levels 3–5, the first letter of the first word in the heading is uppercase, and the remaining words are lowercase (except for proper nouns and the first word to follow a colon).

For more information on headings and seriation in APA 6th edition, go
to http://owl.english.purdue.edu/owl/resource/560/16/

References in APA format (5th ed.):

One Author:

Nathan, A. J. (1990). *China's crisis: Dilemmas of reform and prospects for democracy*. New
York: Columbia University Press.

Two authors:

Simon, M., & Francis, B. (2001). *The dissertation and research cookbook*. Dubuque, IA:
Kendall-Hunt.

Three authors:

Linn, M., Fabricant, S., & Linn, D. (1988). *Healing the eight stages of life*. New York: Paulist
Press.

More than three authors:

Sakakibara, S., Hidetoshi, Y., Hisakatsu, S., Kengo, S., & Shimon, F. (1988). *The Japanese stock
market: Pricing systems and accounting information*. New York: Praeger.

No author:

Diseases. (1983). Springhouse, PA: Nursing 84 Books.

Corporate author:

American Hospital Association. (1988). *American Hospital Association guide to the health care
field*. Chicago: Author.

Editor:

Adams, M. (Ed.). (1987). *The Middle East handbook*. New York: Facts on File.

References in APA format (6th ed.):

One Author:

Nathan, A. J. (1990). *China's crisis: Dilemmas of reform and prospects for democracy*. New
York, NY: Columbia University Press.

Two authors:

Simon, M., & Francis, B. (2001). *The dissertation and research cookbook*. Dubuque, IA:
Kendall-Hunt.

Three authors:

Linn, M., Fabricant, S., & Linn, D. (1988). *Healing the eight stages of life*. New York, NY: Paulist Press.

More than three authors:

Sakakibara, S., Hidetoshi, Y., Hisakatsu, S., Kengo, S., & Shimon, F. (1988). *The Japanese stock market: Pricing systems and accounting information*. New York, NY: Praeger.

No author:

Diseases. (1983). Springhouse, PA: Nursing 84 Books.

Corporate author:

American Hospital Association. (1988). *American Hospital Association guide to the health care field*. Chicago, IL: Author.

Editor:

Adams, M. (Ed.). (1987). *The Middle East handbook*. New York, NY: Facts on File.

Lists (Seriation: APA Section 3.33 (5th ed.) and Section 3.04 (6th ed.)): For listed items within a paragraph like this (a) use letters, not numbers, in parentheses; (b) separate each item with a comma; and (c) use a semicolon if there's already a comma in one of the clauses. When listing items vertically, or breaking them out of the paragraph, use 1, 2, 3, and so forth, each followed by a period. Tab the first number. If sentences run longer than the first line, keep typing back to the left margin.

Numbers (APA 5th ed., Sections 3.42-3.45 and APA 6th ed., Sections 4.31-4.34): In general, numbers less than 10 are written out while numbers 10 and greater appear as Arabic numerals. Exceptions include a series of numbers, numbers preceding elements of time or measurement (e.g., 4 miles; 2 months, 6 decades, and 18 years), and a number beginning a sentence (e.g., Fifty-seven percent of those surveyed disagreed with the statement.). Other exceptions include the number of points in a Likert-type scale (e.g., a 7-point Likert-type scale). In the APA 5th edition, numbers less than 10 should appear as numerals when grouped with numbers greater than 10 and the number of participants should have a numeral as well (e.g., 3 participants). Both these exceptions are removed in the 6th edition. APA 6th edition also indicates approximations of numbers referring to time should not use numerals (e.g., approximately four weeks ago).

Examples: Four companies were selected for the study, including 30 employees and 12 managers who agreed to be interviewed.

Reporting statistics: Statistical abbreviations are usually italicized: *n*, *t*, *SD*, *p*. Uppercase *N* indicates the total population; lowercase *n* is used for samples. The correct form is *t* test, no hyphen, italicized *t*.

Using tables and figures: Permission must be granted by copyright holders if in your dissertation you plan to use tables and figures from published works not in the public domain. (APA 5th ed., Section 3.73 and APA 6th ed., Section 2.12)

Preliminary pages: The order and pagination of the preliminary pages is as follows:

> Abstract title page (no page number)
>
> Abstract (no page numbers)
>
> Title page (no page number)
>
> Dedication (optional) (no page number)
>
> Acknowledgements (optional) (ii)
>
> Table of Contents (iii) (page ii if no Acknowledgments)
>
> List of Tables (   )
>
> List of Figures (   )

Block quotations: Quotations 40 or more words in length must be put in block form. Many universities prefer *single-spaced block quotes*. At the end of block quotations, the final punctuation appears before the citation, as in this example (APA 5th ed., Section 3.34 and APA 6th ed., Section 6.03):

> We are all here to assist each other. Each time you do something to help another person on the planet, think of your action as a drop of water. One drop might not mean much, but without that drop, the ocean would not be the same. (Simon, 2009, p. 49)

ProQuest suggests that permission from the copyright owner be requested for quotes in excess of 150 words.

The list below is *not* exhaustive, but provides a quick list of items you should check for before submitting your manuscript for review.

1. Courier/Times Roman 12-point font used in APA 5th – Only Times New Roman in APA 6th.
2. Document double-spaced throughout
3. Margins at least 1 inch on all sides and ragged right edge
4. Paragraphs indented half an inch; Each paragraph is 3-5 sentences *
5. Headings and subheadings properly formatted (see APA 6th)
6. No end-of-line hyphenation
7. One space after punctuation (5th ed.) or two spaces after sentence-ending periods (6th ed.)
8. No underlined type. In APA 6th edition, bold type is permitted in some heading levels
9. Italics used instead of quotes for emphasis
10. Proper APA in-text citations**
11. Proper formatting of references (see APA 5th ed., chapter 6 and APA 6th ed., chapter 7). Do not indent the first line of a reference, but the second line and thereafter must be indented half an inch (referred to as a *hanging indent*). Check out: http://owl.english.purdue.edu/owl/resource/560/05/
12. The manuscript does not contain colloquial language, slang, jargon, trite expressions, anthropomorphic statements ***(see APA 5th ed., p. 38 and APA 6th ed., pp. 68-69)
13. Numbers 10 and higher appear as numerals; nine and lower are written out (in general; note there are exceptions)
14. Published studies and research that has been conducted are referred to in the past tense. No reference is overcited.
15. If a list is used in a paragraph, then serialization consists of (a), (b), …, and (i). Vertical lists are indented and use numbers: 1. 2.
16. Grammar checked for subject–verb agreement (see APA 5th ed., p. 44 and APA 6th ed., p. 78). Note: A good way to avoid typos and grammatical errors is to have someone else proofread your work. In addition, it might be helpful to read the document out loud. This forces you to read each word individually and increases the odds that you'll find grammatical errors.

* Make certain every paragraph has one, and only one, topic sentence (main idea) and is properly developed. Development in a paragraph is any word, phrase, or sentence that answers one or more of the critical questions—who? what? where? when? why? or how?—about the *main idea of the paragraph.* Paragraphs should flow from one to the other with transition statements. Most paragraphs contain 3-5 sentences.

** The way to cite sources in APA style is to cite the author's last name and year of publication (Simon, 2009) the first time a source is cited in a paragraph. The period comes after the citation, if the citation is at the end of a sentence. If you are quoting directly, add the page number. In APA 5th edition, if you use the same reference in the same paragraph, you do not need the year of publication after the first time the document is cited in that paragraph. In APA 6th edition, a year is not needed after the first citation if that citation is not in parenthesis and a year is always needed in parenthetical citations. We do not use the title of the book, the URL, or the journal article. These are found in the reference section only.

*** Anthropomorphism or personification in your writing occurs when inanimate objects are granted conditions normally reserved for animate (living) objects. Incorrect: The data demonstrated the effect clearly. Research stated that writing is a necessary skill. (Data can't demonstrate anything; they're inanimate. Research can't state anything; it's not alive) Correct: The effect is apparent from the data. One can conclude from research (provide references) that writing is a necessary skill. See APA 5th ed., p. 38 and APA 6th ed., p. 69. An article cannot state anything, but the author of the article can.

On July 1, 2009, the American Psychological Association released a new edition (6th) of the *Publication Manual of the American Psychological Association*. APA subsequently issued an errata sheet for minor errors in the initial publication (http://tinyurl.com/yhzba74). What follows are some changes from APA 5th to APA 6th.

Levels of Heading (3.03)

The formatting for the 5 levels of heading has changed to these current levels within a paper:

1. Spacing after Periods (4.01)

    - The 6th edition has gone back to requiring two spaces after punctuation marks at the end of a sentence.

2. Typeface (8.03)

    - In the 5th edition, either Times New Roman or Courier New 12-point fonts were the preferred typeface for APA. In the 6th edition, *only* Times New Roman is listed as the preferred font.

3. Running Header (8.03)

    - In the 5th edition, the Running Head was presented only on the title page. Now, the Running Head appears on every page of the paper (even the references and appendices) formatted as a header in the top left corner with the page number appearing in the top right corner.

Reducing Bias in Language:

1. Sexual Orientation (3.13)

   - The term *sexual orientation* should be used rather than *sexual preference*. The terms *lesbians*, *gay men*, *bisexual men*, and *bisexual women* are preferable to *homosexual* when one is referring to people who identify this way.

2. Racial and Ethnic Identity (3.14)

   - Use a modifier (such as *ethnic* or *racial*) when using the word *minority*. Racial and ethnic groups should be capitalized as they are designated by proper nouns. Therefore, use *Black* and *White* instead of *black* and *white* (which denotes colors and could be pejorative).

3. Age (3.16)

   - *Girl* and *boy* are the correct terms for individuals under age 12, while *young man* and *young woman* or *female adolescent* or *male adolescent* may be used for ages 13-17. Use *men* and *women* for ages 18 and over. The terms *elderly* and *senior* are not acceptable as nouns; use *older adults* instead.

Retrieval Dates (6.32)

   - Retrieval dates are no longer included except in cases where the source material may change over time (e.g., Wikis, which are usually not acceptable sources in a dissertation or scholarly paper).

Reminder: Each reference cited in the text must appear in the reference list, and each entry in the reference list must be cited in the text. The only exceptions are two kinds of material that would be cited in the text only: references to classical works such as the Bible and personal communications. (However, in a dissertation quotes from the Bible should only be used with the permission of the dissertation committee.)

Citation of Electronic and Internet Material:

1. DOI article identifiers (6.31 and 6.32)

- Digital Object Identifiers (DOIs) are a unique alphanumeric string assigned by a registration agency (the International DOI Foundation) to identify content and provide a persistent link to its location on the Internet. All DOI numbers begin with 10 and contain a prefix and a suffix separated by a slash. APA 6th edition recommends that when a DOI is available, you include them for BOTH print and electronic sources.

- DOIs are typically found on the first page of an electronic journal article near the copyright notice in the top right-hand corner and can also be found on the database landing page for the article (see Figures 6.2 and 6.3 in the 6th edition for location examples).

- Use this format for the DOI in references: doi:xxxxxxxx

When a DOI is used, no further retrieval information is needed to identify or locate the content (i.e., no electronic database name needs to be listed). If no DOI has been assigned to the content, include the home page URL of the journal, the book publisher, or the electronic database.

For a complete list all of the changes presented chapter-by-chapter, please go to the APA Style website www.apastyle.org. This website also has tutorials that you might find useful:

- What's New in the 6th Edition (about 14 minutes): http://tinyurl.com/2v2xfbb

- Basics of APA Style (about 21 minutes): http://tinyurl.com/n2argt

Reference for 6th edition APA Publication Manual (ISBN-10: 1-4338-0561-8 softcover).

PHASE 2

ACCOUTREMENTS

Utensils and Ingredients
[Instruments]
Assistant Chefs
[Population and Sample]
Serving Platters/Spices
[Statistics]

WHAT WILL YOU UTILIZE TO GATHER DATA?

Tests, Inventories, Questionnaires, Interviews, Observations, Archived Documents

In **PHASE 2** of your *Recipes for Success* you will acquire proper utensils for the creation and serving of your *feast*. In addition, during this phase you will be forming the *bulk* of *ingredients* for your *main course*, which you will ultimately complete in **PHASE 3.**

Prepackaged Tests and Inventories

(Just *Stir* and *Serve*)

Prepackaged tests and inventories are among the most useful tools for the *chef*/researcher. They have been seen at many *eloquent banquets* in the past. The benefits of using prepackaged and standardized tests are that the items and total scores have been carefully analyzed and their validity and reliability have most likely been established by careful statistical controls.

Most prepackaged tests have norms based upon the performance of many participants of various ages living in many different types of communities and geographic areas. Among those to choose from are

1. Achievement tests, which attempt to measure what an individual has learned. Achievement tests are designed to quantify an individual's level of performance based on information that has been deliberately taught. Most tests used in schools are achievement

tests. They are used to determine individual or group status in academic learning; to ascertain strengths and weaknesses defined by the test preparer; and as a basis for awarding prizes, scholarships, or degrees.

2. Aptitude tests, which attempt to predict the degree of achievement that may be expected from individuals in a particular activity. They are similar to achievement tests in their measuring of past learning, but differ in their attempt to measure nondeliberate or unplanned learning. They are often used to divide students into relatively homogeneous groups for instructional purposes, identify students for scholarship grants, screen for educational programs, and purport to predict future successes.

FOR YOUR INFORMATION AND EDUCATION

The Buros Institute of Mental Measurements http://buros.unl.edu/buros/jsp/search.jsp provides professional assistance, expertise, and information to users of commercially published tests. The institute's goals are to serve the public interest and contribute positively to the measurement field through the publication of the *Mental Measurements Yearbook* and Tests in Print series; presentation of the Buros-Nebraska Symposium on Measurement and Testing; sponsorship of the journal *Applied Measurement in Education*; and direct professional consultation. The Buros yearbooks contain critical evaluations of tests and provide information concerning costs, availability of alternate forms, administration time required, names of subtests, grade or age levels for which tests were designed, and the name of publishers.

FOR YOUR INFORMATION AND EDUCATION

The case has been made that most achievement and aptitude tests do not accurately predict academic achievement. Many people feel that the questions and concepts being measured by these tests are culturally biased. Efforts are being made to develop culture-free tests that eliminate this undesirable quality, but such tests have yet to meet universal approval.

1. Personality tests or inventories are used by participants to report their own personality traits or tendencies. However, because of many people's inability or unwillingness to report their own actions accurately and objectively, their tendency to withhold

embarrassing responses, and their unwillingness to expose those qualities that are socially unacceptable, the effectiveness and the value of such tests are limited.

2. Psychological tests and inventories are designed to describe and measure certain aspects of human behavior.

To determine if a prepackaged test is right for you, it would be an excellent idea to conduct an in-depth analysis of each question on each test that purports to measure a variable (characteristic) that you are examining. It is your responsibility to provide evidence that the instrument selected is the most appropriate for the purpose at hand.

 ## *Cutting Board*

1. If you are planning to use a prepackaged test, write the name of the test and its reliability and validity information in the space below, and determine how you will obtain the test for use.

   _____

2. List the questions that you feel this test will answer with respect to some variable or characteristic you wish to measure in your study.

Preparing Your Own Questionnaires or Surveys

(Making your meal from scratch)

Questionnaires and surveys are perhaps the most frequently used instruments for gathering data on population variables. Their appeal rests in their ability to get to the heart of the research under investigation. There are subtle differences between a questionnaire and a survey. The questionnaire is more like *fast food* and attempts to gather background (demographic) characteristics such as age, education, and gender. It is used to help feed *hungry* policy makers, program planners, evaluators, and researchers by gathering simple information directly from the people affected. A survey is generally more like good *home cooking*; it is complex and more probing and seeks to elicit the feelings, beliefs, knowledge, experiences, or activities of the respondents. Both are used in research when a sample of participants is drawn from a population and the data obtained are analyzed to make inferences about a population.

Good questionnaires and surveys maximize the relationship between the answers recorded and the variables the researcher is measuring. The answers are valuable to the extent that they can predict a relationship to facts or subjective states of interest. Researchers use three basic types of questions: multiple choice, numeric open end, and text open end or essays.

One means of ensuring that the questions are germane to the study is for the researcher to prepare a working table containing a list of questions related to the hypothesis under investigation. It might help to think of a survey as a test to measure each variable or construct (something that exists theoretically, like intelligence, but cannot be directly observed). To grade the test, you need to create an index to measure each variable and construct. For example, if you were measuring the construct political correctness with 10 questions, scores for each question could be assessed on an index ranging from 0 to 4 on a Likert-type scale, and a total of 0 to 40 points could measure the degree of political correctness, with 0 indicating an absence of political correctness and 40 indicating totally politically correct.

According to Perseus Development Corporation (http://www.perseus.com) , after you have the foundation of your planning—budgets, deadlines, goals, and information uses—it is time to plan the survey itself. This involves five "right" steps.

1.   Choosing the right people (sampling)
2.   Using the right vehicle (survey formation)
3.   Asking the right questions (survey formation)
4.   Obtaining the right interpretations (data analyses)
5.   Persuasively presenting results the right way (writing the report)

You also need to be aware of what constructs you will measure. These include, but are not limited to, the following:

1. Demographics - the categories someone fits into, such as age, marital status, business title, industry, ethnicity, or socioeconomic level
2. Attitude - how people think and feel about something
3. Cognition - the knowledge of subject matter
4. Perception - the way people receive messages and interpret them; insight, intuition, or knowledge gained by perceiving
5. Needs - what people feel are missing from their lives or a program
6. Behavior - how people react to situations and opportunities and also how they think they'd react
7. Efficacy - how effective a program or treatment was

A consideration that needs to be made is the type of data you will obtain. There are four types of data that you can acquire. A mnemonic device used to remember these types of data is found in the French word for black, NOIR (nominal, ordinal, interval, and ratio): Nominal and ordinal data are considered nonparametric data (nonnumerical), whereas interval and ratio are considered parametric (numerical) data.

1. Nominal (name only) data, or levels of measurement, are characterized by information that consists of names, labels, or categories only. These data cannot be arranged in an ordering scheme and are considered to be the lowest level of measurement. There is no criterion by which values can be identified as greater than or less than other values. Researchers cannot, for example, average 12 Democrats and 15 Republicans and come up with 13.5 Independents. We can, however, determine ratios and percentages and compare the results to other groups.
2. Ordinal (or ranked) levels of measurement generate data that may be arranged in some order, but differences between data values either cannot be determined or are meaningless. For example, we can classify income as low, middle, or high to provide information about relative comparisons, but the degrees of differences are not available.

3. Interval level of measurement is similar to the ordinal level, with the additional property that you can determine meaningful amounts of differences between data. This level, however, often lacks an inherent starting point. For example, in comparing the annual mean temperatures of states, the value of 0 degrees does not indicate no heat and it would be incorrect to say that 40 degrees is half as warm as 80 degrees. Grade point averages (GPAs) are also considered interval levels of measuring knowledge. If someone has a 0.0 GPA this does not mean that they have no knowledge.

4. Ratio level of measurement is considered the highest level of measurement. It includes an inherent zero starting point and fractional values. As the name implies, ratios are meaningful for this type of measurement. The heights of children, distances traveled, waiting times, and the amount of gasoline consumed are ratio levels of measurement. A special form of ratio-level measurement is the binary (or dummy) variable of 1,0. This code represents the presence (1) or absence (0) of a certain characteristic.

Ordering of Questions

With regard to the ordering of questions on a survey or questionnaire, the researcher needs to consider ways to encourage the participants to respond and answer honestly. Ideally, the early questions should be easy and pleasant to answer. These kinds of questions encourage people to continue the survey. In telephone or personal interviews they help build rapport with the interviewer. Grouping together questions on the same topic also makes the questionnaire or survey easier to answer. Whenever possible, place difficult or sensitive questions near the end of your survey. Any rapport that has been built up will make it more likely people will answer these questions. If people quit at that point anyway, at least they will have answered some of your questions. Whenever there is a logical or natural order to answer choices, use it. Make certain that *all* possible responses are included in the choices. In general, when using numeric rating scales, higher numbers should mean a more positive or more agreeing answer. However, an obvious answer to a question should be avoided.

A general and important guideline to follow is that statistics based on one level of measurement should not be used for a lower level. Implications made from interval and ratio data can usually be determined through parametric methods, whereas implications from ordinal and nominal data require the use of less sensitive, nonparametric methods.

Another decision that you need to make is whether to use open-ended questions or closed-ended questions. There are several advantages to open-ended questions:

1. You will be able to obtain answers that were unanticipated.
2. They tend to describe more closely the real views of the respondent.
3. Respondents will be able to answer questions in their own words.

However, closed-ended questions are usually an easier way of collecting data:

1. The respondent can perform more reliably the task of answering the question when response alternatives are given.
2. The researcher can perform more reliably the task of interpreting the meaning of answers when the alternatives are given to the respondent.
3. Providing respondents with a constrained number of categories increases the likelihood that there will be enough people in any given category to be analytically interesting.
4. There is a strong belief that respondents find closed-ended questions to be less threatening than open questions.

 *Cutting Board*

If you are planning to create a questionnaire or survey, fill out the information below:

1. List four demographic questions you feel would be helpful to know about your sample:

2. What questions are you seeking answers to in your study?

3. List four other broad questions that you would like to obtain from your sample:

4. Underline the types of measurements you will most likely use:

a. Nominal (name only, certain trait)
b. Ordinal (a ranking system; Likert-type scale)
c. Interval (fixed differences, but no fixed zero—temperature)
d. Ratio (interval with a fixed zero; height, time, weight)

5. Underline the type of questions you will most likely be asking:
   a. Open-ended (subjects fill in the blanks)
   b. Closed-ended (multiple choice)

6. What is the population you are studying? Will you be sending the questionnaire or survey to the whole population or to a subset (sample) of the population?

7. Will the survey administered be cross-sectional (just once) or longitudinal (over time)?

8. How will the survey or questionnaire be administered? Through the mail? Personal interview? Group setting?

9. Approximately how many questions do you plan to have?

10. Will you need permission or help to administer the questionnaire or obtain a mailing list? If yes, how will you obtain this assistance?

The following suggestions can help you to eliminate some obstacles that questionnaire and survey designers often encounter. As you prepare your questions, check to see that each question you create adheres to the warnings given.

____1. Use standardized English when writing your questions.

____2. Keep the questions concrete and close to the respondents' experience.

____3. Be aware of words, names, and views that might automatically bias results.

____4. Use a single thought per question.

____5. Use short questions and ask for short responses if possible.

____6. Avoid words that might be unfamiliar to the respondent.

____7. Define any word whose meaning might be vague.

___8. Avoid questions with double negatives, such as "This class is not the worst math class I have ever taken."

___9. When using multiple-choice questions, make sure all possibilities are covered.

___10. Be as specific as possible.

___11. Avoid questions with two or more parts.

___12. Give points of reference as comparisons. For example, instead of asking, "Do you like mathematics?", you might ask:

Please rank your favorite academic class from most favorite (4), to least favorite (1):

Social studies _____ English _____ Science _____ Mathematics____

___13. Underline or use bold print for words that are critical to the meaning of the questions, especially negative words like **not**.

___14. Ask only important questions since most respondents dislike long questionnaires or surveys that ask too many unimportant questions.

___15. Avoid suggestive questions or questions that contain biases. For example, "Would you support more money in mathematics education if the schools continue to use the same outdated teaching methods?" reflects the writer's bias on mathematics education.

___16. When asking questions regarding ethnic background or political affiliations, it is a good idea to use alphabetical order.

In addition, the following receive high honors in the *culinary* research arts:

___17. Efficiency and brevity - it should only be as long as necessary.

___18. Objectivity - the questions should be as objective as the situation dictates.

___19. Interesting - the questions should be as interesting and as enjoyable as possible.

___20. Simplicity - it should be simple to administer, score, and interpret.

___21. Clarity - it is important that the directions be clear so that each participant can understand exactly the manner in which the test is to be taken.

A widely used type of ordinal measurement used on closed questionnaires is the Likert-type scale, named after its creator, Rensis Likert (1932). Likert's original scale used five categories: *strongly approve, approve, undecided, disapprove*, and *strongly disapprove*. In a Likert-type scale, points are assigned to each of the categories being used. The most favorable response is usually given the most points, that is, favorableness of the attitude, not the response category itself. A Likert-type scale may use fewer or more than five categories. In general, the more categories there are, the better the reliability.

Note: Check out the following URL for more information regarding Likert-type scales: http://www.socialresearchmethods.net/kb/scallik.php

The placement of items should be randomized. Placing all of the favorably worded items first might produce a set or tendency for respondents (e.g., the participants might fill in all 5s without reading the questions).

The score that the individual receives on a Likert-type scale is the sum of the scores received on each item. For example, if 25 items are on a questionnaire and each item contains a minimum of 1 point and a maximum of 5 points, then the highest possible score would be 125, whereas the lowest possible score would be 25 (assuming no items were missing).

FOR YOUR INFORMATION AND EDUCATION

The Visual Analog Scale (VAS) is designed to present to the respondent a rating scale with minimum constraints. Thomeé, Grimby, Wright, and Linacre (1995) used a VAS scale, similar to the one below, to measure the perception of pain for patients with knee problems.

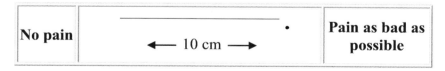

Respondents mark the location on the line corresponding to the amount of pain they are experiencing. This gives the ability to choose the exact intensity of pain that one is experiencing.

VAS data of this type are recorded as the number of millimeters from the left of the line with the range 0–100.

When you report your findings from your survey or questionnaire you will need to include the following:

1. The population you took the sample from.
2. How the people were contacted.
3. The number of people contacted, the number of people who responded, and the response rate.
4. Any evidence that the people who responded are a representative, unbiased sample of the population.
5. How the survey was distributed.
6. The date the survey was conducted.
7. Any caveats that readers should keep in mind as they interpret the findings. These might include cautions about a low response rate, a response group that is not quite representative of the overall population, or anything that has happened since the survey was conducted that might affect the results.

Gay and Airasian (2000) admonished that the best defense to nonresponders to individual items on the questionnaire or survey is the careful examination of the instrument during the pretest or pilot activities. They argued that this is the time that problems with items are most likely to show up. Subjecting the survey or questionnaire to rigorous examination will reduce item nonresponse and lessen significant problems to data and research analysis (Gay & Airasian, p. 290).

Reliability and Validity

Once you have custom-designed or selected your prepackaged instrument, you will need to consider the instrument's reliability and validity. Reliability is concerned with the accuracy (consistency, stability, and repeatability) of a measure in representing the true score of the subject being assessed on a particular dimension. The same results must be achieved, as far as possible, regardless of who is doing the measuring. Reliability of measurement reduces influence or bias on the part of the person(s) doing the measurement to a minimum.

Reliability refers to the consistency of assessment scores. For example, on a reliable test, a student would expect to attain the same score regardless of when the student completed the assessment, when the response was scored, and who scored the response. On an unreliable examination, a student's score might vary based on factors that are not related to the purpose of the assessment.

Many educators are familiar with the terms *test/retest reliability, equivalent-forms reliability, split half reliability*, and *rational equivalence reliability* (Gay, 1987). These terms refer to statistical methods used to establish consistency of student performances within a given test or across more than one test. These types of reliability are of more concern on standardized or high-stakes testing than they are in classroom assessment. In a classroom, students' knowledge is repeatedly assessed and this allows the teacher to adjust as new insights are acquired. Three forms of reliability are typically considered in classroom assessment (good news: they all begin with the letter I!) and in rubric development involve rater (or scorer) reliability and the consistency of different questions or items to measure the same construct. Rater reliability generally refers to the consistency of scores that are assigned by two independent raters and that are assigned by the same rater at different points in time. The former is referred to as *interrater reliability*, while the latter is referred to as *intrarater reliability*. The consistency of questions is considered internal reliability.

Interrater Reliability: Interrater reliability refers to the concern that scores might vary from rater to rater. Students often criticize exams in which their score appears to be based on the subjective judgment of their instructor. For example, one manner in which to analyze an essay exam is to read through the students' responses and make judgments as to the quality of the students' written products. Without set criteria to guide the rating process, two independent raters might not assign the same score to a given response. Each rater has his or her own evaluation criteria. Scoring rubrics respond to this concern by formalizing the criteria at each score level. The descriptions of the score levels are used to guide the evaluation process. Although scoring rubrics do not completely eliminate variations between raters, a well-designed scoring rubric can reduce the occurrence of these discrepancies.

Intrarater Reliability: Factors that are external to the purpose of the assessment can affect the manner in which a given rater scores student responses. For example, a rater might become fatigued with the scoring process and devote less attention to the analysis over time. Certain responses might receive different scores than they would have had they been scored earlier in the evaluation. A rater's mood or *appetite* on the given day or knowing who a respondent is might also impact the scoring process. A correct response from a failing student might be more critically analyzed than an identical response from a student who is known to perform well. Intrarater reliability refers to each of these situations in which the scoring process of a given rater changes over time. The inconsistencies in the scoring process result from influences that are internal to the rater rather than true differences in student performances. Well-designed scoring rubrics respond to the concern of intrarater reliability by establishing a description of the scoring criteria in advance. Throughout the scoring process, the rater should revisit the established criteria to ensure that consistency is maintained.

Internal Reliability: This is the extent to which items in an index or score are correlated with one another and, by extension, the extent to which they measure the same thing. Three main types of reliability coefficients can be measured:

1. Stability - the extent to which individuals maintain their relative standings when the same or similar exam is administered twice over a period of time.

2. Equivalence - correlation of scores on two or more forms of the same test by the same persons.

3. Internal consistency - correlation between questions on the same test to determine if they measure the same trait. Internal consistence on test scores from a single test can be achieved by asking the same question in different ways. The most common measure of

internal reliability or consistency is Cronbach's alpha, which ranges from 0 to 1.0. Scores toward the higher end of this range (above 0.70) indicate that the items in an index are measuring the same thing.

Establishing reliability is a prerequisite for establishing validity (Gay, 1987). Although a valid assessment is usually, by necessity, reliable, the contrary is not true. A reliable assessment is not necessarily valid. A scoring rubric is likely to result in invalid interpretations, for example, when the scoring criteria are focused on an element of the response that is not related to the purpose of the assessment. The score criteria might be so well stated that any given response would receive the same score regardless of the rater or when the response is scored.

As a researcher, you are obligated to select the most reliable instruments. The purpose of the testing determines, in part, the minimum reliability coefficient that can be tolerated. However, reliable tests might not necessarily be valid tests.

Validity refers to the extent to which measurements achieve the purpose for which they are designed. The researcher needs to determine the validity of the content. This is similar to a *chef* who wants to use natural rather than artificial *ingredients*. The main question that a researcher must address to determine validity is, Does an instrument (test, questionnaire, survey, etc.) measure what it is supposed to measure? Validity addresses systematic errors of measurement— for example, a test of music aptitude requiring students to read and write standard music notation would systematically produce higher scores for students with formal music training. There are three main types of validity: content validity, construct validity, and predictive validity.

Content Validity: Content validity refers to whether the questions—called items—included in an instrument cover the whole domain of factors they are intended to address. A measure has content validity when its items accurately represent the construct being measured. This form of validity is often determined by agreement among experts. For example, an instrument intended to measure patterns of alcohol use on a college campus would need to include items covering at least three areas: the proportion of students who drink, how frequently they drink, and how much they drink. If a measure addressed only one of these aspects of college student alcohol consumption, experts would consider it to have poor content validity. Similarly, if a test was given on the Vietnam War and the questions were only about various battles that were fought, this would not be representative of the entire subject.

Construct Validity: Construct validity refers to the extent to which an instrument successfully measures a theoretical concept—called a construct—such as anxiety, peer pressure, bullying, or perceptions of drinking norms. This addresses the question: How well are the variables operationalized? Scores from one instrument can be compared with scores from others that are intended to measure the same construct to assess whether the instruments perform comparably. Moderate or high correlation between instruments designed to measure the same construct indicates that the instruments are performing as intended. A construct, generally, has more validity if it correlates with other constructs that your theoretical framework indicates that it *should* correlate with. This assumes that your theory is correct.

Predictive Validity: Predictive validity indicates an instrument's ability to provide meaningful patterns of results. For instance, student performance on the SAT is used by admissions committees to predict academic performance during the first year of college. How well SAT scores actually do predict success during the first year of college would be an indication of the SAT's level of predictive validity. Predictive validity is also used to refer to an instrument's ability to discriminate among groups of respondents who would be expected to score differently on a particular measure. For example, a researcher could conduct interviews with students about their alcohol consumption and then divide them into two groups, one made up of heavy drinkers and the other of light drinkers, based on the analyses of the interviews. If the researcher then had the students complete a survey on alcohol use, the expectation would be that the heavy drinkers would score differently on the instrument than light drinkers. If the survey could not discriminate between the two groups, it would be considered to have low predictive validity.

The following are some questions that could determine whether a test is valid:

1. Does each item measure a predetermined criterion?

2. Do previously obtained scores accurately predict the criteria measured?

3. Does the behavior or conditions of administrating the test affect the results?

 Cutting Board

This would be an excellent time to create your questionnaire or survey if your study requires the same. Insert a separate sheet of paper and compose your survey or questionnaire now. Check to see that you have incorporated the ideas suggested in this section. Also check out http://owl.english.purdue.edu/owl/resource/559/06/ for more helpful hints.

Enjoy the challenge!

ACCOUTREMENTS TO QUESTIONNAIRES AND SURVEYS
Internet/Intranet (Web Page) Surveys
Pilot Study
Cover Letter
Going the Extra Mile

Internet/Intranet (Web Page) Surveys

Web surveys are quite popular and easy to create. They are expeditious, cost effective, and flexible, but may restrict the groups you can study. Software is available to help you create and analyze online surveys. Two popular sites are found at http://www.surveymonkey.com/ and http://info.zoomerang.com/. The advantage to using an online survey is that you can gather several thousand responses within a few hours. Many people who respond to an e-mail invitation to take a Web survey will do so the first day, and others will do so within a few days. Web page questionnaires or surveys can use complex question-skipping logic, randomizations, and other features not possible with paper questionnaires to ensure the obtainment of better data. On average, people give longer answers to open-ended questions on Web page questionnaire than they do on other kinds of self-administered surveys. However, there are challenges to using online surveys. Although the number of online users keeps growing exponentially, not everyone has regular or reliable access to the Internet. People can easily quit in the middle of taking a survey. They are not as likely to complete a long questionnaire on the Web as they would be if talking with a good interviewer. If you post your survey on a Web page with open access, you will have little or no control over who replies.

There is also little control for people responding multiple times to bias the results. However, if your target population consists entirely, or almost entirely, of Internet users, then an online survey is worthy of consideration. If you do decide to use a Web survey, think about restricting access by requiring a password (good software allows this option) or by putting the survey on a page that can only be accessed directly (i.e., there are no links to it from other pages).

Pilot Study

Before the final form of the survey or questionnaire is constructed, it is useful to conduct a pilot study (or *dress rehearsal*) to determine if the items are yielding the kind of information that is needed. The term *pilot study* is used in two different ways in social science research. It can refer to so-called feasibility studies, which are "small scale version[s], or trial run[s], done in preparation for the major study" (Polit, Beck, & Hungler, 2001, p. 467). It is also used to refer to the pretesting, or trying out, of a particular research instrument (Baker, 1994, pp. 182-183). One of the advantages of conducting a pilot study is that it can give advance warning about where the main research study could fail, where research protocols might not be followed, or whether proposed methods or instruments are inappropriate or too complicated. De Vaus (1993) advised researchers to "check to see if there is any ambiguity, or if the respondents have any difficulty in responding" (p. 54). Surveys are pilot-tested to avoid misleading, inappropriate, or redundant questions. Pilot-testing ensures that the survey or questionnaire can be used properly and that the information obtained is consistent. Fink and Kosekoff (1985) indicated that when pilot-testing, look out for a failure to answer questions, respondents giving several answers to the same question, and written comments in the margin. These may be indications that the questionnaire or survey is unreliable and needs revision.

Administering the questionnaire or survey personally and individually to a small group of respondents is a good way to proceed with your pilot study, but it could be conducted electronically or through other means. Well-designed and well-conducted pilot studies can inform the researcher on the research process and about likely outcomes. It is important to report the findings of the pilot studies (this usually appears in chapters 3 or 4 in the dissertation) and detail the actual improvements made to the study design and the research process as a result of the pilot findings.

The pilot instrument should invite comments about the perceived relevance of each question to the stated intent of the research. It would also be beneficial to provide a means for the respondent to suggest additional questions that the researcher did not include. Check out http://sru.soc.surrey.ac.uk/SRU35.html for more information on pilot studies.

Cover Letter

If a questionnaire or survey is administered to an intact group, such as students in a class or members of a congregation, then you will have the opportunity to inform the respondents of the intent of the study and motivate them to complete the questionnaire or survey. However, when questionnaires or surveys are sent through the mail, it may be difficult to motivate respondents to fill them out and to return them within a reasonable period of time. Unless the potential respondents believe that the questionnaire or survey is of value, it is likely that they will become nonrespondents. For this purpose, a cover letter usually accompanies the questionnaire or survey.

> Note: It is important to inform potential participants that this is part of a doctoral dissertation for your university. This information should be stated in the cover letter since such information often adds credibility to the study.

The cover letter should also state the following:

1. The questionnaire or survey will not take a great deal of time to complete.
2. Each individual's personal attention to the questionnaire or survey is of extreme importance to the study.

In addition, the following *ingredients* would enhance the efficacy of a cover letter:

1. An introduction: The name of the researcher and the company, organization, or university that is requesting or approving this study.

2. A purpose: The reason for conducting the study, the use for this questionnaire or survey, and its value to the investigation should be explained. The sole intention of a study should not be that a student expects to obtain a degree by means of a research study that includes the use of this questionnaire or survey (however important that is). It is unlikely that a potential respondent would take the time to carefully fill out a questionnaire for this goal.

   Note: You must also be careful not to reveal too much. This might bias the study and make the results invalid.

3. A set of directions: Explain how the questions are to be answered, how the questionnaire or survey is to be returned, and if there is some reasonable deadline for returning it. Indicate whether the respondent needs to put his or her name on the form and any other relevant information that should be included with the questionnaire or survey.

4. Return postage: It is unreasonable to ask the respondent to answer your questionnaire and provide postage for its return to you.

5. The researcher should avoid the use of obvious form letters or letters for which the initial salutation is

   Dear _____, or "To Whom it may concern:"

6. You should also sign the letter personally.

Extra attention and personal touches demonstrate the sincerity of the research effort and the importance of the respondents' participation.

Note: Without your taking the aforementioned information into consideration, it is likely that the questionnaire or survey will only make it to the nearest trash receptacle.

 *Cutting Board*

This would be an excellent time to create your cover letter. Insert a separate sheet of paper and compose your cover letter NOW! Check to see that you have incorporated the ideas suggested in this section.

Going the Extra Mile

Some ways to encourage respondents to perform the task of filling out a mailed or online questionnaire or survey include:

1. Making personal contact by phone or in person, prior to sending out the questionnaire.
2. Offering some type of financial compensation or gift.

FOR YOUR INFORMATION AND EDUCATION

One type of incentive to increase response rate is sending a dollar bill along with the survey (or offering to donate a dollar to a charity specified by the respondent). Make certain that you indicate that the dollar is a way of saying thanks, rather than payment for time spent completing the survey. For short questionnaires, you could put a questionnaire on the back of a small check. Another possible incentive is to enroll the people who return completed surveys in a drawing for a prize. You could also offer a copy of the (nonconfidential) result to the participants.

1. Make the cover letter and questionnaire or survey attractive.
2. Make the cover letter personal.
3. Make repeated contact with nonrespondents.

Remember that if you want (or need) a sample of 500 participants, and you estimate a 10% response level, you need to mail 5,000 surveys. You might want to check with your local post office about bulk mail rates—you can save on postage using this mailing method. However, many people associate *bulk* with *junk* and will throw out the survey without opening the envelope, thereby lowering the response rate. Also, bulk mail moves slowly, which increases the time needed to complete your study.

A reasonable sequence of events might be as follows:

1. About 10 days after the initial post or e-mailing, send all nonrespondents a reminder emphasizing the importance of the study and the need for a high response rate.

2. About 10 days after the first reminder, mail the remaining nonrespondents a letter, again emphasizing the importance of a high rate of return and including another questionnaire for those who might have thrown away, or expunged, the first one.

3. If the response rate is still not satisfactory, it would be advisable to call nonrespondents on the telephone.

The challenges of getting the response rate to a reasonable level will depend on the nature of the sample, the nature of the study, the motivation of the people to participate in the study, the ease with which the questionnaire or survey might be completed, and your tenacity.

 Cutting Board

If you are planning to mail out questionnaires or surveys, which of the methods above do you think you will employ to increase the response rate?

The Personal Interview

The personal interview has many similarities to the questionnaire or survey. The major advantages of using an interview instead of a questionnaire or survey are as follows:

1. The response rate is generally high.

2. It is an especially useful technique when dealing with children or an illiterate population.

3. It eliminates the misinterpretation of a question.

4. The participant is more likely to clarify any misunderstandings.

5. It can encourage a relaxed conversation during which questions can be asked in any order depending on the response of the interviewee.

6. It provides an opportunity to find out what people really think and believe about a certain topic through questioning.

7. It is more flexible and allows the interviewer to follow leads during the interview.

8. The interviewer can interpret body language as an extra source of information.

Note: A good interviewer exudes HEARTS: honesty, earnestness, adaptability, reliability, trustworthiness, and sincerity.

Some disadvantages of the interview method are as follows:

1. Time and economy: Questionnaires and surveys can usually be sent through the postal mail or e-mail; thus, for the price of postage and printing the questionnaire or survey, or the time to compose an electronic document, you can reach practically anyone under consideration. Furthermore, the expense and time involved in training interviewers and sending them to interview the respondents needs to be considered.

2. Reliability of information can be questioned because of interviewer bias.

3. Difficulties often arise in quantifying or statistically analyzing data obtained from interviews.

To help you put your participants at ease:

1. Begin with easy nonthreatening questions

2. Follow with increasingly specific questions

3. Follow by questions of a sensitive nature

4. Ensure participants they are free to refuse to respond if questions get too personal

When you conduct a semi-structured or unstructured interview, make certain you have a list of general questions designed to open up conversation about the topic. Often, this includes a series of follow-up questions or probes, prepared in advance, to elicit the information you need from the participant to answer your research questions and obtain the purpose of your study. It is important to recognize a good interviewer is a good listener and that the best probing is that which is responsive, in the moment, and in tune to what the interviewee is saying.

At times you need to be silent to give the interviewee time to think and speak.

After each interview, reflect what kind of talk or discussion emerged when questions were asked, and identify questions that need to be refined. Also, identify new experiences shared by the interviewee that could be incorporated into subsequent interviews. Also reflect on your role as an interviewer and on your preconceptions and behaviors during the interview and make any needed adjustments

All data obtained through questionnaires, surveys, or interviews adhere to the same ethical system: The privacy of the individual is respected and weighed against the public's right to know.

FOR YOUR INFORMATION AND EDUCATION

The results of surveys that deal with sensitive issues are felt by many to be dubious. People are often not willing to reveal private details about their lives.

However, a statistical method can allow investigators to ask questions in a way that is likely to elicit honest responses. It completely protects the privacy of individuals yet provides good survey information. It has been used to improve our understanding of AIDS, the extent of cheating on income tax, and the use of illegal drugs. The method is called randomized response and was invented in 1965 by Stanley Warner of York University in Ontario.

Here is how it works: Suppose the members of the senate ($N = 100$) were asked, Did you ever have sex with a prostitute while in office? The researcher asks the question and has all the participants flip a coin. If the coin turns up heads they are told to write "yes." If the coin turns up tails, they tell the truth. They are not to indicate what the result of the coin toss was. The only true answers are the "no's." If there are 15 "no's," the conclusion is that 30% have not had sex with a prostitute while in office (the 15 that had to get tails to write "no," and then an equal number who happened to get a head on the toss). Those members of Congress who have had sex with a prostitute would be estimated at 70%.

Populations surveyed who are likely to realize that it is in their best interest for investigators to have accurate information, yet do not wish to be identified, are more willing to participate in this type of survey. It is reasonable to expect that if people could be assured anonymity they would give honest answers.

Another example: Suppose Question 10 on a survey is, "Have you used illegal drugs in the past week?" Respondents are told to read the question and flip a coin. They are to answer "no" only if the coin comes up tails and they have not used illegal drugs. Otherwise, they should answer "yes." The proportion of the group that would have answered "no" is then computed to be twice those that actually responded "no." (The other half got heads.) For example, if 40% wrote "no," then 80% of the sample is determined to have not used illegal drugs in the past week, and 20% is determined to have used illegal drugs during the past week.

 Cutting Board

1. If you are planning to use the personal interview, list the reasons for your decision.
2. Who will do the interviewing? Why?

Observation

Obtaining data through observation, both participant and nonparticipant, has become common. It is perhaps the most direct means of finding out information, especially if your study is focused on deeds rather than words. The extent of your personal involvement depends on which of the two methods you choose.

In nonparticipant observation:

1. Your presence might be known or unknown.
2. You might observe through a device such as a one-way glass or rely on observations from video or audio taping.
3. The data obtained tend to be fairly subjective.

The major advantage to using participant observation is that you can experience firsthand the psychological and social conditions that produce different decisions and practices.

The disadvantages to using participant observation are as follows:

1. You could be influenced by your own interpretation and personal experiences.
2. Questions of reliability exist since others might interpret an experience differently than you.
3. Your presence might affect the participants and the situation observed.

One way to reduce the disadvantages is to read your report to the people observed and to ask for comments, additions, or deletions prior to its formalization.

Accuracy is the key to making this type of data collection effective. Special training is needed to move from casual observer to systematic observer. In using structured observation techniques, the researcher usually searches for a relationship between independent variables and a dependent variable. The researcher must thus be able to code and recode data in a meaningful way and be aware of the potential biases he or she brings to research.

Note: A confounding variable is an extraneous variable that is not a focus of the study but is statistically related to (or correlated with) the independent variable. This means that as the independent variable changes, the confounding variable changes along with it. When there is some other variable that changes along with the independent variable, then this confounding variable could be the cause of any difference. Studies that indicate people who eat fast food are less healthy than people who eat gourmet food might neglect confounding variables such as socioeconomic status, which might be the root cause of health status.

Read more: http://tinyurl.com/22ucdcy

Archival Documents

Archival documents are existing records that contain information about the past. Data-based archives are important in social and behavioral research. The National Archives and Records Association, located online at http://www.archives.gov/welcome/index.html, is an independent federal agency that serves as a national record keeper and ensures ready access to essential evidence that documents the rights of American citizens, the actions of federal officials, and the national experience. These records document the common heritage and the individual and collective experiences of U.S. citizens. You can also find a listing of over 5,000 Web sites describing holdings of manuscripts, archives, rare books, historical photographs, and other primary sources for the research scholar at http://tinyurl.com/29gpjdk.

Archival documents can also be obtained from individual organizations. These usually consist of service records, organizational records, lists of names, survey data, and other such records. The investigator has to be careful in evaluating the accuracy of the records before using them. Even if the records are quantitative, they might still not be accurate. In case study research, and to triangulate data from other research methods, documents of interest can be letters, memoranda, agendas, e-mails, administrative documents, newspaper articles, brochures, or any text or record that is germane to the investigation. In the interest of triangulation of evidence, the documents serve to corroborate the evidence from other sources. Documents are also useful for making inferences about events that have taken place and to understand the types of communication and interaction between participants in a study.

FOR YOUR INFORMATION AND EDUCATION

All methods of data collection have advantages and disadvantages compared to other methods. This is comparable to different methods of *cooking—roasting, frying, boiling, baking, barbequing,* etc. The method that you choose should be based upon the aims and objectives of the study and the population being studied. However, when you write your research paper, you should include the advantages and disadvantages of the instrument you chose and explain how you attempted to minimize the disadvantages.

ASSISTANT CHEFS: IDENTIFYING YOUR POPULATION AND CHOOSING YOUR SAMPLE

Most *head chefs* employ a variety of people, or *cooks*, to assist them in producing an *elegant banquet*. Similarly, most researchers depend upon other people to help them obtain the information that they need to prepare their dissertation or research report.

If you are planning to conduct a survey or interview people, one major issue is to get enough people whose views count. Usually it is not practical or possible to study the entire universe or population, so you need to settle for a sample or a subset of the universe. In choosing a sample and a method of data collection, you need to ask yourself certain questions:

1. How quickly are the data needed?
2. What are the resources available?
3. Should probability or nonprobability sampling be used?
4. How large a sample size do I need?

Things to consider when conducting a sample:

Data carelessly collected may be so completely useless or otiose that no amount of statistical torturing can salvage them—*garbage in, garbage out*! There are four points to consider when collecting data.

1. Ensure the sample size is large enough for the required purpose. (This will be discussed in hypothesis testing.)
2. When possible, do the measuring yourself. Self-reporting tends to lead to erroneous, political correctness, wishful thinking, or disproportionate rounding and distorted data.
3. How will data be collected? Mail surveys tend to get lower responses. Personal interviews are time consuming and expensive, but might be necessary for complete data. Telephone interviews are relatively efficient and relatively inexpensive, but consumer concerns about the growing number of unsolicited telephone marketing calls to their homes and the increasing use of automated and prerecorded messages have led to the

Telephone Consumer Protection Act (TCPA). Online surveys also have advantages and disadvantages.

4. Ensure that the sample is representative of the population.

The following are common means of sampling:

1. Random sampling (representative, proportionate) - Members of the population are selected in such a way that each has an equal and nonzero chance of being selected. This needs much planning to avoid haphazard sampling. Telephone directories, for example, leave out unlisted numbers. In Los Angeles, 42.5% of the telephone numbers are unlisted. Computer-generated numbers are better. There is about a 20% refusal rate for telephone intervals, which could bias the study.

2. Stratified sampling - Members of the population are subdivided into at least two subpopulations or strata, for example, gender. Samples are then drawn randomly from each stratum. This procedure requires that the researcher first separate the population from which he or she will sample into the separate groups (based on the characteristic of interest). For example, if the researcher was interested in obtaining a sample of 100 (from a population of 500) that was equal on gender, he or she would separate the 500 possible participants into two separate groups: one female and one male. Then from each group the researcher would randomly select 50 participants.

3. Systematic sampling - Similar to random sampling. Members of the population are listed in some type of roster and then every kth (e.g., 20th) element is chosen.

4. Cluster sampling - Members of the population are divided into sections (or clusters) and a few of those sections are then randomly selected and all the members for the selected sections are chosen. For example, in conducting a pre-election poll, we could randomly select 30 election precincts and survey all people from those precincts. The results might need to be adjusted to correct for any disproportionate representation of groups. This technique is used extensively by government and private research organizations.

5. Snowball sampling - One participant gives the researcher the name of another potential

participant, who in turn provides the name of a third, and so on. This is an especially useful technique when the researcher wants to survey or interview people with unusual characteristics who are likely to know one another. The downside is similar to that in #6 below.

6. Convenience sampling (nonprobability sampling) - Use the results that are readily available. Sometimes this is quite good (e.g., a teacher wanting to know about left-handed students' needs would not include those who are right-handed); sometimes it can be seriously biased when the researcher chooses only those he or she feels comfortable working with.

> Note: The emergent nature of qualitative research requires researchers to employ sampling procedures that will allow for the most insightful data collection in answering a particular question or exploration. This is known as purposeful sampling to meet the criterion under study.

Nonprobability sampling is something we all use in everyday life. If you want to try out a new brand of crackers, you know that you only need to choose one cracker from one box to decide if you like the cracker because the others are expected to taste pretty much the same. Another common form of nonprobability sampling may be carried out when trying to conduct interviews on the street. Researchers will often have some bias toward which people they will sample.

Sometimes nonprobability sampling is done inadvertently. In 1933, a telephone poll indicated that Landon would overwhelmingly become our next president. If you have difficulty remembering President Landon's record, your vexation would be justified. What became apparent, after this study was analyzed, was that it failed to take into account that Republicans had most of the phones in 1933 and that Roosevelt's supporters were the majority without telephones.

If a nonprobability survey is to be conducted, you must be very careful not to generalize too much from it. It is, however, very useful in the early stages of developing your study to obtain some new ideas and in the development of some interview questions, in practicing interviews and surveying techniques, or in a pilot study. At times, only a small sample of the population is available to participate in a study.

Nonprobability samples are usually easier to obtain but the gains in efficiency are often matched with losses in accuracy and generality.

Sometimes thousands of people are sampled to get the data needed; on other occasions, a sample might be as small as one.

The following are some factors affecting the size of a sample:

1. the size of the universe or population being studied,
2. the purpose of the study,
3. the potential application of the result of the study,
4. the type of statistical tests, and
5. the research technique(s) used.

By having a relatively large sample, you are usually able to see the general, overall pattern, but because the significance of measures is a function of sample size in many tests, it is possible to get a statistically significant relation when the strength of the relationship is too small to be used. Under sound statistical practices, using simple random samples obtained through probability means you can often get excellent information from a sample size of 30 or less.

Sometimes a case study of one or two participants is the most appropriate means of conducting an investigation. This enables you to obtain detailed information about a problem in which there is much interest but little information.

Case studies are usually selected by nonprobability sampling according to your judgment about whether the sample is a good representation of the population. For example, most information obtained about the (idiot) savant syndrome has been obtained through individual case studies of these extraordinary people.

Sample Size

Linda Suskie, in her book *Questionnaire Survey Research: What Works* (1996), provides a guide to determine how many people you can survey based on sampling error. A sampling error is an estimate of how a sample statistic is expected to differ from a population parameter in a random sample of the population. If you conducted a random survey of 250 high school students and found that 30% cheated on a test in the past year, then a 5% sampling error would mean that the true number of all high school students who cheated on a test during the past year is between 29.85 and 31.5%.

Random Sample Size	Sample Error
196	7%
264	6%
364	5%
1,067	4%
2,401	2%
9,604	1%

In most studies, 5% sampling error is acceptable. Below are the sample sizes you need from a given population.

Population Size	Sample Size
10,000	370
5,000	357
2,000	322
1,000	278
500	217
250	155
100	80

Note: These numbers assume a 100% response rate.

Gay (1996, p. 125) suggested general rules similar to Suskie's for determining the sample size. He recommended that for small populations ($N < 100$), there is little point in sampling and surveys should be sent to the entire population. If the population size is around 500, approximately 50% of the population should be sampled, if the population size is 1,500, 20% should be sampled, and beyond a certain point (at approximately $N = 5,000$), the population size is almost irrelevant and a sample size of 400 is adequate. Thus, the larger the population, the smaller the percentage needed to get a representative sample.

The following are some other issues to consider when deciding the size of the sample and references that could assist in dealing with these considerations:

Statistical validity. The larger the sample, the more accurate the results.

Characteristics of the sample. Larger samples are needed for heterogeneous populations; smaller samples are needed for homogeneous populations (Leedy & Ormrod, 2001, p. 221).

Cost of the study. A minimum number of participants is needed to produce valid results. http://tinyurl.com/2eqpvqc.

The ability to generalize results from the study to the larger population.

Knowledge of the behavior of the data (variance and standard deviation).

Statistical power needed. Larger samples yield greater the statistical power. In experimental research, power analysis is used to determine sample size (requires calculations involving statistical significance, desired power, and the effect size).

Confidence level desired (reflects accuracy of sample; Babbie, 2001)

Purpose of the study. Merriam (1998) noted, "Selecting the sample is dependent upon the research problem" (p. 67).

Availability of the sample. Convenience samples are used when only the individuals who are convenient to pick are chosen for the sample. A convenience sample is sometimes known as a location sample, as individuals might be chosen from just one area.

Availability of sampling frames (a sampling frame is a list from which a probability sample is selected, e.g., telephone list; Babbie, 2001).

Most important, the sample size must represent the characteristics or behavior of the larger population. More information on sample size can be found at http://tinyurl.com/2eqpvqc.

FOR YOUR INFORMATION AND EDUCATION

Another very important part of sampling is the nonresponse rate, which includes people who could not be contacted or who refused to answer questions. A general rule is to try to keep the nonresponse rate under 25%. To keep the nonresponse rate small, you could ask for the assistance of a community leader and have that person explain the purpose and importance of your study in great detail to potential respondents.

The size of the survey may be decided with statistical precision. A major concern in choosing a sample size is that it should be large enough so that it will be representative of the population from which it comes and from which you wish to make inferences. It ought to be large enough so that important differences can be found in subgroups such as men and women, Democrats and Republicans, groups receiving treatment and control groups, etc.

One major issue to consider when using statistical methods in choosing a sample size is sampling error, also known as margin of error. This is not an error in the sense of making a mistake. Rather, it is a measure of the possible range of approximation in the results because a sample was used. Some small differences will almost always exist among samples and between them and the population from which they are drawn. One approach to measuring sample error is to report the standard error of measurement that is computed by dividing the population standard deviation (if known) by the square root of the sample size. Minimizing the sampling error helps to maximize the sample's representativeness.

Example: If the Stanford-Binet IQ test (where the standard deviation is 15) is administered to 100 participants, then the standard error of the mean would be 15/10 or 1.5.

Note: We can use the following formula to determine the sample size necessary to discover the true mean value from a population.

$$n = \left[\frac{\bar{z}\sigma}{E} \right]^2 ,$$

where $\bar{z}$ corresponds to a confidence level (found on a table or computer program). Some common $\bar{z}$ values are 1.645 or 1.96, which might reflect a 95% confidence level (depending on the statistical hypothesis under investigation), and 2.33, which could reflect a 99% confidence level in a one-tailed test and 2.575 for a two-tailed test. σ is the standard deviation, and E is the margin of error.

Example: If we need to be 99% confident that we are within 0.25 lbs of a true mean weight of babies in an infant care facility, and $s = 1.1$, we would need to sample 129 babies:

$$n = [2.575\,(1.1)/0.25]^2 = 128.3689 \text{ or } 129.$$

Note: A formula that we can use to determine the sample size necessary to test a hypothesis involving percentages is:

$$n = \frac{[\bar{z}]^2}{E^2}\,\hat{p}\hat{q},$$

where n = sample size, $\bar{z}$ = standard score corresponding to a certain confidence level, $\hat{p}$ is an estimate of the population proportion and $\hat{q} = 1 - \hat{p}$. We represent the proportion of sampling error by E, and the estimated proportion or incidence of cases by p.

Example: Suppose that studies conducted 2 years ago found that 18% of drivers talk on a cell phone while driving. We want to do a study to check if this percentage is still true. We want to estimate, with a margin of error of 3 percentage points, the percentage of drivers who talk while driving today. If we need to be 95% confident of our result, how many drivers would we need to survey?

$$n = \frac{[1.96]^2}{0.03^2}\,(.18)(.82) = 1068.$$

 Cutting Board

1. What is the population and sample that you will be studying?

   _____

   _____

2. How will you select your sample? Why?

   _____

   _____

3. What measures will you take to see that your sample size is adequate for your study?

   _____

   _____

SERVING PLATTERS/SPICES

[Statistics]
Featuring: What's Stat? (You Say?)
How to Exhibit Your Date (a)
How to (Ap)praise Your Date (a)

What's Stat? (You Say?)

Statistics is like trying to determine how many different colored M&M's are in a king size bag by looking at only a carefully selected handful.

The Job of a Statistician Involves C O A I P ing Data:

½ cup	**C** OLLECTING
½ cup	**O** RGANIZING
1 cup	**A** NALYZING
1-2 cups	**I** NTERPRETING
1 cup	**P** REDICTING

After data are collected, they are used to produce various statistical numbers such as means, standard deviations, and percentages. These descriptive numbers summarize or describe the important characteristics of a known set of data. In hypothesis testing, descriptive numbers are standardized so that they can be compared to fixed values (found in tables or in computer programs) that indicate how unusual it is to obtain the data you collected. Once data are standardized and significance determined, you may be able to make inferences about an entire population (universe).

Note: Your *Recipes for Success* gives you a substantial *taste* of statistics so that you will feel comfortable with this aspect of your *feast* preparation. You have already *nibbled* on statistics in the last section when you explored different methods of collecting data.

You might wish to seek further *condiments* to add to the knowledge you will acquire from your *Recipes for Success* or consult with a statistician after reading the information in **PHASE 2** to help you decide which statistics, if any, would be applicable to your study. Mario Triola's statistics books are user friendly and offer an excellent foundation for quantitative analyses. You are also encouraged to use statistical programs like SPSS, Excel, or business calculators to perform the hackneyed computations that often arise during statistical testing. Dr. Jim Mirabella has written an excellent manual on how to use SPSS to analyze data for a doctoral dissertation. This is available at http://www.drjimmirabella.com/ebook . Consulting with a statistician is another viable option to help you select the proper statistics.

Remember: You are ultimately responsible for the results. You must be aware of why you are using a certain test, know what assumptions are made when such a test is used, understand what the test results indicate, and understand how this analysis fits in with your study. Good news: This is not as hard as it sounds. ☺

The Role of Statistics

Statistics is merely a tool. It is not the be-all and end-all for the researcher. Those who insist that research is not research unless it is statistical display a myopic view of the research process. These are often the same folks who are equally adamant that unless research is experimental research it is not research. However, without statistics, life would be pretty boring. We would not be able to plan our budgets, evaluate performances, or enjoy sporting events. (Can you imagine your favorite sport without any score keeping or statistics?)

One cardinal rule applies: The nature of the data and the problem under investigation govern which method is appropriate to interpret the data and the tool of research required to process those data. A historian seeking to answer problems associated with the assassination of Dr. Martin Luther King, Jr., would be hard put to produce either a statistical or an experimental study, and yet the research of the historian can be quite as scholarly and scientifically respectable as that of any quantitative or experimental study.

Statistics many times describes a quasi-world rather than the real world. You might find that the mean grade for a class is 81 but not one student actually received a grade of 81. Consider the person who found out that the average family has 1.75 children and with heartfelt gratitude exclaimed, "Boy, am I grateful that I was the first born!" What is accepted statistically is sometimes meaningless empirically. However, statistics is a useful mechanism and, as Ian Stewart noted, *Statistics is a means of panning precious simplicity from the sea of complexity*. It is a tool that can be applied to practically every discipline!

Frequently Asked Questions (FAQs) About Statistics

1. What is the purpose of statistics?

The purpose of statistics is to collect, organize, and analyze data (from a sample); interpret the results; and try to make predictions (about a population). We "do" statistics whenever we COAIP—collect, organize, analyze, interpret, and predict—data. One relies on statistics to determine how close to what one anticipated would happen actually did happen.

2. What is the purpose of descriptive statistics?

Descriptive statistics are used to summarize data in a clear and understandable way and enable the researcher to discern patterns and general trends. For example, suppose a researcher gave a personality test measuring charisma to 200 managers in a Fortune 500 company. There are two basic methods to summarize data: numerical and graphical. Using the numerical approach, she or he might compute descriptive statistics such as the mean, percentages, frequencies, and standard deviation. These statistics convey information about the degree of charisma and the degree to which people differ in charisma*ness*. Using the graphical approach, one might create a stem and leaf display, histogram, pie chart, or box plot. These graphs contain detailed information about the distribution of charismatic scores. Graphical methods are better suited than numerical methods for identifying patterns in the data, whereas numerical approaches are more precise and objective. Check out http://davidmlane.com/hyperstat/A28521.html

3. Why and how would one use inferential statistics?

Inferential statistics are used to draw implications about a population from a sample. In inferential statistics, we compare a numerical result (test value) to a number that is reflective of a chance happening (critical value) and determine how significant the difference between these two numbers is. When we test a hypothesis or create a confidence level, we are doing inferential statistics.

4. Are predictions indisputable in statistics?

Statistics can be used to predict, but these predictions are not certainties. Statistics offers us a best guess. The fact that conclusions might be incorrect separates statistics from most other branches of mathematics. If a fair coin is tossed 10 times and 10 heads appear, the statistician would incorrectly report that the coin is biased. This conclusion, however, is not certain. It is only a likely conclusion, reflecting the very low probability of getting 10 heads in 10 tosses.

5. What are hypotheses?

Hypotheses are educated guesses (definitive statements) derived by logical analysis using induction or deduction from one's knowledge of the problem and from the purpose for conducting a study. They can range from very general statements to highly specific ones. We can translate our claims into substantive hypotheses (what you are trying to substantiate) and then turn this claim into null and alternative hypotheses.

FOR YOUR INFORMATION AND EDUCATION

Deductive reasoning involves a hierarchy of statements or truths. From these statements, hypotheses are tested. You likely studied deductive geometry in mathematics, where you started with a few principles and then proved various propositions using those principles and some defined and undefined terms. To prove more complicated propositions, you used propositions that you had already proved along with the original principles. In more formal logic terms, deductive reasoning is reasoning from stated premises to conclusions formally or necessarily implied by such premises. The Pythagorean theorem, for example, can be proven from propositions, definitions, and previously proved theorems. Deduction is like using your grandma's *recipe to bake apple pie* and having the *pie* turn out exactly like grandma's.

Inductive reasoning is the opposite of deductive reasoning. Inductive reasoning involves trying to *create* general principles by starting with specific examples. If you were to start with 10 random triangles and find that the sum of the measures of the interior angles all equal 180 degrees, you would probably conclude that the sum of the interior angles of *all* triangles equal 180 degrees. However, if someone were to show you another triangle (in non-Euclidean geometry there are triangles that are made with circle arcs) where the sum is not 180, then your conclusion would be incorrect. [Note: In Euclidean geometry we can prove that all triangles have angle sum of 180 degrees, but this requires Euclid's 5th postulate, which is a whole other story!]. Induction is like trying to make a unique *apple pie* without a *recipe* but using ingredients that you feel will *blend* well together, using your intuition and knowledge about what would be *tasty*. Much to the surprise of many doctoral students, statistics is an inductive branch of mathematics. That is why we really do not PROVE anything with statistics. However, we do test theories based on specific cases and laws of probability. Since probability IS a deductive branch of mathematics, the "truths" we discover are likely to be true or can be quantified regarding the degree of truth.

When it comes to quantitative studies, they are more deductive than qualitative studies. In quantitative studies, we use the laws of statistics and probability to test theories; in qualitative studies, we use inductive techniques to develop theories.

Broad Area	Hypothesis (or Hypotheses)
Employee Motivation	The implementation of an attendance bonus is related to employee attendance. There is a difference in motivation between Gen X and Baby Boomers in the information technology industry.
Employee Satisfaction	There is a relationship between employee satisfaction and management style. There is a relationship between employee satisfaction and the frequency of communication management delivers to employees.
Marketing	Implementation of the product placement campaign has increased sales at EZ Computers.

Customers have a significantly higher preference for the XYZ Bank's location in a grocery store to traditional bank locations.

Quality   Schools that have rejected No Child Left Behind (NCLB) have a more authentic reading program than schools that have embraced NCLB.

6. What is statistical hypothesis testing?

Statistical hypothesis testing, or tests of significance, is used to determine whether the differences between two or more descriptive statistics (such as a mean, percentage, proportion, or standard deviation) are statistically significant or more likely due to chance variations. It is a method of testing claims made about populations by using a sample (subset) from that population. To help formulate your hypothesis, check out http://tinyurl.com/2eta485.

In hypothesis testing, descriptive numbers are standardized so that they can be compared to fixed values, which are found in tables and in computer programs, and indicate how unusual it is to obtain the data collected. A statistical hypothesis to be tested is always written as a null hypothesis (no change). Generally the null hypothesis will contain the symbol "=" to indicate the status quo, or no change. An appropriate test will tell us to either reject the null hypothesis or fail to reject (in *essence* accept) the null hypothesis.

Note: Some people refer to the null hypothesis as the "no" hypothesis; *no* relationship, *no* change; *no* difference. If the null hypothesis is not rejected, this does not lead to the conclusion that no association or differences exist, but instead that the analysis did not detect any association or difference between the variables or groups. Failing to reject the null hypothesis is comparable to a finding of not guilty in a trial. The defendant is not declared innocent. Instead, there is not enough evidence to be convincing beyond a reasonable doubt. In the judicial system, a decision is made and the defendant is set free. Check out http://tinyurl.com/y7jpbh to see out how simple it is to perform a hypothesis test and compute the results.

7. Once I find an appropriate test for my hypothesis, is there anything else I need to be concerned about?

Certain conditions are necessary prior to initiating a statistical test. One important condition is the distribution of the data. Once data are standardized and the significance level determined, a statistical test can be performed to analyze the data and possibly make inferences about a population (universe).

8. What are p values?

A p value (or probability value) is the probability of getting a value of the sample test statistic that is at least as extreme as the one found from the sample data, assuming the null hypothesis is true. Traditionally, statisticians used alpha (α) values that set up a dichotomy: reject/fail to reject null hypothesis. A p value measures how confident we are in rejecting a null hypothesis. If a p value is less than 0.01, we say this is highly statistically significant, and there is very strong evidence against the null hypothesis. A p value between 0.01 and 0.05 indicates that there is statistically significant and adequate evidence against the null hypothesis. For a p value greater than 0.05, there is, generally, insufficient evidence against the null hypothesis, and the null hypothesis is not rejected.

p value	Interpretation
$p < 0.01$	Very strong evidence against H0
$p < 0.05$	Moderate evidence against H0
$p < 0.10$	Suggestive evidence against H0
$p > 0.10$	Little or no real evidence against H0

Note: If the null hypothesis is not rejected, this does not lead to the conclusion that no association or differences exist, but instead that the analysis did not detect any association or difference between the variables or groups. Failing to reject the null hypothesis is comparable to a finding of not guilty in a trial. The defendant is not declared innocent. Instead, there is not enough evidence to be convincing beyond a reasonable doubt. In the judicial system, a decision is made and the defendant is set free.

9. What is the connection between hypothesis testing and confidence intervals?

There is an extremely close relationship between confidence intervals and hypothesis testing. When a 95% confidence interval is constructed, all values in the interval are considered plausible values for the parameter being estimated. Values outside the interval are rejected as implausible. If the value of the parameter specified by the null hypothesis is contained in the 95% interval, then the null hypothesis cannot be rejected at the 0.05 level. If the value specified by the null hypothesis is not in the interval, then the null hypothesis can be rejected at the 0.05 level. If a 99% confidence interval is constructed, then values outside the interval are rejected at the 0.01 level.

10. What does statistically significant mean?

In English, *significant* means important. In statistics, it means *probably true*. Significance levels show you how likely a result is due to chance. The most common level, which usually indicates "good enough," is 0.95. This means that the finding has a 95% chance of being true. However, this is reported as a 0.05 level of significance, meaning that the finding has a 5% (0.05) chance of *not* being true, which is the converse of a 95% chance of being true. To find the significance level, subtract the number shown from 1. For example, a value of 0.01 means there is a 99% (1 - 0.01 = 0.99) chance of it being true.

11. What is data mining?

Data mining is an analytic process designed to explore large amounts of data in search of consistent patterns or systematic relationships between variables and then to validate these findings by applying the detected patterns to new subsets of data. There are three basic stages in data mining: exploration, model building or identifying patterns, and validation and verification. If the nature of available data allows, it is typically repeated until a model is identified. However, in business decision making, options to validate the model are often limited. Thus, the initial results often have the status of general recommendations or guides based on statistical evidence (for example, soccer moms appear to be more likely to drive a minivan than an SUV).

12. What are the different levels of measurement?

Data come in four types and four levels of measurement, which can be remembered by the French word for black:

NOIR: nominal (lowest), ordinal, interval, and ratio highest

Nominal Scale	Measures in terms of name of designations or discrete units or categories. Example: gender, color of home, religion, type of business.
Ordinal Scale	Measures in terms of such values as more or less, larger or smaller, but without specifying the size of the intervals. Example: rating scales, ranking scales, Likert-type scales.
Interval Scale	Measures in terms of equal intervals or degrees of difference but without a true zero point. Ratios do not apply. Example: temperature, GPA, IQ.
Ratio Scale	Measures in terms of equal intervals and an absolute zero point of origin. Ratios apply. Example: height, delay time, weight.

A general and important guideline is that the statistics based on one level of measurement should not be used for a lower level, but can be used for a higher level. An implication of this guideline is that data obtained from using a Likert-type scale (a scale in which people set their preferences from say 1 = *totally agree* to 7 = *totally disagree*) should, generally, not be used in parametric tests. However, there is controversy regarding treating Likert-type scales as interval data (see below). The good news is that if you cannot use a parametric test, there is almost always an alternative approach using nonparametric tests.

FOR YOUR INFORMATION AND EDUCATION

Can Likert-type scales be considered interval? Likert-type scales are used to quantify results and obtain shades of perceptions. Choices (or categories of responses) usually range from *strongly disagree* to *strongly agree*. As the categories move from one to the next (e.g., from *strongly disagree* to *disagree*), the value will increase by one unit. The Likert-type scale has equal units as the categories move from most negative to most positive. This allows measurement of attitudes, beliefs, and perceptions, providing an efficient and effective means of quantifying data. Although Likert-type scales are ordinal data, they are commonly used with interval procedures, provided the scale item has at least five and preferably seven categories. Most researchers would not use a 3-point Likert-type scale with a technique requiring interval data. The fewer the number of points, the more likely the departure from the assumption of normal distribution required for many tests. Here is a typical footnote inserted in research using interval techniques with Likert-type scales:

> *In regard to the use of (insert name of test – such as t test or Pearson test), which assumes interval data, with ordinal Likert-type scale items, in a review of the literature on this topic, Jaccard and Wan (1996, p. 4) found, "for many statistical tests, rather severe departures (from intervalness) do not seem to affect Type I and Type II errors dramatically when scales of five or seven categories are used."*

Note: Under certain circumstances, there is general consensus that ranked data are interval. This would happen, for instance, in a survey of children's allowances if all children in the sample got allowances of $5, $10, or $15 exactly and these were measured as low, medium, and high. That is, interval*ness* is an attribute of the data, not of the labels.

13. What type of distributions can be found when data are collected?

One of the most important characteristics related to the shape of a distribution is whether the distribution is skewed or symmetrical. Skewness (the degree of asymmetry) is important. A large degree of skewness causes the mean to be less acceptable and useful as the measure of central tendency. To use many parametric statistical tests requires a normal (symmetrical) distribution of the data. Graphical methods such as histograms are very helpful in identifying skewness in a distribution. Check out http://www.stat.sc.edu/webstat/.

If the mean, median, and mode are identical, then the shape of the distribution will be unimodal, symmetric, and resemble a normal distribution. A distribution that is skewed to the right and unimodal will have a long right tail, whereas a distribution that is skewed to the left and unimodal will have a long left tail. A unimodal distribution that is skewed has its mean, median, and mode occur at different values. For highly skewed distributions, the median is the preferred measure of central tendency, since a mean can be greatly affected by a few extreme values on one end.

Kurtosis is a parameter that describes whether the particular distribution concentrates its probability in a central peak or in the tails, or how pointed or flat a distribution looks. Kurtosis explains how outlier-prone a distribution is. The kurtosis of the normal distribution is 3. Distributions that are more outlier-prone than the normal distribution have kurtosis greater than 3; distributions that are less outlier-prone have kurtosis less than 3. Platykurtic means flatter than a normal curve; leptokurtic means pointier than a normal curve.

14. What is the difference between a parametric and a nonparametric test?

Most of the better known statistical tests use parametric methods. These methods generally require strict restrictions such as the following:
1. The data should be ratio or interval.
2. The sample data must come from a normally distributed population.

Good things about nonparametric methods are as follows:
1. They can be applied to a wider variety of situations and are distribution free.
2. They can be used with nominal and ranked data.
3. They use simpler computations and can be easier to understand.

Not so good things about nonparametric methods are as follows:
1. They tend to waste information since most of the information is reduced to qualitative form.
2. They are generally less sensitive, so stronger evidence is needed to show significance, which could mean larger samples are needed.

How to Exhibit Your Data (a)

Data that are collected but not organized are often referred to as *raw* data. It is common to seek a means in which the human mind can easily assimilate and summarize raw data. Frequency tables and graphs *delectably* fulfill this purpose. However we need to be aware that unscrupulous practices could lead to distortion and a misrepresentation of data.

FOR YOUR INFORMATION AND EDUCATION

A frequency table is so named because it lists categories of scores along with their corresponding frequencies. This is an extremely simple and effective means of organizing data for further evaluation. For a large collection of scores, it is best to use a statistical program such as Statview, SPSS, GBSTAT, EXCEL, MINITAB, etc., where you enter the raw data into your computer and then with the mere press of a button or two, a frequency table is constructed.

If the data you obtained were demographic (about personal characteristics or geographical regions), then it would be beneficial to present the percentages of these characteristics within the sample (e.g., 24% of the participants studied were Hispanic). If you determined an arithmetic mean in your study, then both the mean and the standard deviation should be presented.

Data are often represented in pictorial form by means of a graph. Some common types of graphs include pie charts (if you are picturing the relationship of parts to a whole) and histograms (if you are displaying the different types of numerical responses with respect to the frequency in which they occur. A histogram is similar to a bar graph, which is often used to represent the frequency of nominal data, ogives (if you are displaying cumulative frequencies such as incomes under $10,000), or stem and leaf plots (if you wish that the actual data be preserved and used to form a picture of the distribution). However, make sure that the graph adds value to the study. If you are simply using descriptive data like means, medians, modes, range, and standard deviation, a chart is likely otiose.

 *Cutting Board*

1. Arrange your data in a frequency table. If you have administered a questionnaire or survey, you might wish to list the different responses to each question in conjunction with the frequency that they were selected.

2. Construct appropriate graphs to picture the distributions determined by your frequency table.

3. Compute any statistical numbers that are descriptive of your data such as means, standard deviations, proportions, percentages, or quartiles. (You may wish to use a calculator or a computer that is programmed to determine your mean and standard deviation with the mere press of a button once information has been entered in a befitting manner. The manual that comes with the machine or computer program could prove helpful for this task.)

Definitions

One of the keys to understanding a specialized field is getting to know its technical vocabulary. As you continue to put together your research project, you might come across unfamiliar words. The following words often appear in quantitative studies. Remember to refer to them as needed.

Alternative hypothesis: The hypothesis that is accepted if the null hypothesis is rejected.

Analysis of variance (ANOVA): A statistical method for determining the significance of the differences among a set of sample means.

Aggregated data: Data for which individual scores on a measure are combined into a single group summary score.

Central limit theorem: A mathematical conjecture that informs us that the sampling distribution of the mean approaches a normal curve as the sample size, n, gets larger.

Chi-square (χ^2) distribution: A continuous probability distribution used directly or indirectly in many tests of significance. The most common use of the chi-square distribution is to test differences between proportions. Although this test is by no means the only test based on the chi-square distribution, it has come to be known as the chi-square test. The chi-square distribution has one parameter, its degrees of freedom (*df*). It has a positive skew; the skew is less with more degrees of freedom. The mean of a chi-square distribution is its *df*, the mode is $df - 2$, and the median is approximately $df - 0.7$.

Confidence interval: A range of values used to estimate some population parameter with a specific level of confidence. In most statistical tests, confidence levels are 95% or 99%. The wider the confidence interval, the higher the confidence level will be.

Confidence level: A desired percentage of scores (often 95% or 99%) that the true parameter would fall within a certain range. If a study indicates that the Democratic candidate will capture 75% of the vote with a 3% margin of error (or confidence interval) at the 95% level of confidence, then the Democratic candidate can be 95% sure that she will capture between 72 and 75% of the votes.

Confounding variable: An extraneous variable that is not a focus of the study but is statistically related to (or correlated with) the independent variable. This means that as the independent variable changes, the confounding variable changes along with it.

Correlation: A relationship between variables such that increases or decreases in the value of one variable tend to be accompanied by increases or decreases in the other.

Correlation coefficient: A measurement between -1 and 1 indicating the strength of the relationship between two variables.

Critical region: The area of the sampling distribution that covers the value of the test statistic that is not due to chance variation. In most tests it represents between 1 and 5% of the graph of the distribution.

Critical value: The value from a sampling distribution that separates chance variation to variation that is not due to chance.

Cronbach's alpha: This is a measure of internal reliability or consistency of the items in an index. Used often with tests that employ Likert-type scales. Values range from 0 to 1.0. Scores toward the high end of that range (above 0.70) suggest that the items in an index are measuring the same thing.

Data: Facts and figures collected through research. The word data is plural, just like the word "toys." Data are us. :) Datum is the singular form of data.

Degrees of freedom (*df*): The number of values that are free to vary after certain restrictions have been imposed on all values. The *df* depends on the sample size (*n*) and dimensionality (number of variables (*k*)).

Dependent variable: The variable that is measured and analyzed in an experiment. In traditional algebraic equations of the form $y = \underline{\quad} x + \underline{\quad}$, it is usually agreed that *y* is the dependent variable.

Dependent samples: The values in one sample are related to the values in another sample. Before and after results are dependent samples.

Descriptive statistics: The methods used to summarize the key characteristics of known population and sample data.

Effect size: The degree to which a practice, program, or policy has an effect based on research results, measured in units of standard deviation. If a researcher finds an effect size of $d = .5$ for the effect of a test preparation program on SAT scores, this means the average student who participates in the program will achieve one-half standard deviation above the average student who does not participate. If the standard deviation is 20 points, then the effect size translates into eight additional points, which will increase a student's score on the test.

Experiment: Process that allows observations to be made. In probability an experiment can be repeated over and over under the same conditions.

External validity: The degree to which results from a study can be generalized to other participants, settings, treatments and measures.

Exploratory data analysis: Any of several methods, pioneered by John Tukey, of discovering unanticipated patterns and relationships but presenting quantitative data visually.

F distribution: A continuous probability distribution used in tests comparing two variances. It is used to compute probability values in the ANOVA. The F distribution has two parameters: degrees of freedom numerator (dfn) and degrees of freedom denominator (dfd).

Goodness of fit: Degree to which observed data coincide with theoretical expectations.

Histogram: A graph of connected vertical rectangles representing the frequency distribution of a set of data.

Hypothesis: A statement or claim that some characteristic of a population is true.

Hypothesis test: A method for testing claims made about populations; also called the test of significance. In your *Recipes for Success*, the CANDOALL method is presented to help you understand how to test hypotheses.

Independent variable: The treatment variable. In traditional algebraic equations of the form $y =$ ___ $x +$ ___, it is usually agreed that x is the independent variable.

Inferential statistics: The methods of using sample data to make generalizations or inferences about a population.

Interval scale: A measurement scale in which equal differences between numbers stand for equal differences in the thing measured. The zero point is arbitrarily defined. Temperature is measured on an interval scale.

Kurtosis: The shape (degree of peakedness) of a curve that is a graphic representation of a unimodal frequency distribution. It indicates the degree to which data cluster around a central point for a given standard deviation. It can be expressed numerically and graphically.

Kruskal-Wallis test: A nonparametric hypothesis test used to compare three or more independent samples. It is the nonparametric version of a one-way ANOVA for ordinal data.

Left-tail test: Hypothesis test in which the critical region is located in the extreme left area of the probability distribution. The alternative hypothesis is the claim that a quantity is less than (<) a certain value.

Level of significance: The probability level at which the null hypothesis is rejected. Usually represented by the Greek letter alpha (α).

Linear Structural Relations (LISREL): A computer program developed by Jöreskog that is used for analyzing covariance structures through structural equation models. It can be used to analyze causal models with multiple indicators of latent variables and relationships between the latent variables. It goes beyond more typical factor analysis.

Mean: A measure of central tendency, the arithmetic average; the sum of scores divided by the number of scores.

Median: A measure of central tendency that divides a distribution of scores into two equal halves so that half the scores are above the median and half are below it.

Mode: A measure of central tendency that represents the most fashionable, or most frequently occurring, score.

Multiple regression: Study of linear relationships among three or more variables.

Nominal data: Data that are names only, with no real quantitative value. Often numbers are arbitrarily assigned to nominal data, such as male = 0, female = 1.

Nonparametric statistical methods: Statistical methods that do not require a normal distribution or that data be interval or rational.

Normal distribution: Gaussian curve. A theoretical bell-shaped, symmetrical distribution based on frequency of occurrence of chance events.

Null hypothesis: The null hypothesis is a hypothesis about a population parameter. It assumes no change or status quo (=). The purpose of hypothesis testing is to test the viability of the null hypothesis in the light of the data. Depending on the data, the null hypothesis either will or will not be rejected as a viable possibility. We do not use the term accept when referring to the results of a statistical test.

Odds in favor: The number of ways an event can happen compared to the number of ways that it cannot happen.

Ogive: A graphical method of representing cumulative frequencies.

One-tailed test: A statistical test in which the critical region lies in one tail of the distribution. If the alternative hypothesis has a $<$, then you will conduct a left-tailed test. If it contains a $>$, then it will be right-tailed test.

One-way ANOVA: Analysis of variance involving data classified into groups according to a single criterion.

Operational definition: A concise definition of a term characterized by the functional use of that term. Operational definitions focus on prototypical usage or usage in practice. Operational definitions need to be concise and no more than one to three sentences in length.

Ordinal scale: A rank-ordered scale of measurement in which equal differences between numbers do not represent equal differences between the things measured. The Likert-type scale is a common ordinal scale.

Outlier: A single observation far away from the rest of the data. One definition of "far away" is less than $Q1 - 1.5 \times IQR$ or greater than $Q3 + 1.5 \times IQR$ where $Q1$ and $Q3$ are the first and third quartiles, respectively, and IQR is the interquartile range (equal to $Q3 - Q1$). These values define the so-called inner fences, beyond which an observation would be labeled a mild outlier. Outliers could be indicative of the occurrence of a phenomenon that is qualitatively different than the typical pattern observed or expected in the sample; thus, the relative frequency of outliers could provide evidence of a relative frequency of departure from the process or phenomenon that is typical for the majority of cases in a group.

Parameter: Some numerical characteristic of a population. If the mean score on a midterm exam for a statistics class was 87%, this score would be a parameter. It describes the population composed of all those who took the test. Population parameters are usually symbolized by Greek letters, such as μ for the mean and σ for standard deviation.

Parametric methods: Types of statistical procedures for testing hypotheses or estimating parameters based on population parameters that are measured on interval or rational scores. Data are usually normally distributed.

Pie chart: Graphical method of representing data in the form of a circle containing wedges.

Population: All members of a specified group.

Probability: A measure of the likelihood that a given even will occur. Mathematical probabilities are expressed as numbers between 0 and 1.

Probability distribution: Collection of values of a random variable along with their corresponding probabilities.

p value: The probability that a test statistic in a hypothesis test is at least as extreme as the one actually obtained. A p value is found after a test statistic is determined. It indicates how likely the results of an experiment were due to a chance happening.

Qualitative variable: A variable that is often measured with nominal data.

Quantitative variable: A variable that is measured with interval and rational data.

Random sample: A subset of a population chosen in such away that any member of the population has an equal chance of being selected.

Range: The difference between the highest and the lowest score.

Ratio scale: A scale that has equal differences and equal ratios between values and a true zero point. Heights, weights, and time are measured on rational scales.

Raw score: A score obtained in an experiment that has not been organized or analyzed.

Regression line: The line of best fit that runs through a scatterplot.

Right-tailed test: Hypothesis test in which the critical region is located in the extreme right area of the probability distribution. The alternative hypothesis is the claim that a quantity is greater than (>) a certain value.

Sample: A subset of a population.

Sampling error: Errors resulting from the sampling process itself.

Scattergram: The points that result when a distribution of paired values are plotted on a graph.

Sign test: A nonparametric hypothesis test used to compare samples from two populations.

Significance level: The probability that serves as a cutoff between results attributed to chance happenings and results attributed to significant differences.

Skewed distribution: An asymmetrical distribution.

Spearman's rank correlation coefficient: Measure of the strength of the relationship between two variables.

Spearman's rho: A correlation statistic for two sets of ranked data.

Standard deviation: The weighted average amount that individual scores deviate from the mean of a distribution of scores, which is a measure of dispersion equal to the square root of the variance. At least 75% of all scores will fall within the interval of two standard deviations from the mean. At least 89% of all scores will fall within three standard deviations from the mean. The 68, 95, 99.7 rule (applies generally to a variable X having normal (bell-shaped or mound-shaped) distribution with mean μ (the Greek letter mu) and standard deviation σ (the Greek letter sigma). However, this rule does not apply to distributions that are "very" nonnormal. The rule states: approximately 68% of the observations fall within one standard deviation of the mean; approximately 95% of the observations fall within two standard deviations of the mean; and approximately 99.7% of the observations fall within three standard deviations of the mean. Another general rule is this: If the distribution is approximately normal, the standard deviation is approximately equal to the range divided by 4.

Standard error of the mean: The standard deviation of all possible sample means.

Standard normal distribution: A normal distribution with a mean of 0 and a standard deviation equal to 1.

Statistic: A measured characteristic of a sample.

Statistics: The collection, organization, analysis, interpretation, and prediction of data.

t distribution: Theoretical, bell-shaped distribution used to determine the significance of experimental results based on small samples. Also called the Student *t* distribution.

t test (Student *t* test): Significance test that uses the *t* distribution. A Student *t* test deals with the problems associated with inference based on small samples.

Test statistic: Used in hypothesis testing, it is the sample statistic based on the sample data. We obtain test statistics by plugging in data we gathered into a formula.

Two-tailed test of significance: Any statistical test in which the critical region is divided into the two tails of the distribution. The null hypothesis is usually a variable equal to a certain quantity. When the alternative hypothesis is not equal, this implies < or > as alternatives. This yields a two-tailed test.

Type I error: The mistake of rejecting the null hypothesis when it is true.

Type II error: The mistake of failing to reject the null hypothesis when it is false.

Uniform distribution: A distribution of values evenly distributed over the range of possibilities.

Variable: Any measurable condition, event, characteristic, or behavior that is controlled or observed in a study.

Variance: The square of the standard deviation; a measure of dispersion.

Wilcoxon rank-sum test: A nonparametric hypothesis test used to compare two independent samples.

z score: Also known as a standard score. The *z* score indicates how far and in what direction an item deviates from its distribution's mean, expressed in units of its distribution's standard deviation. The mathematics of the *z* score transformation are such that if every item in a distribution is converted to its *z* score, the transformed scores will necessarily have a mean of 0 and a standard deviation of 1.

How to (Ap)praise your Date (a)

Statistical Hypothesis Testing

1 cup	Analyzing
1 cup	Interpreting
1 cup	Predicting

Featuring:

Essential Steps in Hypothesis Testing S³d²CANDOALL
How to Choose Desirable *Spices* (Tests)
Testing Claims About: Means, Standard Deviations, Proportions, and Relations
Nonparametric Tests

In this section you will explore statistical hypothesis testing to determine how much of what you anticipated would happen actually did happen. For another opinion or viewpoint, you might also wish to check out http://tinyurl.com/379u8gv.

Hypotheses are educated guesses derived by logical analysis using induction or deduction from your knowledge of the problem and from your purpose for conducting the study. They can range from very general statements to highly specific ones. Most quantitative research studies focus on testing hypotheses.

After the data are collected and organized in some logical manner, such as a frequency table, and a descriptive statistic (mean, standard deviation, percentage, etc.) is computed, then a statistical test is often utilized to analyze the data, interpret what this analysis means in terms of the problem, and make predictions about a population based on these interpretations.

You might wish to visit this section once before all your data are collected and then plan to revisit once your data are known.

> Note: When you use statistics, you are comparing your numerical results to a number that is reflective of a chance happening and determining the significance of the difference between these two numbers. If you are planning to use statistical hypothesis testing as part of your dissertation, thesis, or research project, you should read this section slowly and carefully, paying close attention to key words and phrases. Make sure you are familiar with all the terminology employed.

There is a myth that statistical analysis is a difficult and unpleasant process that requires a thorough understanding of advanced mathematics. This is not the case. Statistical hypothesis testing can be fun and easy. Although many esoteric tests exist (just as there are many exotic *spices* in the universe), most researchers use mundane tests (the way most *chefs prepare delicious meals with common spices*). The mundane *spices* for statistical hypothesis testing are z tests, t tests, chi-square tests, ANOVA (F tests), and rho tests. As you carefully and cheerfully read this section, you will learn which of these *spices* might best complement your *meal*. Just as in *cooking*, sometimes you will find more than one *spice* that could be apropos and could enhance your *dishes*. In analyzing your data, you will likely find more than one type of statistical test that would be appropriate for your study, and the choice is often yours to make.

Testing a Claim About a Mean

The example in this section will be testing a claim about a mean obtained from a sample. If you can answer yes to one or more of the questions below, you could use this statistical test in your study:

Are you claiming that:

____1. A new product, program, or treatment is better than an existing one?

____2. An existing product, program, or treatment is not what it professes to be?

____3. A group is under- (or over-) achieving?

____4. A new product, program, or treatment has met (or not met) its goals?

____5. A new product, program, or treatment is effective?

Note: The *recipe* in this section can be used to check any statistical hypothesis (not just a statistical hypothesis about a mean), so it would behoove you to read the following example with eager anticipation and note any similarities between this study and your study.

Example: Ms. R has found a new method of teaching reading (NMTR) that she claims is better than traditional methods. The average seventh grader reads at a 7.5 reading level by mid-year. Ms. R claims that NMTR will increase the average reading level significantly by mid-year.

To test her claim, Ms. R samples 36 students ($n = 36$) who have been using NMTR and finds that by mid-year the mean average of this group is 7.8. However, since the standard deviation of the population is 0.76, this could indicate that the sample students are just within normal boundaries.

Statistical hypothesis testing will be used to determine if the sample mean score of 7.8 represents a statistically significant increase from the population mean of 7.5 or if the difference is more likely due to chance variation in reading scores.

Before the eight-step statistical test (CANDOALL) *recipe* is employed, you need to procure five preliminary pieces of information: three begin with the letter "s" and two with the letter "d": $\mathbf{S^3 d^2}$

(s) What is the **s**ubstantive hypothesis?

(What does the researcher think will happen based on a sound theoretical framework?)

Ms. R claims that NMTR will significantly increase the average reading level of seventh-grade students by mid-year.

 Cutting Board

Write one substantive hypothesis that is apropos to your study, i.e., what do you think (claim) that your study will reveal?

(s) How large is the **s**ample that was studied?

 Ms. R sampled 36 seventh-grade students ($n = 36$) who have been using NMTR.

(s) What descriptive **s**tatistic was determined by the sample?

The mean average of the sample, $\overline{x}$, was 7.8.

(d) What type of **d**ata was collected?

Ms. R used interval data.

(If data were nominal or ordinal then a nonparametric test would be called for.)

(d) What type of **d**istribution did the data form? To use parametric statistical tests usually requires a normal (or close to normal) distribution of the data. Graphical methods such as histograms are very helpful in identifying skewness in a distribution. If the statistic you are testing is a mean and the data type is ratio or interval, then a *z* test or *t* test will likely be applied. These tests are pretty robust and can be applied even if the data are skewed.

Ms. R will not need to be concerned about the distribution of her data.

 Cutting Board

1. Determine the sample size for your study ($n =$ _____).
2. What descriptive statistic was obtained from your study? _____
   (You may wish to give an approximate value or result that you think you might obtain from your study to practice applying this process.) _____

Now we are ready to take the information obtained by the three **S**s and two **D**s and employ an eight-step *recipe* to create a *delectable* statistical test.

We will determine if Ms. R's claim, "NMTR increases the reading level of seventh graders," is statistically correct.

1. Identify the claim (**C**) to be tested and express it in symbolic form. The claim is about the *population* and that is reflected by the Greek letter μ:

$$\mu > 7.5.$$

That is, Ms. R claims that the mean reading score, μ, of the seventh-grade students who could use NMTR is greater than the population mean, 7.5.

Write your claim in symbolic form.

2. Express in symbolic form the statement that would be true, the alternative (**A**), if the original claim is false. All cases must be covered.

$$\mu \leq 7.5$$

Write the opposite of your claim in symbolic form (remember to cover all possibilities).

_____

3. Identify the null (**N**) and alternative hypothesis.

Note: The null hypothesis should be the one that contains no change (an equal sign)

H0: $\mu \leq 7.5$ (Null hypothesis)
H1: $\mu > 7.5$ (Alternative hypothesis)

Determine the null and alternative hypotheses in your study.

_____

Note: A statistical test is designed to reject or fail to reject the statistical null hypothesis being examined.

4. Decide (**D**) the level of significance, α, based on the seriousness of a type I error, which is the mistake of rejecting the null hypothesis when it is in fact true. Make α small if the consequences of rejecting a true α are severe. The smaller the α value, the less likely you will be to reject the null hypothesis. Alpha values 0.05 and 0.01 are very common. The default α is 0.05.

Ms. R chooses $\alpha = 0.05$

FOR YOUR INFORMATION AND EDUCATION

Some researchers do not use α values (which are predetermined at the beginning of a statistical test and indicate acceptable levels of significance). Instead, they prefer to use only p values (which indicate actual levels of significance of a claim and leave the conclusion as to whether this is "significant enough" to the reader). It is possible to do both (set α and compute p) and then compare the two values when reporting the findings.

Before a test of hypotheses is employed, we are certain that only four possible things can happen. These are summarized in the table that follows.

		Claim is tested	
		H_O	H_1
Decision	H_O	**Correct Fail to Reject Null**	Type II Error β
	H_1	Type I Error α	**Correct Reject Null**

Note that two kinds of errors are represented in the table. Many statistics textbooks present a point of view that is common in business decision making: α, the type I error, must be kept at or below 0.05, and that, if at all possible,

β, the type II error rate, must be kept low as well. *Statistical power*, which is equal to $1 - \beta$, must be kept correspondingly high. Ideally, power should be at least .90 to detect a reasonable departure from the null hypothesis.

5. Order (**O**) a statistical test relevant to your study—see Table 1. Since the claim involves a sample mean and $n > 30$, we can compute a z value and use a z test. A z value, or test value, is a number we compute that can be graphed as a point on the horizontal scale of the standard normal distribution (bell-shaped) curve. This point indicates how far from the population mean

(expected mean under the null conditions) our sample mean is and thus enables us to determine how unusual our research findings are.

FOR YOUR INFORMATION AND EDUCATION

The *central limit theorem* (the distribution of a mean will tend to be normal as the sample size increases, regardless of the distribution from which the mean is taken) implies that for samples of sizes larger than 30 ($n > 30$), the sample means can be approximated reasonably well by a normal (z) distribution. The approximation gets better as the sample size, n, becomes larger. Do not confuse the CLT with a BLT (*Bacon/Lettuce/Tomato sandwich*) ☺.

When you compute a z value, you are converting your mean to a mean of 0 and your standard deviation to a standard deviation of 1. This allows you to use the standard normal distribution curve and its corresponding table to determine the significance of your values regardless of the actual value of your mean or standard deviation.

A standard normal probability distribution is a bell-shaped curve (also called a Gaussian curve in honor of its discoverer, Karl Gauss) for which the mean, or middle value, is 0 and the standard deviation, the place where the curve starts to bend, is equal to 1 on the right and -1 on the left. The area under every probability distribution curves is equal to 1 or 100%). Since a Gaussian curve is symmetric about the mean, it is important to note that the mean divides this curve into two equal areas of 50%. Approximately 68% of the data are within one standard deviation of the mean.

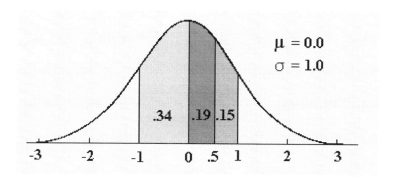

Blood cholesterol levels, heights of adult women, weights of 10-year-old boys, diameters of apples, scores on standardized test, etc., are all examples of collections of values whose frequency distributions resemble the Gaussian curve.

If you were to record all the possible outcomes from the toss of 100 different coins by graphing the number of heads that could occur on the horizontal axis (0,1,2,3...100) and the frequency with which each of the number of heads could occur on the vertical axis, you will produce a graph resembling the normal distribution. (The most frequent results would cluster around 50 heads and become less and less frequent as you consider values further and further from 50.)

6. Do the Arithmetic (**A**): Determine the test statistic, the critical value, or values, and the critical region.

The sample mean, $\bar{x}$, of 7.8 is equivalent to a z value of 2.37. This z value is the test statistic and was computed using the following formula:

$$z = \frac{\bar{x} - \mu}{\sigma / \sqrt{n}},$$

where $\bar{x}$ = sample mean, μ = population mean, n = size of sample, and σ = population standard deviation.

Thus, z = (7.8 - 7.5) / (0.76)/6 = 2.37 (to the nearest hundredth).

Note: z values usually vary between -3 and +3. If they are outside this range, the null hypothesis will almost always be rejected (or an error was made).

Note: $\sigma / \sqrt{n}$ is often called the standard error of the mean or the standard deviation of the sample means.

Note: Sometimes you can substitute the standard deviation of the sample, s, for the population standard deviation, σ, if sigma (σ) is unknown.

The $\alpha = 0.05$ level requires us to find a z value that will separate the curve into two unequal regions: the smaller one with an area of 0.05 (5%) and the larger one with an area of 100% - 5% or 95% (0.95, often referred to as a 95% confidence level).

Z values indicate the percentage of area under the bell-shaped curve from the mean (middle) toward the right tail of the curve. Thus, for an alpha of 0.05, we need to determine what z value will cut off an area of 45% (0.4500) from the mean toward the right tail (we already know that 50% of the area is on the left side of the mean. We obtain 95% by adding 45% to 50%).

Hunting through the vast array of four-digit numerals in the table, we find our critical value to be between 1.6 (see z column) + .04 (1.64), which (reading down the .04 column) determines an area of .4495, and 1.6 +.05 (1.65), which determines an area of .4505. Thus, if we take the mean average of 1.64 and 1.65, we can blissfully determine the critical value to be 1.645 and the critical region to be all z values greater than 1.645. This determination requires us to reject the null hypothesis if our test statistics (z value) is greater than 1.645.

Note: Because there is only one alternative hypothesis (H1), $\mu > 7.5$, we call this is a one-tailed (right-tailed) test. If our alternative hypothesis was $\mu \neq 7.5$, a two-tailed test would be used since there would be two alternatives: $\mu < 7.5$ or $\mu > 7.5$.

An entry in the table is the proportion of the area under the entire standard normal curve, which is between $z = 0$ and a positive value of z. Areas for negative values are obtained by symmetry.

Standard Normal (Z) Distribution Table

Z	0	0.01	0.02	0.03	0.04	0.05	0.06	0.07	0.08	0.09
0	0.00000	0.00399	0.00798	0.01197	0.01595	0.01994	0.02392	0.02790	0.03188	0.03586
0.1	0.03983	0.04380	0.04776	0.05172	0.05567	0.05962	0.06356	0.06749	0.07142	0.07535
0.2	0.07926	0.08317	0.08706	0.09095	0.09483	0.09871	0.10257	0.10642	0.11026	0.11409
0.3	0.11791	0.12172	0.12552	0.12930	0.13307	0.13683	0.14058	0.14431	0.14803	0.15173
0.4	0.15542	0.15910	0.16276	0.16640	0.17003	0.17364	0.17724	0.18082	0.18439	0.18793
0.5	0.19146	0.19497	0.19847	0.20194	0.20540	0.20884	0.21226	0.21566	0.21904	0.22240
0.6	0.22575	0.22907	0.23237	0.23565	0.23891	0.24215	0.24537	0.24857	0.25175	0.25490
0.7	0.25804	0.26115	0.26424	0.26730	0.27035	0.27337	0.27637	0.27935	0.28230	0.28524
0.8	0.28814	0.29103	0.29389	0.29673	0.29955	0.30234	0.30511	0.30785	0.31057	0.31327
0.9	0.31594	0.31859	0.32121	0.32381	0.32639	0.32894	0.33147	0.33398	0.33646	0.33891
1	0.34134	0.34375	0.34614	0.34849	0.35083	0.35314	0.35543	0.35769	0.35993	0.36214
1.1	0.36433	0.36650	0.36864	0.37076	0.37286	0.37493	0.37698	0.37900	0.38100	0.38298
1.2	0.38493	0.38686	0.38877	0.39065	0.39251	0.39435	0.39617	0.39796	0.39973	0.40147
1.3	0.40320	0.40490	0.40658	0.40824	0.40988	0.41149	0.41309	0.41466	0.41621	0.41774
1.4	0.41924	0.42073	0.42220	0.42364	0.42507	0.42647	0.42785	0.42922	0.43056	0.43189
1.5	0.43319	0.43448	0.43574	0.43699	0.43822	0.43943	0.44062	0.44179	0.44295	0.44408
1.6	0.44520	0.44630	0.44738	0.44845	**0.44950**	**0.45053**	0.45154	0.45254	0.45352	0.45449
1.7	0.45543	0.45637	0.45728	0.45818	0.45907	0.45994	0.46080	0.46164	0.46246	0.46327
1.8	0.46407	0.46485	0.46562	0.46638	0.46712	0.46784	0.46856	0.46926	0.46995	0.47062
1.9	0.47128	0.47193	0.47257	0.47320	0.47381	0.47441	0.47500	0.47558	0.47615	0.47670
2	0.47725	0.47778	0.47831	0.47882	0.47932	0.47982	0.48030	0.48077	0.48124	0.48169
2.1	0.48214	0.48257	0.48300	0.48341	0.48382	0.48422	0.48461	0.48500	0.48537	0.48574
2.2	0.48610	0.48645	0.48679	0.48713	0.48745	0.48778	0.48809	0.48840	0.48870	0.48899
2.3	0.48928	0.48956	0.48983	0.49010	0.49036	0.49061	0.49086	**0.49111**	0.49134	0.49158
2.4	0.49180	0.49202	0.49224	0.49245	0.49266	0.49286	0.49305	0.49324	0.49343	0.49361

Note: The p value is .0089. We arrived at this value quite easily. Recall, in step 6, when we did the arithmetic, we computed the z value between scores to be 2.37. If you go down the left side of the table and find a z value of 2.3, then go across to the .07 column, you will find the number **.4911.** This indicates an area of 49.11% from the mean z value of 0 to the z value of 2.37. Thus, 50% + 49.11% or 99.11% of the area of the curve is to the left of 2.37 and the small tail to the right of 2.37 has an area of 100% - 99.11% = 0.89% **or 0.0089**, which is our p value.

Check out http://tinyurl.com/2a2vvza

7. Look (**L**) to reject the null hypothesis if the test statistic is in the critical region. Fail to reject the null hypothesis if the test statistic is not in the critical region.

Ms. R's *z* value is in the critical region since 2.37 > 1.645. Thus we will reject the null hypothesis.

8. Restate the previous decision in lay (**L**) or simple nontechnical terms.

We have reason to believe that NMTR improves the reading level of seventh-grade students.

FOR YOUR INFORMATION AND EDUCATION

If your sample size, *n*, is less than 30 and the population standard deviation is unknown, but there is a normal distribution in the population, then you can compute a *t* statistic

$$t = \frac{\bar{x} - \mu}{s / \sqrt{n}},$$

where s is the standard deviation of the sample, μ is the mean under contention, and n is the size of the sample.

Notice that *z* and *t* statistics are computed exactly the same way; the only difference is in their corresponding values of significance when you (or your computer) checks these values on the graph or table.

In this example, we tested a claim about a numerical value mean test score on a standardized test. The sample data came from a population known to have a normal distribution. We were thus able to use parametric methods in our hypothesis testing.

In general, when you test claims about interval or rational parameters (such as mean, standard deviation, or proportions), and some fairly strict requirements (such as the sample data has come from a normally distributed population) are met, you should be able to use parametric methods.

If you do not meet the necessary requirements for parametric methods, do not despair. It is very likely that there are alternative techniques, appropriately named nonparametric methods, that you will be able to use instead.

Because they do not require normally distributed populations, nonparametric tests are often called distribution-free tests. Some advantages to using nonparametric methods include the following:

1. They can often be applied to nominal data that lack exact numerical values.
2. They usually involve computations that are simpler than the corresponding parametric methods.
3. They tend to be easier to understand.

Unfortunately, there are the following disadvantages:

1. Nonparametric methods tend to waste information, since exact numerical data are often reduced to a qualitative form. Some treat all values as either positive (+) or negative (-). (A dieter using this test would count a loss of 50 pounds as the same as a loss of 2 pounds.)
2. They are generally less sensitive than the corresponding parametric methods. This means that you need stronger evidence, or larger sample sizes, before rejecting the null hypothesis.

 Cutting Board

1.   My data are best described as

   A. Parametric (deal only with numbers that are integers or ratios)
   B. Nonparametric (deal with ordered numbers, rankings, or names only)

2.   Checking with Table 1, I find the appropriate statistical test(s) to check the validity of my hypothesis will be:

   _____

Note: The nonparametric counterparts of both the *t* and *z* tests are the sign test or the Mann Whitney U test.

TABLE 1   Recommended Methods of Cooking HYPOTHESIS TESTING

My Claim Is About a	Claim	Assumption	Parametric Test/Statistic	Nonparametric Test/Statistic
Mean	Class A has a higher IQ than average	$n \geq 30$, or s.d. known $n < 30$, s.d. unknown	z t	Sign test Wilcox/Mann-Whitney U (U)
Proportion	75% of voters prefer candidate	$np > 5$ and $nq > 5$	z	
Standard deviation	This instrument has less errors than others	Normal population	χ^2	Kruskal-Wallis H (H)
Two means	EZ diet is more effective than DF diet? The percent of cures is the same for those using Drug A as Drug B.	Dependent Independent	t t or z	Sign test (U)
		(A low t or U value would indicate that the proportions are similar)		
Two standard deviations	The ages of Group A are more homogeneous than the ages of Group B.		F	(H)
Two proportions	There are more Democrats in Chicago than in L.A.		z	Sign test
Relationship between two variables	Smoking is related to cancer. (If r is close to 0, then no relation)		Pearson r	Spearman r
Are two variables dependent?			F	H
How close do expected values agree with observed (aka goodness of fit)	k variables		χ^2 $df = k - 1$	
ANOVA	Comparing three or more means	(Compute: variances between sample means/ total variances)	F	Kruskal-Wallis (H)

Contingency table (two-way ANOVA, cross tabulation): A table of observed frequencies in which the rows correspond to one variable and the columns another. It is used to see if two variables are dependent but cannot be used to determine what the relationship is between the two variables.

df: num: $= (k - 1)$ den $= k(n - 1)$; $K =$ no. of groups; $n =$ amount in each group

Assumptions for ANOVA: normal distribution, equal variances from each sample. However, George E. P. Box demonstrated that as long as the sample sizes are equal (or almost equal) the variances can be up to nine times as large and the results from ANOVA will continue to be essentially reliable. However, if the data do not fit these basic assumptions we can always use the nonparametric version (Kruskal-Wallis). If a significant F ratio is found, another test can be employed to determine where the significance lies. One of these is Tukey's HSD (honestly significant difference).

The CANDOALL *recipe* can be used to assist you in your hypothesis testing.

(s^3d^2)CANDOALL

Sample Size: n= _____

Substantive Hypothesis:
What are we trying to substantiate?_____

_____

Data level of measure (NOIR) - _____   **Distribution (normal or not) –** _____

Statistic:
What statistic gathered from the sample data?_____

_____

Claim:
Always state the claim in symbolic form $<, >, =, \neq, \leq, \geq$ (against population Greek letters)

_____

_____

Alternate:
Just the alternate or opposite of the claim

_____

Null Hypothesis: $H_o =$_____

                         $H_1 =$_____

Always state the claim in symbolic form (population form). Whoever has the *equal* is the null (H_o). (H_1) tells you what type of tail this test is.

Decide Level of Significance:
$\alpha = .05$ (default unless otherwise noted)

_____

Order a Test:
Look at statistic, sample size. Choose between *z, t,* chi-square, Spearman, Pearson, proportions, etc.

_____

Arithmetic:

Test Value – From Equation: _____

Critical Value – From Table: _____

Look to reject (or not) the null:

Stated as *fail to reject the null* or *reject the null*. Test Value - Check the tail, draw a graph, plot critical and test value. Null gets the large part, alternative the tail.

_____

Lay Terms:

Was the claim supported? _____

_____

By Marilyn K. Simon and Vincent Saldano

We are now going to examine some *flavorsome* applications for other statistical tests. You might wish to scan the list and see if you can identify similarities between the examples given and any of the hypotheses that you are planning to test.

_____

 *Cutting Board*

Testing Claims About Two Means

In this section we will discuss a claim made about two means (such that the mean of one group is less than, greater than, or equal to the mean of another group). The researcher will first need to determine if the groups are dependent, i.e., the values in one sample are related to the values in another sample. This includes before and after tests, tests involving spouses, relationships between an employer and an employee, or if the groups are independent, i.e., the values in one sample are not related to the values in another sample. This includes comparing an experimental group to a control group or samples from two different populations such as the eating habits of people in Michigan versus Hawaii.

If the researcher can answer "yes" to one of the questions below, then the identical statistical test described in this section can be employed. Is the researcher claiming

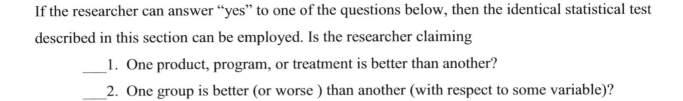

_____ 1. One product, program, or treatment is better than another?

_____ 2. One group is better (or worse) than another (with respect to some variable)?

_____ 3. An experimental program was effective?

Many real and practical situations involve testing hypotheses made about two population means. For example, a manufacturer might want to compare output on two different machines to see if they obtain the same result. A nutritionist might wish to compare the weight loss that results from patients on two different diet plans to determine which is more effective. A chef might want to decide which *entrée* goes better with a *meal*. A psychologist mightwant to test for a difference in mean reaction times between men and women to determine if women respond quicker than men in an emergency situation.

If the two samples (groups) are dependent—the values in one sample are related to the values in the other in some way—a t statistic is computed and a simple paired t test may be used to test your claim. Computing the differences between the related means and then obtaining the mean of all these differences leads to this t statistic.

If the two samples are independent, i.e., the values in one sample are not related to the values in the other, and the size of each group, $n, \geq 30$, or the standard deviations of the population are known, then a simple z statistic might be computed and a paired z test could be ordered. In this case, the differences in the population means are computed and subtracted from the differences in the sample means. The result is divided by the square root of the sum of each variance divided by the respective sample size.

BUT if the two samples are independent, the sample size (n) < 30 for each group, and the population standard deviation is not known, then whom do you call? Answer: The F (team) test. The F test is used first to see if the standard deviations are equal. (A relatively small F value indicates that the standard deviations are the same.) If the F value is relatively small, then the researcher, or much more likely a computer, would need to perform a t test to test the claim. This involves a very hackneyed computation. However, if the F test was to yield a relatively large F value, this would lead to a more benign t test.

Once the mean and standard deviation are computed for each sample, it is customary to identify the group with the larger standard deviation as Group 1 and the other sample as Group 2.

The nonparametric counterpart of the paired z or t test is the Wilcoxon signed-rank test if samples are dependent and the Wilcoxon rank-sum test if samples are independent.

Testing Claims About Three or More Means

If you can answer yes to one of the questions below, you can use the identical statistical test described in this section. Are you claiming the following?

____ 1. There is a difference between three or more products, programs, or treatments?

____ 2. There is a different outcome from the same program, product, or treatment among three or more groups?

Claims about three or more means require the creation of an F statistic and the performing of an F test is on the menu. Here you, or hopefully your computer, will compare the variances between the samples to the variances within the samples. This is called ANOVA. It is an extension of the t test, which is used for testing two means. The null hypothesis is that the means are equal. An F value close to 1 would indicate that there are no significant differences between the sample means. A relatively large F value will cause you to reject the null hypothesis and conclude that the means in the samples are not equal. There are some important things to know about the F distribution:

1. It is not symmetric; it is skewed to the right.
2. The values of F can be 0 or positive, but cannot be negative.

3. There is a different F distribution for each pair of degrees of freedom for the numerator and denominator.

Note: If you are asking yourself or your *Recipes for Success,* "Why are we dealing with variances when the claim is about means?" you would be asking a very good question. The answer is that the variance, or the standard deviation squared, is determined by, and dependent on, the mean, so it is actually all in the family!

FOR YOUR INFORMATION AND EDUCATION

The method of ANOVA owes its beginning to Sir Ronald A. Fisher (1890–1962) and received its early impetus because of its applications to problems in agricultural research. It is such a powerful statistical tool that it has since found applications in just about every branch of scientific research, including economics, psychology, marketing research, and industrial engineering.

The following example will be testing a claim about 3 means obtained from a sample using the s^3d^2 CANDOALL model. A report on the findings follows the example.

Example: A study was conducted to investigate the time in minutes for 3 police precincts to arrive at the scene of a crime. Sample results from similar types of crimes are:

A: 7   4   4   3
       sample size: $n = 4$, mean $x = 4.5$, variance, $s^2 = 3.0$

B: 9   5   7
       sample size: $n = 3$, mean $x = 7.0$, variance, $s^2 = 4.2$

C: 2   3   5   3   8
       sample size: $n = 5$, mean $x = 4.2$, variance, $s^2 = 5.7$

At the $\alpha = 0.05$ significance level, test the claim that the precincts have the same mean reaction time to similar crimes.

What are the pretest assumptions?

Assumptions for ANOVA: normal distribution and equal variances from each sample. However, George E.P. Box demonstrated that as long as the sample sizes are equal (or near equal), the variances can be up to nine times as large and the results from ANOVA will continue to be essentially reliable.

    (a) What is the substantive hypothesis?

      (What does the researcher think will happen?)

      The reaction times are similar in the three precincts.

    (b) How large is the sample size that was studied?

      The 3 groups have sample sizes 4, 3, and 5, respectively.

    (c) What descriptive statistic was determined by the sample?

      The means and variances for each group were determined.

Now we are ready to take the information obtained in (a), (b), and (c) and employ the 8-step CANDOALL recipe to test this hypothesis.

    We will determine if the claim "the reaction times are similar" is statistically correct.

    1. Identify the **claim** (C) to be tested and express it in symbolic form.

$$\mu_a = \mu_b = \mu_c$$

That is, there is a claim that the mean reaction time in each precinct is the same

    2. Express in symbolic form the **alternative** (A) statement that would be true if the original claim is false.

$$\mu_a \neq \mu_b \neq \mu_c$$

Remember we must cover all possibilities.

    3. Identify the **null** (N) and alternative hypotheses.

Note: The null hypothesis should be the one that contains no change (an equal sign).

        H_0: $\mu_a = \mu_b = \mu_c$ (Null hypothesis)
        H_1: $\mu_a \neq \mu_b \neq \mu_c$ (Alternative hypothesis)

Remember: A statistical test is designed to reject or fail to reject (accept) the statistical null hypothesis being examined.

4. **Decide** (D) on the level of significance (α) based on the seriousness of a type I error.

Note: This is the mistake of rejecting the null hypothesis when it is in fact true. Make α small if the consequences of rejecting a true α are severe. The smaller the α value, the less likely you will be to reject the null hypothesis. Alpha values 0.05 and 0.01 are very common.

$$\alpha = 0.05$$

5. **Order** (O) a statistical test and sampling distribution that is relevant to the study (see Table 1).

Note: Since the claim involves data from 3 groups and we wish to test the hypothesis that the differences among the sample means are due to chance, we can use the ANOVA test.

Note: The following assumptions apply when using the ANOVA: The population has a normal distribution, the populations have the same variance (or standard deviation or similar sample sizes), and the samples are random and independent of each other.

6. Perform the **arithmetic** (A) and determine the test statistic, the critical value, and the critical region.

Note: It would be best for this to be performed on a computer.

To perform an ANOVA test we need to compute the following:

The number of samples, k,

$$k = 3.$$

The mean of all the times, x:

$$x = 5.0.$$

The variance between the samples, which is found by subtracting the mean (5.0) from the variance of each sample, squaring the differences, multiplying each by the sample size, and finally adding up the results for each sample.

The variance within the samples, which is found by multiplying the variance of each sample by 1 less than the number in the sample and adding the results, which equals 39.8, and then dividing by the total population minus the number of samples, 9.

The variance within the samples = 4.4222.

The test statistic is $F = \dfrac{\text{variance between samples}}{\text{variance within samples}}$

$$F = 1.8317$$

The variance between the samples = 8.1.

The degrees of freedom in the numerator = $k - 1 = 3 - 1 = 2$. The degrees of freedom in the denominator = $n - k = 12 - 3 = 9$.

Note: Degrees of freedom (*df*) are the number of values that are free to vary after certain restrictions have been imposed on all values. For example, if 10 scores must total 80, then we can freely assign values to the first 9 scores, but the 10th score would then be determined so that there would be 9 degrees of freedom. In a test using an F statistic, we need to find the degrees of freedom in both the numerator and the denominator.

The critical value of $F = 4.2565$. (This can be found on a table or from a computer program.)

7. **Look** (L) to reject or fail to reject the null hypothesis.

Note: This is a right-tailed test since the F-statistic yields only positive values.

Because the test statistic of $F = 1.8317$ does not exceed the critical value of $F = 4.2565$, we fail to reject the null hypothesis that the means are equal.

Note: The shape of an F distribution is slightly different for each sample size n. The $\alpha = 0.05$ level employs us to find an F value that will separate the curve into two unequal regions: the smaller one with an area of 0.05 (5%) and the larger one with an area of 100% - 5% or 95% (0.95, often referred to as a 95% confidence level).

---

8. In **Lay** terms (L), write what happened.

There is not sufficient sample evidence to warrant rejection of the claim that the means are equal.

Note: In order for statistics to make sense in research, it is important to use a rigorously controlled design in which other factors are forced to be constant. The design of the experiment is critically important, and no statistical calisthenics can salvage a poor design.

Writing About This Study in a Research Paper

If this study were to be published in a research journal, the following script could be used to summarize the statistical findings. This information usually appears in the data analysis section of a document, but could also be properly placed in the section in which the conclusion of the study is found or even in the methodology section. This information would also be very appropriate to place in the abstract.

A study was conducted to investigate the time in minutes for 3 police precincts to arrive at the scene of a crime. Sample results from similar types of crimes were found to be as follows:

A: 7 4 4 3
   sample size: $n = 4$, mean, $x = 4.5$, variance, $s^2 = 3.0$

B: 9 5 7
   sample size: $n = 3$, mean, $x = 7.0$, variance, $s^2 = 4.2$

C: 2 3 5 3 8
   sample size: $n = 5$, mean, $x = 4.2$ variance, $s^2 = 5.7$

At the $\alpha = 0.05$ significance level, the claim that the precincts have the same mean reaction time to similar crimes was tested. The null hypothesis is the claim that the samples come from populations with the same mean:

$$H_0: \mu_a = \mu_b = \mu_c \text{ (Null hypothesis)}$$
$$H_1: \mu_a \neq \mu_b \neq \mu_c \text{ (Alternative hypothesis)}$$

To determine if there are any statistically significant differences between the means of the 3 groups, an ANOVA test was performed. The groups were similar in size and the level of measurement was ratio data. An F distribution was employed to compare the two different estimates of the variance common to the different groups (i.e., variation between samples and variation within the samples). A test statistic of $F = 1.8317$ was obtained. With 2 degrees of freedom for the numerator and 9 degrees of freedom for the denominator, the critical F value of 4.2565 was determined. Because the test F does not exceed the critical F value, the null hypothesis was not rejected. There is not sufficient sample evidence to reject the claim that the mean values were equal.

The nonparametric counterpart of ANOVA is the Kruskal-Wallis test.

Testing A Claim About Proportions/Percentages

If the answer to one of the questions below is "yes," then the identical statistical test described in this section could be employed. Is the researcher claiming that

_____1. A certain percentage or ratio is higher or lower than what is believed?

_____2. There is a characteristic of a group that is actually prevalent in a higher or lower percentage?

Data at the nominal (name only) level of measurement lack any real numerical significance and are essentially qualitative in nature. One way to make a quantitative analysis when qualitative data are obtained is to represent such data in the form of a percentage or a ratio. This representation is useful in a variety of applications, including surveys, polls, and quality control considerations involving the percentage of defective parts.

A z test will work fine here provided that the size of the population is large enough. The condition is that

$$np \geq 5 \text{ and } nq \geq 5,$$

where, as usual, n = sample size, p = population proportion, and $q = 1 - p$.

Note: The p in the test of proportions is different than the p value we use to determine significance in hypothesis testing. It is important to be aware that in mathematics oftentimes the same symbol can have more than one interpretation. While doing mathematics, keep this in mind and remember to learn the meaning of a symbol in its context.

Example: If a manager believes that less than 48% of her employees support the company's dress code, the claim can be checked based on the response of a random sample of employees. If 720 employees were sampled and 54.2% actually favored the dress code, then to check the manager's claim, the researcher could perform a test of the hypothesis to determine if the actual value of 0.542 is significantly different from the value of 0.48. Here, $n = 720, p = 0.48, q = 0.542$. The conditions $np \geq 5$ and $nq \geq 5$ are met since $720(0.48) = 345.6$ and $720(0.542) = 390.24$. The z value would be 3.33. This would lead us to reject the null hypothesis and conclude that this is probably a low estimate.

Testing Claims About Standard Deviations And Variability

Many real and practical situations demand decisions or inferences about variances and standard deviations. In manufacturing, quality control engineers want to ensure that a product is on the average acceptable but also want to produce items of consistent quality so there are as few defects as possible. Consistency is measured by variances.

FOR YOUR INFORMATION AND EDUCATION

During World War II, 35,000 American engineers and technicians were taught to use statistics to improve the quality of war material through the efforts of Dr. W. Edwards Deming (born in Sioux City, Iowa, on October 14, 1900). Deming's work was brought to the attention of the Union of Japanese Scientists and Engineers (JUSE). JUSE called upon Deming to help its members increase productivity. Deming convinced the Japanese people that quality drives profits up. The rebirth of Japanese industry and its worldwide success are attributed to the ideas and the teachings of Deming. In gratitude, the late Emperor Hirohito awarded Japan's Second Order Medal of the Sacred Treasure to Deming.

If you can answer "yes" to one of the questions below, you can use the identical statistical test described in this section. Are you claiming that

     ___1. A product, program, or treatment has more or less variability than the standard?

     ___2. A product, program, or treatment is more or less consistent than the standard?

To test claims involving variability, the researcher usually turns to a chi-square (χ^2) statistic.

FOR YOUR INFORMATION AND EDUCATION

Both the t and chi-square (χ^2) distributions have a slightly different shape depending on n, the number in the sample. For this reason, the researcher needs to determine the degrees of freedom to find out what shape curve will be used to obtain the test statistics.

Note: When the researcher uses a sample size of n to investigate one parameter, e.g., a mean or standard deviation, the degrees of freedom equals $n - 1$. When investigating a relationship between two variables, the degrees of freedom are $n - 2$. The test statistics used in tests of hypotheses involving variances or standard deviations is chi-square (χ^2).

Example: A supermarket finds that the average checkout waiting time for a customer on Saturday mornings is 8 minutes with a standard deviation of 6.2 minutes. One Saturday management experimented with a single queue. They sampled 25 customers and found that the average waiting time remained 8 minutes, but the standard deviation went down to 3.8 minutes.

To test the claim that the single line causes lower variation in waiting time, a computed chi-square value would be $\chi^2 = 9.016$ and there would be 24 degrees of freedom since $n = 25$. The null hypothesis would be that the new line produced a standard deviation of waiting time greater than or equal to 6.2, and this would yield a one-tail (left) test. The critical value would be 13.48, and we would reject the null hypothesis if the computed value were less than the critical value. Since $9.016 < 13.48$ we would reject the null hypothesis and conclude that this method seems to lower the variation in waiting time.

Testing a Claim About the Relation Between Two Variables (Correlation and Regression Analysis)

Many real and practical situations demand decisions or inferences about how data from a certain variable can be used to determine the value of some other related variable. For example, researchers of a Florida study of the number of powerboat registrations and the number of accidental manatee deaths confirmed that there was a significant positive correlation. As a result, Florida legislators created coastal sanctuaries where powerboats are prohibited so that manatees could thrive.

Researchers of a study in Sweden found that there was a higher incidence of leukemia among children who lived within 300 meters of a high-tension power line during a 25-year period. This led Sweden's government to consider regulations that would reduce housing in close proximity to high-tension power lines.

If you can answer yes to both questions below, you can use the identical statistical test described in this section. Are you claiming that

___ 1. There is a relationship or correlation between two factors, two events, or two characteristics?, **and**

___ 2. The data are at least of the interval measure?

To perform regression and correlational analyses:

1. Record the information in table form.
2. Create a scatter diagram see any obvious relationship or trends.
3. Compute the correlation coefficient r, also known as the Pearson correlation coefficient factor, to obtain objective analysis that will uncover the magnitude and significance of the relationship between the variables.
4. Determine if r is statistically significant. If r **is** statistically significant, then regression analysis can be used to determine the relationship between the variables.

Example: Suppose a randomly selected group of teachers is given the Survey on Calculator Use (SOCU) to measure how they integrate calculators in their classrooms and then tested for their levels of math anxiety using the Math Anxiety Rating Scales or MARS test:

1. The results for each participant is recorded in table form (some of these values appear below):

MARS	SOCU
123.00	15.00
145.00	12.00
154.00	11.00
121.00	16.00
230.00	5.00
300.00	4.00
145.00	10.00
124.00	17.00
145.00	11.00
165.00	12.00
138.00	14.00
312.0	4.00

The researcher's hypothesis is that teachers who have lower levels of math anxiety are more likely to use calculators in their classes. (Note: The independent variable (x) is the math anxiety level, determined by MARS, and is being used to predict the dependent variable (y), the use of calculators, as measured by SOCU.)

$H_0: r = 0$ (there is no relationship)
$H_1: r \neq 0$ (there is a relationship)

Note: These will usually be hypotheses in regression analysis.

2. Draw a scatter diagram:

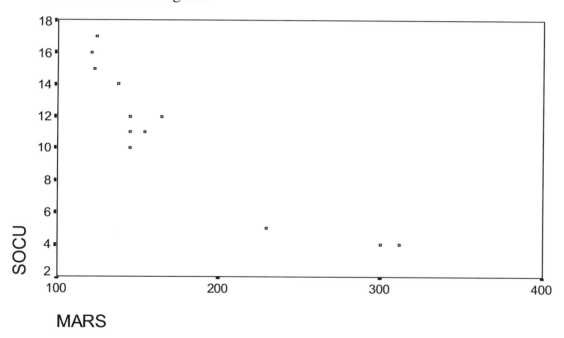

The points in the figure above seem to follow a downward pattern, so we suspect that there is a relationship between level of math anxiety and the use of calculators by teachers surveyed, but this is somewhat subjective.

3. Compute r.

217

To obtain a more precise and objective analysis we can compute the linear coefficient constant, r. Computing r is a tedious exercise in arithmetic but practically any statistical computer program or scientific calculator would willingly help you along. In our example, the very user-friendly program SPSS determined that $r = -0.882$.

Some of the properties of this number r are as follows:

1. The computed value of r must be between -1 and +1. (If it's not then someone or something messed up.)

2. A strong positive correlation would yield an r value close to +1; a strong negative linear correlation would be close to -1.

3. If r is close to 0, we conclude that there is no significant linear correlation between x and y.

Checking the table, we find that with a sample size of 10 ($n = 10$), the value $r = -0.9169$, indicating a strong negative correlation between the use of calculators and measures of math anxiety levels. The r-squared number (0.779) indicates that a person's math anxiety might explain 84% of his or her calculator usage (or nonusage).

4. If there is a significant relation, then regression analysis is used to determine what that relationship is.

5. If the relation is linear, the equation of the line of best fit can be determined. (For two variables, the equation of a line can be expressed as $y = mx + b$, where m is the slope and b is the y–intercept.)

Thus, the equation of the line of best fit would be
$$S = -.9169 \, M + 21.614.$$
The nonparametric counterpart to the Pearson r is the Spearman rank correlation coefficient (r_s), Spearman's rho, or Kendall's tau (τ).

FOR YOUR INFORMATION AND EDUCATION

The full name of the Pearson *r* is the Pearson product-moment correlation coefficient. It is named for Karl Pearson (1857–1936), who originally developed it. It is called product-moment because it is calculated by multiplying the *z* scores of two variables by one another to get their product and then calculating the average or mean value, which is called a moment of these products. Also check out http://www.socialresearchmethods.net/kb/statcorr.php

 Cutting Board

How alike are two people's tastes in television shows? The following activity will employ the nonparametric, Spearman rank correlation coefficient test to help determine the answer to this question. You will need a friend or a relative to perform this activity.

1. In Column I of the chart provided in Step 3, list 10 different TV shows that you and a friend or relative are familiar with. Try to have at least one news show, a situation comedy, a mystery, a variety show, a talk show, and a drama. Include shows that you like as well as those that you dislike.
2. In Column II, rank the shows that are listed, where 1 is your favorite (the one you would be most inclined to watch) and 10 is your least favorite (the one you would be least inclined to watch).
3. Have your friend or relative do a similar ranking in Column III.

I TV Shows	II Your Ratings	III IV F/R Ratings	d	V d^2
A				
B.				
C.				
D.				
E.				
F				
G.				
H.				
I.				
J.				

4. Use the graph below to plot the ordered pairs consisting of the two rankings. Label the points with the letters corresponding to the shows in the list. If the two rankings were identical, the points would be on a starting line pointing northeast and forming a 45-degree angle with both axes. If you were in total disagreement, then the points would be on a straight line pointing southeast and also form a 45-degree angle with both axes.

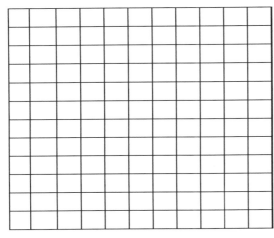 Friend's Rating

Your Rating

5. Although the scattergram you created might give you an impression of how the two ratings match or correlate with each other, it is probably not very definitive. To determine how closely correlated these rankings are, we can use the r statistics and the Spearman rank correlation coefficient, which we will compute in the steps that follow.
6. Go back to the chart in step 3 and compute d, the difference between the two ratings for each show, and d^2, that is, $(d)(d)$. After you have all the d^2, add them up.
7. The formula for finding the rank correlation is

$$r_s = 1 - \frac{6\sum d^2}{n(n^2 - 1)}.$$

8. To do this on your calculator, multiply the sum of your d^2 numbers by 6. Divide this product by 990, which is the denominator, (10)(99). Store this number in memory +. Compute 1 minus memory recall. The number in the display is your r number. It should be between -1 and +1.
9. A Spearman table indicates that for your sample size of 10, an r value of .564 or greater would indicate a positive correlation with an alpha of 0.10, or a negative value less than -.564 would indicate a negative correlation with an alpha value of 0.10. The closer r is to 1 or -1, the stronger the relation. An r value close to 0 indicates no particular relation. What can you conclude from this test? Should you and this other person turn on the tube when you are together or would it be better to find a different activity?

Critical Values of Spearman's Rank Correlation Coefficient: $r_{s \text{ (rho)}}$

n	$\alpha = 0.10$	$\alpha = 0.05$	$\alpha = 0.02$	$\alpha = 0.01$
10	.564	.648	.745	.794

More on Correlational Statistics

Warning: Correlation does not imply CAUSATION!

The purpose of correlational research is to find co-relationships between two or more variables with the hope of better understanding the conditions and events we encounter and with the hope of making predictions about the future. (From the Annals of Chaos Theory: Predictions are usually very difficult—especially if they are about the future; Predictions are like diapers, both need to be changed often and for the same reason!)

As was noted previously, the linear correlation coefficient, r, measures the strength of the linear relationship between two paired variables in a sample. If there is a linear correlation, that is, if r is large enough between two variables, then regression analysis is used to identify the relationship with the hope of predicting one variable from the other.

Note: If there is no significant linear correlation, then a regression equation *cannot* be used to make predictions.

A regression equation based on old data is not necessarily valid now. The regression equation relating used car prices and ages of cars is no longer usable if it is based on data from the 1960s. Often a scattergram is plotted to get a visual view of the correlation and possible regression equation.

Note: Nonlinear relationships can also be determined, but due to the fact that more complex mathematics is used to describe and interpret data, they are used considerably less often. The following are characteristics of all linear correlational studies:

1. Main research questions are stated as null hypotheses, i.e., no relationship exists between the variables being studied.
2. In simple correlation, there are two measures for each individual in the sample.
3. To apply parametric methods, there must be at least 30 individuals in the study.

221

4. Can be used to measure the degree of relationships, not simply whether a relationship exists.
5. A perfect positive correlation is 1.00; a perfect negative (inverse) is -1.00.
6. A correlation of 0 indicates no linear relationship exists.
7. If two variables, x and y, are correlated so that $r = .5$, then we say that $(0.5)(2)$ or 0.25 or 25% of their variation is common, or variable x can predict 25% of the variance in y.

Bivariate correlation is when there are only two variables being investigated. These definitions help us determine which statistical test can be used to determine correlation and regression.

Continuous scores: Scores can be measured using a rational scale
Ranked data: Likert-type scales, class rankings
Dichotomy: Participants classified into two categories—Republican versus Democrat
Artificial – Pass/ fail (arbitrary decision); true dichotomy (male/female).

The Pearson product-moment correlation coefficient (that is a mouthful!), or Pearson r, is the most common measure of the strength of the linear relationship between two variables. The Spearman rank correlation coefficient, or Spearman r (which we performed above), used for ranked data or when you have a sample size less than 30 ($n < 30$), is the second most popular measure of the strength of the linear relationship between two variables. To measure the strength of the linear relationship between test items for reliability purposes, Cronbach alpha is the most efficient method of measuring the internal consistency. Table 2 below can be used to determine what statistical technique is best used with respect to the type of data the researcher collects.

TABLE 2. Types of Correlations

Technique	Symbol	Variable 1	Variable 2	Remarks
Pearson	r	Continuous	Continuous	Smallest standard of error
Spearman rank	r_s	Ranks	Ranks	Also called Spearman rho; used when $n < 30$
Kendall's tau	τ	Ranks	Ranks	Used for $n < 10$
Biserial Correlation (Cronbach)	a/bis	Artificial dichotomy	Continuous	Sometimes exceeds 1; often used in item analysis
Widespread biserial correlation	r/wbis	Artificial dichotomy	Continuous interval	Looking for extremes on Variable 1
Point-biserial correlation	r/pbis	True dichotomy	Continuous interval	Yields lower correlation than r/biserial
Tetrachoric correlation	r/t	Artificial dichotomy	Artificial dichotomy	Used when Variables 1 and 2 can be split arbitrarily
(example: self-confidence vs. Internal Locus of Control)				
Phi coefficient	ϕ	True dichotomy	True dichotomy	
Correlation ratio eta	h	Continuous	Continuous	Nonlinear relationships

Multivariate Correlational Statistics

If you wish to test a claim that multiple independent variables might be used to make a prediction about a dependent variable, several possible tests can be constructed. Such studies involve *multivariate correlational statistics*.

Discriminant Analysis – This is a form of regression analysis designed for classification. It is used to determine the correlation between two or more predictor variables and a dichotomous criterion variable. The main use of discriminant analysis is to predict group membership (e.g., success/nonsuccess) from a set of predictors. If a set of variables is found that provides satisfactory discrimination, classification equations can be derived, their use checked out through hit/rate tables, and if good, they can be used to classify new participants who were not in the original analysis. In order to use discriminant analysis, the following *ingredients*, or assumptions (conditions), are needed:

1. At least twice the number of participants as variables in study
2. Groups have the same variance/covariance structures

3. All variables are normally distributed

For more information, check out http://tinyurl.com/33snxtz

Canonical Correlation – This is also a form of regression analysis used with two or more independent variables and two or more dependent variables. It is used to predict a combination of several criterion variables from a combination of several predictor variables. For example, suppose a researcher was interested in the relationship between a student's conation and school achievement. She or he may wish to use several measures of conation (number of hours spent on homework, receiving help when needed, class participation) and several measures of achievement (grades, cores on achievement tests, teacher evaluation). The two clusters of measurement could be studied with canonical correlations.

Path Analysis – A type of multivariate analysis in which causal relations among several variables are represented by graphs or path diagrams showing how causal influences traveled. It is used to test theories about hypothesized causal links between variables that are correlated. Researchers can calculate direct and indirect effects of independent variables that are not usually done with ordinary multiple regression analysis.

Factor Analysis – Used to reduce a large number of variables to a few factors by combining variables that are moderately or highly correlated with one another. Factor analysis is often used in survey research to see if a long series of questions can be grouped into shorter sets of questions, each of which describes an aspect or factor of the phenomenon being studied.

Differential Analysis – Used to examine correlation between variables among homogeneous subgroups within a sample; can be used to identify moderator variables that improve a measure's predictive validity.

Multiple Linear Regression – Used to determine the correlation between a criterion variable and a combination of two or more predictor variables. The coefficient for any particular predictor variable is an estimate of the effect of that variable while holding constant the effects of the other predictor variables. As in any regression method we need the following conditions to be met: We are investigating linear relationships; for each x value, y is a random variable having a normal distribution. All of the y variables have the same variance; for a given value of x, the distribution of y values has a mean that lies on the regression line.

> Note: Results are not seriously affected if departures from normal distributions and equal variances are not too extreme.

The following example illustrates how a researcher might use different multivariate correlational statistics in a research project:

Example: Suppose a researcher has, among other data, scores on three measures for a group of teachers working overseas:

1. Years of experience as a teacher
2. Extent of travel while growing up
3. Tolerance for ambiguity

Research Question: Can these measures (or other factors) predict the degree of adaptation to the overseas culture they are working on?

Discriminant Analysis - Hypothesis 1: The outcome is dichotomous between those who adapted well and those who adapted poorly based on these three measures. Hypothesis 2: Knowing these three factors could be used to predict success.

Multiple Regression - Hypothesis: Some combination of the three predictor measures correlates better with predicting the outcome measure than any one predictor alone.

Canonical Correlation - Hypothesis: Several measures of adaptation could be quantified, i.e., adaptation to food, climate, customs, etc. based on these predictors.

Path Analysis - Hypothesis: Childhood travel experience leads to tolerance for ambiguity and desire for travel as an adult, and this makes it more likely that a teacher will score high on these predictors, which will lead them to seek an overseas teaching experience and adapt well to the experience.

Factor Analysis - Suppose there are five more (a total of eight) adaptive measures that could be determined. All eight measures can be examined to determine whether they cluster into groups such as education, experience, personality traits, etc.

Example: To compute the correlation between gender (male/female) and employment status (employed/unemployed), you could use a phi coefficient. You couldn't use it for age and income, however, because these are not dichotomous variables.

Example: Kendall's tau could be used to compute the correlation between feelings about a new health plan (not in favor/in favor/highly in favor) and health of a patient (unhealthy/healthy/very healthy).

Example: A point biserial correlation can be used when females and males applying for a job report the total number of years of education they have had and we want to know whether there is any correlation between gender and years of education.

Analysis of Covariance

A "yes" on one of the questions below will lead you to a different type of statistical test involving bivariate data. Are you claiming that

____1. Two groups being compared come from the same population and contain similar characteristics?

____2. There is a covariate source of variation that is not controlled for in the design of the experiment, but which does affect the dependent variable?

If you are planning to divide your participants into two groups (perhaps a control group and an experimental group), or if you are planning to use two different treatments on two different groups, then problems in randomization and matching the groups might be a concern.

A statistical process called analysis of covariance (ANCOVA) has been developed to equate the groups on certain relevant variables identified prior to the investigation. Researchers often use pretest mean scores as covariates.

The following guidelines should be used in the ANCOVA:

1. The correlation of the covariate (some variable different than the one you are testing) and the response variable should be statistically and educationally significant.
2. The covariate should have a high reliability.
3. The covariate should be a variable that is measured prior to any portions of the treatments.
4. The conditions of homogeneity of regression should be met. The slopes of the regression lines describing the linear relationships of the criterion variable and the covariate from cell to cell must not be statistically different.
5. All follow-up procedures for significant interaction or post-hoc comparisons should be made with the adjusted cell or adjusted marginal means.

ANCOVA is a transformation from raw scores to adjusted scores that takes into account the effects of the covariate. ANCOVA allows us to compensate somewhat when groups are selected by nonrandom methods.

The nonparametric counterpart of ANCOVA is the runs test.

If your hypothesis is that many variables or factors are contributing to a certain condition, you might wish to use multiple regression analysis. This is similar to linear regression analysis with a significant increase in number crunching. If this is not how you wish to spend several hours of your day, we recommend that you employ a computer to calculate the numerical information necessary to use multiple regression analysis.

Contingency Tables

If you only want to test whether or not two variables are dependent on one another (e.g., are death and smoking dependent variables? Are SAT scores and high school grades independent variables?), consider using a contingency table.

The null hypothesis would be that the variables are independent. Setting up a contingency table is easy; the rows are one variable and the columns another. In contingency table analysis, you determine how closely the amount in each cell coincides with the expected value of each cell if the two variables are independent.

The following contingency table lists the response to a bill pertaining to gun control.

	In favor	Opposed
Northeast	10	30
Southeast	15	25
Northwest	35	10
Southwest	10	25

Notice that Cell 1 indicates that 10 people in the northeast were in favor of the bill.

Example: In the previous contingency table, 40 out of 160 (1/4) of those surveyed were from the northeast. If the two variables were independent, you would expect half of that amount (20) to be in favor of the amendment because there were only two choices.

To determine how close the expected values are to the actual values, the test statistic chi-square (χ^2) is determined. Small values of chi-square support the claim of independence between the two variables. That is, chi-square will be small when observed and expected frequencies are close. Large values of chi-square would cause the null hypothesis to be rejected and reflect significant differences between observed and expected frequencies.

Note: As in all tests of hypotheses, there are certain assumptions that need to be met prior to conducting the test. In this case, we require the expected value of each cell to be 5 or greater. While contingency tables are most commonly analyzed using χ^2, there is an exact method (Fisher's exact test) that avoids the concerns of small expected values, but which is more difficult to compute. For more information, check out http://tinyurl.com/2atcepc.

Before you move into your final **PHASE**, use the Cutting Board below to assist you in deciding what *spices* you can use in your study.

 Cutting Board

1. Underline the terms that best complete the sentence. I will be testing a claim about

   a mean, a standard deviation, a proportion, 2 means, 2 variances, a relationship between 2 variables, the independence of 2 variables, relationship between more than 2 variables.

2. If you will be using nonparametric testing, underline the test(s) that you think you will use (you might wish to read the information on nonparametrics first).

   Sign test, Wilcoxon signed-rank test, Wilcoxon rank-sum test, Kruskal-Wallis test, Spearman rank correlation, runs test, Friedman, McNemar, Mann-Whitney U, Fisher

3. If you plan to use parametric testing, underline the test(s) that you plan to use:

   Z test, t test, paired t or z test, χ^2, r, F test, Pearson r, other: _____

4. Why did you choose the test(s) in (2) and/or (3)?

   After your data are collected, make sure you visit this section again and fill out all information that is relevant to your research study. Once this is accomplished, you will be able to fully *digest* chapter 4 of your dissertation.

5. What assurance do you have that you have met the assumptions and prerequisites to use this test?

TEST YOUR QUANTITATIVE ACUMEN

1. Descriptive Statistics

2. Ex Post Facto

3. Inferential Statistics

4. Factorial Design

5. A Priori

6. Validity

7. Reliability

8. Rosenthal effect

9. Hawthorne Effect

10. Quasi-Experimental

11. Covariant Analysis

12. Evaluative Research

A) The consistency in which the same results occur.

B) Experimental studies that are not double-blinded and might cause bias on the part of the researcher.

C) A mode of inquiry in which a theory is proposed and hypotheses are made in advance of gathering data about a specific phenomenon. Hypothetical-deductive theory.

D) A form of descriptive research in which the investigator looks for relationships that may explain phenomena that have already taken place.

E) A method used to depict systematically the facts and characteristics of a given population or area of interest.

F) Differences in independent variables relevant to a study are controlled.

G) A method that rigorously explores the efficacy of a program, treatment, or product.

H) A method used to study the effects of more than one independent variable on more than one dependent variable.

I) A set of procedures used to test hypothesis or estimate the parameters in a population.

J) Participants appear to make progress just because they are in a study.

K) A method in which a sample of convenience is used and then treated to determine if there is any significant differences pre- and post-treatment.

L) The extent to which data measure what they purport to.

Answers: 1- E, 2-D, 3-I, 4-H, 5-C, 6-L, 7-A, 8-B, 9-J, 10-K, 11-F, 12-G

Nonparametric Tests

To understand the idea of *nonparametric* statistics (the term *nonparametric* was first used by Wolfowitz, 1942) first requires a basic understanding of parametric statistics that we have just studied in some detail. The concept of statistical significance testing is based on the sampling distribution of a particular statistic as well as a basic knowledge of the underlying distribution of a variable. Once these are known, then we can make predictions about how, in repeated samples of equal size, this particular statistic will behave, that is, how it is distributed. For example, if we draw 100 random samples of 100 female children aged 10, each from the general population, and compute the mean height in each sample, then the distribution of the standardized means across samples will likely approximate the normal distribution. Now imagine that we take an additional random sample in a particular city ("Kiddysville") where we suspect that 10-year-old children are taller than the average population. If the mean height in that sample falls outside the upper 95% tail area of the z distribution, then we conclude that the 10-year-old children of Kiddysville appear to be taller than the average population or with 95% confidence we conclude that the children of Kiddysville are taller than normal.

In the above example, we relied on our knowledge that, in repeated samples of equal size, the standardized means (for height) will be distributed following the z distribution (with a particular mean and variance). However, this will only be true if in the population the variable of interest (height in our example) is normally distributed, that is, if the distribution of people of particular heights follows the normal distribution (the bell-shaped distribution).

For many variables of interest, we simply do not know for sure that this is the case. For example, is income distributed normally in the population? Probably not. The incidence rates of AIDS are not normally distributed in the population. The number of car accidents is also not normally distributed, and neither are many other variables in which a researcher might be interested. Another factor that often limits the applicability of tests based on the assumption that the sampling distribution is normal is the size of the sample of data available for the analysis (sample size, *n*). We can assume that the sampling distribution is normal even if we are not sure that the distribution of the variable in the population is normal, as long as our sample is large enough (e.g., 100 or more observations). However, if our sample is very small, then those tests can be used only if we are sure that the variable is normally distributed, and there is often no way to test this.

Hopefully, after this somewhat lengthy overture, the need is evident for statistical procedures that allow us to process data of low quality, from small samples, on variables about which little is known (concerning their distribution). Specifically, nonparametric methods were developed to be used in cases when the researcher knows nothing about the parameters of the variable of interest in the population (hence the name *nonparametric*). In more technical terms, nonparametric methods do not rely on the estimation of parameters (such as the mean or the standard deviation) describing the distribution of the variable of interest in the population. Therefore, these methods are also sometimes (and more appropriately) called *parameter-free* or *distribution-free* methods.

Advantages of Nonparametric Methods

1. Can be applied to a wide variety of situations since they do not require normally distributed populations.
2. Can be applied to nominal data.
3. Computations are usually simpler.
4. Tend to be easier to understand.

Disadvantages of Nonparametric Methods

1. They tend to waste data. Exact numerical data are reduced to qualitative form.
2. The tests are less sensitive; therefore, we need stronger evidence to reject the null hypothesis.
3. A few of the most popular parametric tests, their nonparametric equivalence, and the efficacy of the nonparametric test are found in the table that follows.

TABLE 3. **Parametric and Nonparametric Tests**

Application	Parametric Test	Nonparametric Test	Efficacy of Nonparametric Test with Normal Population
Two dependent samples	t test or z test	Sign test or Wilcoxon signed-rank	0.63
Two independent samples	t test or z test	Wilcoxon rank-sum	0.95
Several independent samples	ANOVA (F test)	Kruskal-Wallis test	0.95
Correlation	Linear - Pearson	Rank Correlation - Spearman	0.95
One sample against a population	t test or z test	Mann Whitney U	
Change in nominal data		McNemar test	

The sign test is the oldest of all nonparametric statistical tests and one of the easiest nonparametric tests to use. It is also considered crude and insensitive because it has a tendency to waste information. Using this test, for example, a person who lost 80 pounds on a diet would be considered the same as a person who lost 1 pound! The level of significance can be estimated without the help of a calculator or table. If the sign test indicates a significant difference and another test does not, you should seriously rethink whether the other test is valid. It may be of use when it is only necessary (or possible) to know if observed differences between two conditions are significant. It is commonly used in a before-and-after experiment where the researcher can simply assign a + to each case where the results were higher after treatment and a − when the opposite were true or where two treatments are being compared for the same participants.

To use the sign test, we need two dependent samples. The sign test can be used with any type of data where a change can be determined.

Example: 14 right-handed pilots were tested to determine if there was a difference between reaction times using their right and left hand. Use a 0.05 significance level to test the claim of no difference in reaction times.

Right: 189   97   116   165   116   129   171   155   112   102   188   158   121   133

Left: 220   171   121   191   130   134   168   187   123   111   180   186   143   156

Sign of -   -   -   -   -   -   +   -   -   -   +   -   -   -   difference:

Using the s^3d^2 CANDOALL *recipe:* We will decide on the sign test. We perform the arithmetic to determine x, the number of times the less frequent sign occurs: 12 negative and 2 positive gives us $x = 2$. This is a two-tailed test since we are testing to see if there is a difference between using the right or the left hand. The table below comes from a critical sign test chart. We will look to reject or fail to reject the null hypothesis if x is less than or equal to the value in the table. Since $2 < 3$, we reject the null and in lay terms we can conclude that there is reason to believe there is a difference in reaction time.

Critical values for the sign test

n	0.005 (one tail) or 0.01 (two tails)	0.01 (one tail) or 0.02 (two tails)	0.025 (one tail) or 0.05 (two tails)	0.05 (one tail) or 0.10 (two tails)
14	1	2	2	3

Example: A sign test can be used to compare participants' attitudes about purchasing a software program (interested or not interested) before and after having viewed a demonstration of the software.

The Wilcoxon Rank-Sum Test

The Wilcoxon rank-sum test is a nonparametric equivalent of the unpaired *t* test. It is used to test the hypothesis that two independent samples have come from the same population. Because it is nonparametric, it makes no assumptions about the distribution of the data.

The *t* test tests the hypothesis that the means of the two groups differ. The Wilcoxon rank-sum test tells us more generally whether one group is better than the other.

The way the test works is to rank all the data from both groups. Thus, the smallest value will be given a rank of 1, the second smallest will have a rank of 2, and so on. Where values are tied, they are given an average rank. The ranks for each group are added together (hence the term rank-sum test). The sums of the ranks used to be compared with tabulated critical values to generate a *p* value, although now computer programs are better suited for the job. For small sample sizes, it is still perfectly feasible to do the test manually if you don't have the necessary software or if you like to get in and work with the data at a more basic level.

The Wilcoxon Signed-Rank Test

The Wilcoxon signed-rank test is a nonparametric equivalent of the paired *t* test. It is used to test the hypothesis that two paired samples have come from the same population. Because it is nonparametric, it makes no assumptions about the distribution of the data.

For example, suppose we are interested in whether a particular drug given for depression affects the liver enzyme ALT. If we measure the study participants' ALT before and after they take the drug, we have matching pairs of data. We might think of testing the data with a paired *t* test, but this would not be appropriate because ALT values are not normally distributed. The Wilcoxon signed-rank test can be used instead.

The test works as follows: For each participant, we subtract the post-drug ALT value from the pre-drug value. This gives us a number for each participant, which may be positive, negative, or zero. We then rank all those numbers in order, ignoring the sign. Finally, we add the ranks of the positive numbers and the ranks of the negative numbers (in a similar way to the ranks of the two groups in the Wilcoxon rank-sum test). The summed ranks can then, if necessary, be compared with tabulated critical values to generate a *p* value, although it would be far more likely that the test would be done by appropriate software like with your SPSS program.

Example: A comparison of student attitudes about school (very excited, moderately excited, neutral, moderately bored, very bored) before and after taking a course on study habits.

Examples of Other Nonparametric Statistical Tests

The McNemar Test

- The philosophy of the McNemar test is similar to that of the chi-square test. It assumes that you are dealing with research questions where two variables are related. Here, our hypothesis usually is that the difference is significant between the precondition and postcondition in the same groups.

- The McNemar test can be used with either nominal or ordinal data and is especially useful with before-and-after measurements of the same participants.

- The McNemar test determines the significance of any observed change by setting up a fourfold table of frequencies to represent the first and second responses.

Example: Suppose a group was interested in the support for a new mental health clinic in a certain area. A town meeting was held to discuss the pros and cons of such a clinic in the area. Participants were surveyed before and after the town meeting.

In the table that follows, A represents those who were in favor before and not in favor after, B represents those who were in favor before and after, C represents those not in favor before and not in favor after, and D represents those not in favor before and in favor after. $A + D$ represents the number who changed their mind. Since the data are nominal and the study involves before-and-after measurements of two related samples, the McNemar test can be used to see if the change from one point of view is different from the change to the other point of view (i.e., is there is a difference between A and D). The null hypothesis would be that there is no change. If the test value is higher than the critical value, we would reject the null hypothesis.

Before/After	Do Not Favor	Favor
Favor	A	B
Oppose	C	D

The chi-square distribution is used for this test. The test value is

$$\chi^2 = \frac{(|A - D| - 1)^2}{A + D} \text{ with } df = 1.$$

Compute the test chi-square = $[(|A - D| - 1)^2 / (A + D)]$ and compare the value obtained to the critical value of 3.84. If the test value >3.84, reject the null; otherwise, fail to reject the null.

Example: High school students are surveyed on their knowledge of family planning and birth control. Half the group is given a workshop on this topic. The survey is readministered to both groups after the seminar to assess the knowledge gained.

Kruskal-Wallis Test

We used ANOVA to test hypotheses that influences among several (k) sample means are due to chance. The parametric F test requires that all the involved populations possess normal distributions with variances that are approximately equal. The Kruskal-Wallis test is a nonparametric alternative that does not require normal distributions or equal variances. Like many nonparametric tests, the Kruskal-Wallis test uses the ranks of the data rather than their raw values to calculate the statistic. In using the Kruskal-Wallis test (also called the H test) we test the null hypothesis that independent and random samples come from the same or identical populations. We compute the test statistic, H, which has a distribution that can be approximated by the chi-square distribution with $k - 1$ degrees of freedom, as long as there are at least three random samples and each sample has at least five observations.

The computation of an H value involves considering all observations as if they came from the same group, ranking the entire group from lowest to highest, and in cases of ties, assigning to each observation the mean of the ranks involved. Then return each number to its sample and find the sum of the ranks and the sample size.

Example: The income from a random sample of 50 parents from five different schools (10 parents from each school) in one school district is collected to test the claim that the income level of the schools are equal.

Fisher's Exact Test

In Fisher's exact test, we compute a test statistic for measures of association that relate two nominal variables. It is used mainly in 2 x 2 frequency tables when the expected frequency is too small to use the chi-square test. A phi (ϕ) coefficient can be generated, which is a symmetric measure equivalent to a Pearson's correlation coefficient.

One of the limitations of Fisher's exact test is that the data must be dichotomous and the elements must originate from two different sources. To compute the correlation between sex (male/female) and employment status (employed/unemployed), you could use a phi coefficient. However, this cannot be used with age and income, per se, since these are not dichotomous variables.

A 2 x 2 contingency table is constructed and usually set up as follows:

	Accepted into SW Program	Rejected from SW Program	Total
From the East	9	2	11
From the West	7	6	13
Total	16	8	24

TABLE = [9 , 2 , 7 , 6]

Left: p value = 0.9725849149728539

Right: p value = 0.15574101494144757

Two-tail: p value = 0.21079553102705903

Conclusion: There would be no reason to believe that, based on the data, a person from the west was more likely to be accepted into an SW program. Computations are based on factorials, which become prohibitive if the numbers get large. 8! = 40,320!!!

Example: Compare attitudes toward marijuana (harmful or not harmful) of 12th graders who did ($n = 9$) and did not ($n = 6$) complete a DARE program in elementary school.

Chi-Square Test of Independence

The most familiar use of the chi-square test is when a researcher wants to see if there are statistically significant differences between the observed (actual) frequencies and the expected (hypothesized) frequencies of two variables presented in a cross-tabulation or contingency table. The larger the observed frequency is in comparison with the expected frequency, the larger the chi-square statistic is and the more likely the difference is statistically significant.

For example, suppose a researcher gave a pass-fail test on knowledge of drug abuse to a sample of 100 participants (42 men and 58 women), and 61 participants passed and 39 failed. Suppose the researcher was interested in whether the differences in knowledge were related to gender. She could use a chi-square analysis to test the null hypothesis of no statistically significant differences between sexes.

The following tables could be tabulated:

Expected Frequencies

	Pass	Fail	Total
Men	27	15	42
Women	35	23	58
Total	62	38	100

Observed Frequencies

	Pass	Fail	Total
Men	18	24	42
Women	42	16	58
Total	61	39	100

Comparing these tables, we see immediately that they are not identical, but the question the researcher asks is whether these differences were statistically significant. A chi-square test would tell us that the differences are significant at the 0.01 level of significance, leading us to reject the null hypothesis and conclude that the differences are greater than what could be expected by chance alone.

Note: The null hypothesis states there is no association between these variables, while the alternative hypothesis states a relationship does exist between the two variables. This chi-square statistic has a distribution and degrees of freedom associated with it. The degree of freedom for the chi-square is calculated by multiplying the number of rows minus 1 by the number of columns minus 1. Since this example has two rows and two columns, the **df** = 1. The Pearson chi-square is evaluated as statistically significant when the probability of the statistic is .05 or less. The formula for computing the chi-square statistic is

$$\chi^2 = \Sigma \; \frac{(\text{observed} - \text{expected})^2}{\text{expected}}$$

Calculate the chi-square statistic (χ^2) test value by completing the following steps:

For each observed number in the table, subtract the corresponding expected number (O - E). Square the difference [$(O - E)^2$].

Divide the squares obtained for each cell in the table by the expected number for that cell [$(O - E)^2 / E$].

Sum all the values for $(O - E)^2 / E$. This is the chi-square statistic.

Assumptions in using the chi-square test of goodness of fit:

- The sample values are independent and identically distributed.
- The sample values are grouped in categories, and the counts of the number of sample values occurring in each category are recorded.
- The hypothesized distribution is specified in advance, so that the number of observations that should appear each category, assuming the hypothesized distribution is the correct one, can be calculated without reference to the sample values.

The chi-square test involves using the chi-square distribution to approximate the underlying exact distribution. The approximation becomes better as the expected cell frequencies grow larger and may be inappropriate for tables with very small expected cell frequencies. For tables with expected cell frequencies less than 5, the chi-square approximation might not be reliable.

A standard (and conservative) rule to follow is to avoid using the chi-square test for tables with expected cell frequencies less than 1, or when more than 20% of the table cells have expected cell frequencies less than 5.

Koehler and Larntz (1980) suggested that if the total number of observations is at least 10, the number of categories is at least 3, and the square of the total number of observations is at least 10 times the number of categories, then the chi-square approximation should be reasonable.

A key assumption of the chi-square test of independence is that each participant contributes data to only one cell. Therefore the sum of all cell frequencies in the table must be the same as the number of participants in the experiment. Consider an experiment in which each of 12 participants threw a dart at a target once using their preferred hand and once using their nonpreferred hand. The data are shown below:

	Hit	Missed
Preferred hand	9	3
Non-preferred hand	4	8

It would not be valid to use the chi-square test of independence on these data because each participant contributed data to two cells: one cell based on their performance with their preferred hand and one cell based on their performance with their nonpreferred hand. The total of the cell frequencies in the table is 24, but the total number of participants is only 12.

In the test for independence, the claim is that the row and column variables are independent of each other. This is the null hypothesis. The multiplication rule states that if two events were independent then the probability of both occurring is the product of their probabilities. This is the theory upon which the test of independence is based. If we reject the null hypothesis, then the assumption is assumed wrong and the row and column variables are dependent. There is an excellent application of this test at http://tinyurl.com/39k32gj.

Mann Whitney U

This is a nonparametric test to determine if there is a difference between two independent groups. It is used when the data for two samples are measured on at least an ordinal scale in rank order. It is the nonparametric equivalent of the t test. Although ordinal measures are used, it is assumed that data are continuously distributed. The test assesses whether the degree of overlap between the two observed distributions is less than would be expected by chance on the null hypothesis that the two samples are drawn from a single population.

The Mann-Whitney U test is one of the most popular of the nonparametrics. There is no such thing as a free lunch, of course, so the Mann-Whitney U is less powerful (more conservative or less likely to find a difference if a real difference exists) than a *t* test.

It is for

1. Independently drawn random samples, the sizes of which need not be the same.
2. Sample sizes where the larger is $n \geq 9$.

(If both sample sizes are eight or fewer measures, then other tests can be applied.)

Like a Kruskal-Wallis, the Mann-Whitney U works by first ranking the data.

The way it works is that the scores in both groups are combined into one data set ranked from lowest to highest. The rank of each score is recorded and when two or more scores are tied, all of the tied scores get the same rank—a rank equal to the average of the positions in the ordered array. For example, if three scores are tied for positions 3, 4, and 5, all would be assigned the rank of 4. If the sums of the ranks are very different, the p value will be small.

The p value answers the following question: If the populations really have the same median, what is the chance that random sampling would result in a sum of ranks as far apart (or more so) as observed in this experiment?

Example: A group of students were given a sensitivity test and their scores were ranked by gender as follows:

Rank numbers for males: 1,2,3,7,8,9,10,13,14,15,23,24,26,27
Rank numbers for females: 4,5,6,11,12,16,17,18,19,20,21,22,25,28,29,30,31

The sum of the rank numbers for males equals 182 (1+2+3+7+8+...+26+27), while the sum of the rank number for females equals 314 (4+5+6+11+....+30+31).

The expected sums for males and females are 224 and 272, respectively; the standard deviation of the expected sums is 25.19; and the p value of the observed divergence equals 0.04779. Thus, at the 0.05 level of significance, we can conclude that females tend toward the higher rank numbers while males tend toward the lower rank numbers.

Example: Determine if the level of physical abuse (minor, moderate, or severe) inflicted by fathers ($n = 50$) is different from those inflicted by mothers ($n = 50$) on their court-dependent children.

The Cochran Q Test and the Friedman Test

Recall that the philosophy of the McNemar test is similar to that of the chi-square test. It assumes that you are dealing with research questions in which two variables are related. Here, our hypothesis usually is that the difference is significant between the precondition and the postcondition in the same groups' responses. The Cochran Q test is an extension of these tests for studies having more than two dependent samples. It tests the hypothesis that the proportion of cases in a category is equal for several related categories. The object of the Cochran Q test is to investigate the significance of the differences between many treatments (k) on the same n elements with a binomial distribution. Some of the limitations of this test are that it is assumed that there are k series of observations on the same n elements. The observations are dichotomous and 0 or 1 represents the observations in the two classes. In addition, the number of elements must be sufficiently large, usually greater than 10.

The test statistics computed is referred to as a Q value. This approximately follows a chi-square distribution with $k - 1$ degrees of freedom. The null hypothesis that the k samples come from one common dichotomous distribution is rejected if Q is larger than the critical value.

When the data are at least ordinal, the Friedman two-way ANOVA is appropriate. The object of the Friedman test for multiple treatments of a series of participants is to investigate the significance of the differences in responses for several treatments (k) applied to several participants (n). It tests matched samples, ranking each case and calculating the mean rank for each variable across all cases. It uses these ranks to compute a test statistic. The product is a two-way table where the rows represent participants and the columns represent the treatment conditions.

Characteristics

The Friedman test is frequently called a *two-way analysis on ranks*. It is at the same time a generalization of the sign test and the Spearman rank correlation test. The Friedman test models the ratings of n (rows) judges on k (columns) treatments. One popular application of the Friedman test is found in wine tastings, where each judge rates a collection of wines independently of the other judges. The null hypothesis would be that the ratings of the judges are not related (e.g., they cannot distinguish the wines).

The limitation of the Friedman test is that we need to assume that a participant's response to one treatment is not affected by the same participant's response to another treatment and that the response distribution for each participant is continuous. The test statistic is often referred to as a

G value. If this value exceeds the critical chi-square value obtained from a chi-square table with $k - 1$ degrees of freedom, the null hypothesis that the effects of the k treatments are all the same is rejected.

If ties occur in the ranking procedure, one has to assign the average rank for each series of equal results. For example, four entries can be assigned the rank of 12.25.

How the Friedman Test Works

The Friedman test is a nonparametric test that compares three or more paired groups. The Friedman test first ranks the values in each matched set (each row) from low to high. Each row is ranked separately. It then sums the ranks in each group (column). If the sums are very different, the p value will be small (and the null hypothesis will be rejected). The whole point of using a matched test is to control for experimental variability between participants, thus increasing the power of the test. Some factors you don't control in the experiment will increase (or decrease) all the measurements in a participant. Because the Friedman test ranks the values in each row, it is not affected by sources of variability that equally affect all values in a row (since that factor won't change the ranks within the row).

Example: If clinical therapists take part in a new intervention program on drug abuse and their attitudes about this program are measured before, during, and after the program, and they are asked if this program is worthwhile, Cochran's Q could test the hypothesis that the proportion of *strongly agree* responses will differ for the clinicians taking part in the intervention depending on which of the three time periods is being considered. The Friedman test could be used to test the hypothesis: There will be at least one difference among the median attitude scores at preintervention, at postintervention, and at a 6-month follow-up for the clinicians who took part in the intervention.

Example: Children who are living in a residential treatment program return to their families after staying for 3 months, 6 months, or 12 months. Cochran's Q test can be used to determine if there is a difference in the level of comfort in taking home a family member after these time periods. Friedman's test could be used to determine whether there is a difference in the family satisfaction scores of 64 children who were discharged from the residential treatment center at these different time intervals.

Qualitative Analysis

Bogdan and Biklen (1982) defined qualitative data analysis as "working with data, organizing it, breaking it into manageable units, synthesizing it, searching for patterns, discovering what is important and what is to be learned, and deciding what you will tell others" (p. 145). Qualitative researchers tend to use inductive analysis of data, meaning that the critical themes emerge from the data (Patton, 1990). If you are planning to use qualitative analysis in your dissertation, you need to place the raw data into logical, meaningful categories, examine them in a holistic fashion, and find a way to communicate this interpretation to others.

Sitting down to organize a pile of raw data can be a daunting task. It can involve literally hundreds of pages of interview transcripts, memos, e-mails, documents, field notes, and documents. The mechanics of handling large quantities of qualitative data can range from physically sorting using Post-its, index cards, or slips of paper to using one of the several computer software programs designed to aid in this task. To save time, it is highly recommend that you consider one of the programs like NVivo, Qualrus, or Atlas.ti. There is a bit of a learning curve when using these software programs. Excellent information on NVivo is at http://tinyurl.com/2wamayr. You might also want to consider getting a qualitative analysis coach.

Analysis begins with identification of the themes emerging from the raw data, a process sometimes referred to as *open coding* (Strauss & Corbin, 1990). During open coding, you will identify and tentatively name the conceptual categories into which the phenomena observed will be grouped. The goal is to create descriptive, multidimensional categories that form a preliminary framework for analysis. Words, phrases, or events that appear to be similar can be grouped into the same category. These categories may be gradually modified or replaced during the subsequent stages of analysis.

As the raw data are broken down into manageable chunks, you should also devise an *audit trail*—that is, a method for identifying these data chunks according to the source and the context. If the data are generated from a participant, it is a good idea to acknowledge this in the research report. Most participants, however, are provided with code names such as P1, P2, etc. Qualitative research reports are characterized by the use of voice in the text; that is, participant quotes that illustrate the themes being described.

The next stage of analysis involves a reexamination of the categories identified to determine how they are linked, a process sometimes called *axial coding* (Strauss & Corbin, 1990). During this stage, the categories identified in open coding are compared and combined in new ways as the researcher begins to assemble the "big picture." Coding serves a dual purpose—to describe and to acquire a new understanding of a phenomenon of interest. During axial coding, you will build a conceptual model and determine whether sufficient data exist to support that interpretation.

Finally, you will translate the conceptual model into the story line that will be read by others. Ideally, the analysis will be a rich account and "closely approximates the reality it represents" (Strauss & Corbin, 1990, p. 57).

Although the stages of analysis appear to be linear, in practice they may occur simultaneously and repeatedly. When you are conducting axial coding, you might determine that the initial categories identified must be revised, leading to a reexamination of the raw data. Additional data collection might be needed if you uncover gaps in the data. Informal analysis begins the moment you begin your data collection, and this will help guide subsequent data collection.

An interesting data analysis exercise was presented by Marsha Court, and is found in the *Academic Exchange Quarterly* (Spring 2005): http://tinyurl.com/2uyxolq. Court asks students to review the items in their recycling bins and suggests the following scenario: Imagine you are an archeologist in the year 3000 visiting your geographical location. This area has been unoccupied for hundreds of years, but recent excavations have revealed that there was a thriving civilization here until some natural or human disaster forced the population to abandon the city. Little is known of these people's way of life. The data in this bag (recycled items) recovered from the site appear to represent the contents of a home or neighborhood refuse site. Due to special conditions in the soil, these items have been preserved in remarkably good condition.

Your job is to sort these items into from three to seven categories to shed light on the general research question: "What was the culture of these people like?" Give each category a name and be prepared to present your categories to the class, explaining and interpreting them in order to arrive at a tentative description and analysis of this culture. This activity can elucidate an understanding of the potential of carefully conducted qualitative research to uncover cultural meanings, to build theory, and to provide recommendations for further study.

Excellent information on NVivo is at http://tinyurl.com/2wamayr and at http://tinyurl.com/yz9lezj.

An excellent NVivo expert is Karen I. Conger, Ph.D., DataSense, LLC, Research Consultant Specialists in QSR Software Ph: (661) 831-3521 Fax: (661) 215-9379 Email: kconger@datasense.org Web: http://www.datasense.org/

The 5 P's
Preliminary Preparation: Proposal Planning - Prospectus
(A *recipe* for the construction of a dissertation research proposal)

Before you actually do your research (prepare for your *feast*), most graduate programs require that you first put together a research proposal. When done properly, this could provide you with a plan and most of the *ingredients* you will need to *cook up* a high-quality dissertation. Most universities require that you submit a three-chapter proposal, which can later be transformed (with modifications) into the first three chapters of your dissertation.

A dissertation proposal must contain sufficient detail to convince faculty readers that the proposed investigation (a) has potential to contribute valuable knowledge to a profession, (b) is sufficiently planned to ensure that the project can be completed (answers research questions) as described in the proposal document, and (c) will possess the level of intellectual rigor commonly expected at the graduate level of study.

In the proposal, you will discuss things that you are *going to do* (use the future tense); in the dissertation, you write about things you *have done* (past tense). According to Dr. Robert E. Hoye of Walden University,

> The most important aspects of writing a proposal is solving a real problem and ensuring that all of the parts of the proposal fit together. You cannot change your methodology without adjusting the purpose and the significance. The review of literature, for example, has to be related to the problem, purpose, theoretical framework, and the hypotheses.

Warning! Any time you change one thing in your proposal (or dissertation), you must make sure that any other parts of your design with which it is associated are appropriately modified.

In **PHASE 3**, we will examine how to *cook up* both a terrific proposal (what you will do) and a *delectable* dissertation (what you did do). Many of the suggestions presented here were first seen in **PHASE 1**. Be sure to check back as needed.

Many universities and research-granting agencies require a prospectus (an *appetizer* to *whet the appetite* of your guests) before reviewing a research proposal. A prospectus provides a clear statement of the problem the study is intended to resolve, accompanied by a detailed description of the procedures to be used, the practical or theoretical significance of the problem, the research questions, and the methodology that will guide the study. A prospectus indicates that your research project fits the required parameters. The audience for the prospectus is the readers who will determine whether your research should be undertaken. The readers might be members of your research committee, a graduate degree committee, a funding agency, or the management of the company or agency for whom you will conduct the study.

 ### *Cutting Board*

Carefully examine the following sample prospectus and then vigilantly put together a prospectus for your research proposal. Make sure you share this with the members of your committee and those who will be closely involved with approving your research.

Sample *Bill of Fare* (Prospectus) for a Proposal

Title: The Application of the 12-Step Programs by Alcoholics Who Have Been Successful in Aftercare: A Descriptive Study

Problem Statement: Alcohol abuse is one of the most critical problems facing society (Parker & Parker, 2003). The 12-step program has been purported to be the primary model for the treatment of alcoholism (Brooks & Penn, 1999). Yet, to date, there has been little, if any, formal evaluation as to the actual use and application of this program for those who are able to maintain abstinence. In order to provide the most effective and expeditious treatment for alcoholics, it is necessary that a descriptive study be conducted to determine to what extent those who have been successful in aftercare have utilized the 12-step program.

Introduction: Quote from Kaminer's *I'm Dysfunctional, You're Dysfunctional* questioning the efficacy and discussion of the overuse of 12-step programs. Kaminer seems to suggest that AA is beyond reproach.

Purpose: The purpose of this study is to evaluate a group of successful participants in Alcoholics Anonymous with respect to their degree of use of the program's 12 steps. Since the

12-step program is hailed as the paramount means of successfully treating those suffering from chemical dependency, it is imperative to ascertain the actual use of the program for those who have been successful in aftercare.

Theoretical Framework: The researcher is taking a postmodern constructivist view. To maintain sobriety, the knowledge obtained in the treatment program is likely to be invented or constructed in the minds of people who have participated in the program. People create knowledge, ideas, and language, not because they are true, but rather because they are useful. Perhaps those who are successful in care have constructed a modified theory based on the information they have received.

Research Question: To what extent is the 12-step program being used by those who have been successful in care for at least 1 year?

Significance: This study will be able to reach people that have not been reached before. The researcher will elaborate on his personal qualifications to obtain the desired information. If the study reveals that successful patients only practice part of the program, then this information could aid counselors in seeking a more concentrated and abridged treatment regime, thus saving patients, their family, and society both time and money.

Background: 12-step program development; alcoholism as a disease.

Nature of the Study: This will primarily be a descriptive study but the researcher will also utilize ethnographic and evaluative techniques. The researcher believes that in order to elicit accurate information from this population, the investigator must have personal knowledge of this disease. The researcher plans to discover what the participants believe or perceive they have experienced. The investigator further believes that nothing can be understood apart from the context within which it was experienced.

Literature/Research Review: Aftercare, alcoholism, the 12-step program, AA, alcohol as a disease, other programs for recovery and treatment of substance abuse, evaluation of other recovery programs. (Proposal: 20–40 pages, Dissertation: 50–70 pages.)

Scope: The participants will be alcoholics who have maintained sobriety for at least 1 year. Abusers of substances other than alcohol will not be included in the study.

Limitation: The researcher will only work with adults who have completed the AA 12-step program. The researcher will need to rely on self-reporting of what steps were employed.

Delimitations: The study will be narrowed to include only graduates of an alcoholic treatment center in Southern California who currently reside in the Southern California area. Only the 12-step program will be evaluated.

Assumptions: There is an assumption that people will answer truthfully. Since participation will be voluntary and anonymity will be preserved, this is a reasonable assumption. Voluntary participation, encouraging participants to voice their own views, and assurances that there are no right or wrong answers helps overcome the need to give socially acceptable answers.

Methodology: This study will use a descriptive research design that includes ethnographic and evaluative components to describe the way things are. Descriptive research involves observation and description of variables as they are distributed throughout a population (Crowl, 1993). Quality observation (i.e., measurement) is at the heart of descriptive research (Heppner et al., 1992). Both qualitative and quantitative data will be collected.

The intent of this study is to determine how the 12-step program is actually being utilized. The population to be studied is alcoholics who have maintained sobriety for at least 1 year. The sample will come from graduates of an outpatient alcohol treatment center in Southern California and will include approximately 50 men and 50 women, ages 20–60. Participants will be selected with the help of personnel from the center and the willingness of patients to participate in the study. The researcher will construct a survey designed to answer the research question and also conduct personal interviews to triangulate the findings. The survey will make use of a visual analog scale with multiple means of assessing the utilization of each step of the 12-step program. A panel of experts in the field will validate the instruments. A pilot study will be used to test for reliability. Permission to conduct the study will be obtained. Using descriptive statistics, the researcher will report on the step(s) most utilized by the group as a whole and by other criteria such as age and gender. The researcher will attempt to determine if there is a linear correlation between gender, ethnic group, age, occupation, and other factors and rankings of the 12 steps by the frequency of their use through the use of nonparametric statistics and multiple regression.

Definitions: sobriety, abstinence, 12-step program, successful treatment.

Social Impact of Study: Perhaps crime caused by alcoholism could be curtailed if there was an effective treatment for alcoholics. In this day of *instant everything* and *fast food*, there is a constant search to condense and distill effective programs for the most expeditious implementation. If this study shows that successful patients do not utilize certain steps in the 12-step program, then an investigation of those steps might be studied in greater detail to determine their fruitfulness.

Proposal Outline - Blueprint - Prospectus for YOUR Study

Title:

Problem Statement: (Write in full)

Introduction: (sketch)

Purpose: (sketch)

Significance: (sketch)

Limitations/Scope:

Delimitations:

Assumptions:

Theoretical Framework:

Background: (sketch)

Nature of the Study: (select type(s)): Provide a rationale for the paradigm (qualitative/quantitative/mixed), as well as your reasons for choosing a particular methodology.

Definitions: Make sure these are unique connotations for terms in the study. Provide references for each definition.

Literature Review: (areas to investigate)

Methodology: (Research questions and/or hypotheses).

Population/sample

Instrument(s) (how to validate?)
Data :
How will you:
    Collect?
    Organize?
    Analyze?
    Interpret?
    Predict?

Social Impact: (give details)

PHASE 3

THE FEAST

(Your Dissertation/Research Paper)

CHAPTER 1

Appetizer

(Introduction)

CHAPTER 2

Soup/Salad

(Research Review)

CHAPTER 3/CHAPTER 4

Main Course

(Methodology and Presentation)

CHAPTER 5

Dessert

(Conclusions and Recommendations)

You are now ready to skillfully *dish* out a fastidiously prepared *feast* for your distinctive guests to *delectably digest*. Carefully follow the directions in **PHASE 3** of your *Recipes for Success,* and *knead* the critical ingredients together. As you present your research project, you will be describing to your readers the importance and background of your problem, the way others have examined this problem, and your unique contribution and solution to the problem you framed. You will describe how you examined this problem and why you chose the particular method of inquiry to guide you through answering your research questions and obtaining your purpose. Finally, you will explain the *fruits* of your investigation and the recommendations that you want to make to others who will be finding solutions and understandings to other aspects of this problem.

Most universities require that the dissertation proposal consist of three *courses*: the first three chapters of the dissertation. However, proposals are speculative and written in the future tense. Dissertations are reflective and indicate what you did and are written in the past tense. It is important that the dissertation be viewed as a cogent whole. This means when you are ready to submit your dissertation you need to go back through your proposal and make changes to report on what you "did do" not what you "thought you would do." The Council of Graduate Schools (CGS) did a study regarding the role of the mentor in the successful completion of the dissertation. Check it out at http://www.cgsnet.org/?tabid=377

CHAPTER 1
APPETIZER
(INTRODUCTION

½ cup Introduction	1 cup Research Questions/Hypotheses
¼ cup Problem Statement	1 teaspoon Irony
2 cups Background	5 teaspoons Creativity
½ cup Purpose	1 teaspoon Drama
1 cup Significance	2 teaspoons Definitions
1½ cups Nature of Study	½ cup Assumptions
1 cup Theoretical Framework	
1 cup Conceptual Framework	

Combine all ingredients together carefully in a word processor. Simmer over all thoughts until mixture comes to a boil, stirring frequently with inspiration and ingenuity.

½ cup Introduction

The purpose of an Introduction is to capture the attention of the reader or set the stage for the courses to follow. An Introduction will acquaint the reader with the problem you are studying, the approach that you have chosen to study the problem, and your style of writing. It is the place where your begin to *dish* out your ideas and *whet the appetite* of your readers. An Introduction gives the reader a PEAC (peek) at your study. It usually

1. **Puts** your study in some perspective

2. **E**stablishes the need for your study

3. **A**lerts the reader to what will follow

4. **C**atches the attention and interest of the reader

As suggested by the proportion, ½ cup, the Introduction section is usually brief (one or two pages at most). Below you will find some attention-getting ways to introduce the reader to your study and thus begin your research paper.

____1. A dramatic illustration of the problem. Consider the worst-case scenario of the problem you are investigating or the best-case scenario if this problem did not exist.

____2. A quote from a passage that captures the problem. Share with the reader a study that calls attention to the problem you have researched or a quotation from a famous person that supports, or contradicts, your point of view.

____3. A narration describing how your interest in the problem was first piqued and how your convictions have changed since you have become aware of the problem and have conducted your study.

____4. Data that attest to the seriousness of the problem you will investigate.

FOR YOUR INFORMATION AND EDUCATION

Most research papers and, thus, dissertations, are written in the past tense and in the third person. When relating an anecdotal story or a personal observation, it is usually proper etiquette to say "the researcher found" in lieu of "I find." However, an even better approach is to recast the entire sentence so that the need to write "the researcher" is avoided. Dissertation proposals are written in the future tense since you are proposing what you plan to accomplish.

> Note: The first page of each chapter **does not** have a page number.

 Cutting Board

1. Which of the methods (1-4) above would you be most comfortable using in your introduction?_____

2. Put yourself in the position of the reader. What about this study would capture your interest? Why is it important?

3. On a separate piece of paper, do a mind map of your introduction and attach it here:

¼ cup Problem Statement

The Problem Statement section is the heart of the research paper. The mind seems to follow its own equivalent of Newton's law of inertia and becomes aroused to intense analysis only when some dilemma presents itself. Systematic thought is driven by the failure of established ideas, by a sense that something is wrong, by a belief that something needs closer attention, or by old ideas and methods that are no longer adequate. The problem statement provides the logical foundation upon which you will build the rest of the study. The scope of your study, its ability to make a point, and the amount of research you need to do to make that point depend heavily on the initial specification of the problem or problems under investigation. The Problem Statement section deals with the reality of the problem you are investigating or the necessity of a program you are analyzing. The objective of a problem statement is

1. To persuade your reader that the project is feasible, appropriate, and worthwhile
2. To capture and maintain your reader's attention

The research methodology being employed often helps to dictate the problem statement. The following are drafts of potential problem statements that can be used in conjunction with the research methodologies specified for investigating the relationship between socioeconomic class and education. It is important that references and citations be included in the actual problem statement when appropriate.

Historical Research. Following the Civil War, teachers perceived children from the low socioeconomic strata of society as less intelligent. Such perceptions have had a detrimental effect on children in this group (check out http://cie.asu.edu/volume3/number3/). It is important that a historical study be conducted to learn about causes, effects, or trends after the Civil War that caused this problem to arise in order to explain present events and anticipate future events.

257

Phenomenological Research. *Excerpt from *A Phenomenological Study of Female Executives in Information Technology Companies in the Washington, D.C., Area*: Dissertation by Dr. Tammie Page (2005), University of Phoenix, School of Advanced Studies.

… Despite equal opportunity and antidiscrimination laws, less than 4% of executive-level positions are held by women (Meyerson & Fletcher, 2004). Discriminatory practices, collectively known as the glass ceiling, contributed to the current situation (van Vianen & Fischer, 2002). This is particularly evident in the IT industry, where only 5.1% of executives are women (Melymuka, 2000). According to Ngo, Foley, Wong, and Loi (2003), gender inequity violates the principle of equal treatment for all employees and often leads to problems with retention, morale, and performance. Focusing on executive-level women's perceived gender inequity rather than actual gender inequity is beneficial because perceptions of organizational conditions affect work-related attitudes and behaviors (Sanchez & Brock, 1996). This phenomenological study identified skill sets, coping mechanisms, and strategies used by executive-level women in IT companies to sustain their positions within such companies. Although various studies have found males and females to be equal in leadership competence (Maher, 1997; Pounder & Coleman, 2002; Thompson, 2000), women often face socially prompted stereotypes about masculinity and femininity that undermine their credibility as organizational leaders (Carli & Eagly, 2001).

Check to see if the Problem Statement you developed in **PHASE 1** seeks an answer to one or more of the questions listed below:

My research will determine or examine the following:

____1. What is wrong with society, or with one of its institutions, that has caused this problem or allowed this problem to exist?

____2. What has failed in society that has caused this problem?

____3. What is missing in society that has allowed this problem to develop?

____4. What happened that has become interesting and important enough to study?

____5. What historical description of an event has become open to reexamination?

____6. A program that was in need of studying, evaluating, or analyzing.

____7. A need to develop a program that could contribute to society or one of its institutions.

____8. A need to analyze a current theory in light of new events.

____9. A relationship between the problem and a factor or factors that could be contributing to the problem.

____10. An inequity that exists in society.

Despite this lengthy description of how to develop the Problem Statement, and as we saw in **PHASE 1**, the crafting of the statement itself, when complete, should be relatively brief (one or two paragraphs). There is much to think about, but not a great deal to write. In fact, as long as it adequately conveys what you intend, the shorter the problem statement, the better.

 Cutting Board

1. Which of the question(s) above does your study address?

2. What research methodology best describes your study? (Check back to **PHASE 1**— What's Cooking ?)

3. In **PHASE 1** you created a problem statement prior to conducting your research. Rewrite that statement in the space below:

   _____

   _____

4. Make sure that you have stated the problem precisely and concisely. If that is not the case, rewrite the problem sentence with your new insight:

   _____

---

2 cups Background

The Background section offsets the brevity of the Problem Statement section. Here you will elaborate on why the problem you will investigate is of pressing societal concern or theoretical interest. This is the place in your paper where you want to make your reader as interested in the problem as you are and help elucidate the need to shed further light on this problem. Try to find a natural starting point. For example, the call for educational change is often traced back to the 1983 document "A Nation at Risk" (Check out http://www.ed.gov/pubs/NatAtRisk/risk.html). Follow this with germinal or classical works that have contributed to furthering the problem or added to the solution of the problem.

Carefully read the statements below. Put a check next to the ones that apply to your research project and could potentially be used in the Background section of your paper.

_____ 1. There are knowledgeable observers (political figures, theorists, newscasters, professional in the field, etc.) who have attested to the importance of this problem.

_____ 2. There are statistics that attest to the depth and spread of this problem.

_____ 3. There is documentation of the failure of certain aspects of society that have contributed to this problem and call for further examination.

_____ 4. There are theoretical issues in need of reexamination.

_____ 5. There are programs, events, mandates, rulings, and/or documents that have called attention to this problem.

 Cutting Board

1. When was the problem first acknowledged?
2. Which statement(s) above pertain to your problem?
3. How will (did) you obtain information to support these statements (books, videos, articles, consulting with authorities)?
4. Give at least three reasons why the problem you chose is (was) important and valid to you, society, or some institution in society:
5. If applicable, give at least two concrete examples of the problem:
6. If applicable, what programs, documents, rulings, or mandates have addressed similar issues?
7. To what public statistics, political trends, theoretical controversy does your study relate?
8. What group has been adversely affected by this problem?
9. How was attention first called to the problem? (Name any key figure or figures that assisted in bringing this problem into focus.)
10. What are the most important critical events related to this problem?

½ cup Purpose

The Purpose Statement section deals with the reason the study was or will be conducted and describes what your study will accomplish or has accomplished. It succinctly creates direction, scope, and the means of data collection. The purpose statement includes a list of specific objectives accomplished. The objectives should be stated as outcomes, not as procedures; however, the procedures will enable the outcomes to be realized or to be found unattainable (COEHS, 2005).

If the intent of the problem statement is to appeal to the heart, the intent of the purpose statement is to appeal to the brain. The purpose statement is like a compass; changes in the purpose statement change the direction, and in turn the focus, of the study. The purpose of the study needs to be described in a logical, explicit manner. The purpose statement is also like a menu that focuses your reader's attention on the essentials and intentions of your study (feast). Thus, the reader will be better able to judge whether your approach is or was effective.

Purpose statements are usually supplemented with additional information for clarification, but a single, succinct sentence that captures the essence of the study should identify the (a) research method, (b) the problem investigated, (c) the audience to which the problem is significant, and (d) the setting of the study. A sample purpose statement that illustrates the above elements follows: "The purpose of this (a) qualitative, descriptive research study is (was) to analyze (b) the personal value patterns and profiles of (c) Generation X and Generation Y managers at an (d) information technology company in the Pacific Northwest." In most proposals and dissertations, the section relating to the purpose is about ½ to ¾ of a page.

Put a check next to the phrases that could best be used to complete the statement:
The purpose of this research is to

____1. advance knowledge by understanding cause and effect;

____2. provide new answers to old problems;

____3. elucidate what makes the program under investigation successful or unsuccessful;

____4. change a regretful situation and make it better;

_____5. interpret, evaluate, or analyze existing conditions that lead to an unacceptable situation;

_____6. determine to what extent certain factors contributed to the problem;

_____7. determine the need for a particular program or study;

_____8. describe a problem that has been given little attention up until this point, but could have a great impact on society;

_____9. understand why a particular condition exists and who is affected by this condition;

_____10. elucidate what aspects of a program are successful and what aspects are not successful.

Cutting Board

1. Which of the statements above apply to your study? _____

2. State briefly and precisely what your study intended to do about the problem you have specified by completing the following sentence: The purpose of this study was (is) to:

    _____

    _____

3. Who (sample) or what will be part of your study? _____

    _____

4. Where did (will) your study take place? _____

5. What variables are measured in your study?_____

    _____

Purpose Checklist	√
1. Key identifier words are used to signal the reader, such as 'The purpose of this study is…" This purpose is in accord with the problem statement. A descriptive study would use words like *determine*, a phenomenological study would use words like *understand the perception of lived experiences around a phenomenon*, a grounded theory study would use words like *develop a theory regarding a phenomenon*.	
2. The type of paradigm(s) (qualitative/quantitative/mixed) is indicated or implied and appropriate for this purpose.	
3. The type of method (phenomenological, correlational, grounded…) is indicated or implied and appropriate for this purpose.	
4. The central phenomena being explored are explicated. The variables, if quantitative, are clearly defined.	
5. The intent of the study (to analyze, determine, evaluate…) is delineated with words that reflect higher order thinking skills.	
6. The participants in the study (sample and population) are mentioned.	
7. The setting (including geographic location) of the study is explained.	
8. Words are well chosen; statements are free from contradiction; the statement is free of jargon and clichés. No unnecessary words are used.	
9. The writing has cadence and flows easily; the reader can sense the person behind the words.	

1 cup Significance

Just as the Background section elaborates on the problem statement, the Significance section provides *garnishing* for the purpose statement. A significant piece of work provides information that is useful to other scholars in the field and, ideally, is of such importance that it alters the thinking of scholars in your profession and society at large. In the Significance section you will justify why you chose to investigate this problem and the type of research methodology you chose.

Besides your personal desire and motivation to do research, your wish to obtain a degree, your need for a good grade, and your craving to get something published, there needs to be a more global reason for doing a worthwhile study. You should state who, besides yourself, your immediate family, your teachers, and close friends, cares that this research is conducted or not conducted. You should use about ¾ of a page to explain why this is such a unique approach and who will be thrilled (besides yourself, your family, your teachers, and friends!) that this study is done. Here is where you tell us what type of contribution you will be making to your profession and to society.

The statements below are valid reasons for doing research. Put a check next to the ones that apply to your research project and can potentially be used in the Significance section of your paper.

___ 1. This study is able to reach people that were not reached by other similar studies (i.e., a different population was studied).

___ 2. This study gives a different perspective on an established problem.

___ 3. This is an appropriate approach to this particular research problem although it had not been embraced before.

___ 4. There was an important benefit to doing the study this way so that there could be a better understanding of the problem.

___ 5. If this study were not done, some aspect of society would be in danger.

___ 6. This is the first time an important problem was examined in this vein.

___ 7. This study has the potential to effect social change.

___ 8. This program was needed to rectify certain wrongs in society.

___ 9. This study provided an objective measure of the success or failure of an important program.

___ 10. This study will add to the scholarly literature in your field.

___ 11. Policy makers need this information to right a wrong or make better decisions.

Thus, the significance section addresses the *so what* of the study and report. It describes or explains the potential value of the study. This section should identify the audience for the study and how the results will be beneficial to them. Remember, a dissertation is conducted to add to the existing knowledge base and solve a problem – how your particular research will do this should be articulated in this section.

 ## *Cutting Board*

1. Which statement(s) above pertain to your study?
2. State in your own words why this study is so important.
3. To whom is your study important, other than yourself?
4. How will society benefit from your study?
5. How will policy makers benefit from your study?
6. How would you respond (in a nice way) to a person who says, "So what?" to your project?
7. How would you provide a persuasive rationale to the person who says, "So what?"
8. Write down several reasons why you chose to study the problem in this way, and what or who will benefit from the results of the study.

1½ cups Nature of the Study

The Nature of the Study section (about 2–3 pages) presents the rationale for choosing your research design. Here you will address the appropriateness of the research methodology you chose and how you plan to answer your research questions and solve the problem you posed based on the tenets of the selected method. This is the place where you defend your selected methodology and distinguish it from other research methodologies that have been, or could be, conducted to investigate the problem. It gives the reader a synopsis of the *meal you are cooking up* and places your study with similar types—case study, historical, correlational, evaluative, phenomenological, experimental, quasi-experimental, etc., or the way you plan to prepare your *feast*. Thus, this is where you will elaborate on the methodology you have chosen and justify why this is (was) such a great way to investigate this problem. If you chose a qualitative research method you will probably need to do a little more explaining than if you chose a quantitative design. Provide details connecting the type of methodology to the theoretical framework guiding your study. The quantitative researcher will generally test theories and hypotheses with the intent of generalizing results, whereas the qualitative researcher will seek to determine patterns to help explain a phenomenon.

In **PHASE 1**, we discussed different types of research methodologies. Refer to this section now, and then answer the questions on the Cutting Board.

 Cutting Board

1. From what perspective did you view your problem: past, present, or future?
2. Which subset(s) of the past, present, or future perspective seemed to apply the most to your study (e.g., descriptive, correlational, ground theory, action, heuristic, etc.)?
3. Within the perspective of 1 and 2 above, which of the following do (did) you do?

     a) Describe facts

     b) suggest causes

     c) Analyze changes

     d) Investigate relationships

     e) Test causal hypotheses

     f) Evaluate efficiency or effectiveness

     g) Develop a program

     h) Develop a theory

4. To summarize, complete the following statement: The methodology that I used in my study could best be classified as a (an) _____ study because I

_____

5. Name another type of methodology that could have been used to study the problem. _____Why did you reject this methodology?

_____

---

1 cup Theoretical Framework

A theoretical framework enables a researcher to frame and solve problems, as well as understand and explain social reality. It is a bit more specific than a worldview and should be clearly discernible in a research project. A theoretical framework places the study in perspective among other relevant studies and describes the important issues, perspectives, and controversies in the field under investigation. Along a continuum, the theoretical framework fits between a researcher's values, beliefs, hunches, assumptions, and worldview and formal theories (Creswell, 2005, p. 127; Lierr & Smith, n.d., para. 12). Many use the term conceptual framework and theoretical framework interchangeably, but Eisenhart (2001) purported that "a conceptual framework is more of a justification, or an argument, that the concepts chosen for investigation or interpretation, and any anticipated relationships among them, will be appropriate and useful, given the research problem under investigation" (p. 209). A conceptual framework provides an overall path from problem definition to problem resolution.

In chapter 1 you will present a theoretical framework that includes a sketch of existing theories that are closely related to your research topic and upon which you will build your study. Choose the theories that best apply to your research design and the unique problem you are solving. It is not enough that you find the topic interesting: you need to demonstrate that it addresses important questions that interest those already researching the field. You should make clear how your research relates to existing theories. You should make your own theoretical assumptions and allegiances as explicit as possible. According to Borgatti, Everett, and Freeman (1999), in a qualitative study, the theoretical framework is generally the set of assumptions or fundamental beliefs that the researcher possesses that affects the conclusions drawn. Borgatti et al. suggested that an implicit framework (the assumptions and beliefs held) provides the reader with the tools to better judge the validity of the conclusions.

In chapter 3, when you discuss your methodology, you will link the method you chose to this theoretical framework. In chapter 2, in your literature review, you will elaborate on these theories and how they have affected the problem you are addressing. You need to explain other studies and theories that substantiate the importance and significance of your investigation and that connect the problem, purpose, research questions, and hypotheses in your study. Conversely, your research might be significant enough to determine that a particular theory is invalid. Every discipline is built on a foundation of theories or postulates that are accepted as foundational to the discipline. In chapters 4 and 5 you will go back to these theories to determine if your findings are consistent or inconsistent with these theories. Your study will *macerate*, or *soak*, with other studies to *absorb* the essence of what others have done to solve the problem.

Educators base much research on learning theories such as cognitive learning, constructivism, behaviorism, observational learning, and intelligence theories. These theories and perspectives explain how and why people learn and are used as premises or rationales for educational researchers to draw conclusions. For example, the theory of multiple intelligences (MI) is a theoretical framework that suggests there are a number of distinct forms of intelligence that each individual possesses in varying degrees. Gardner (1983) initially proposed seven primary forms: linguistic, musical, logical-mathematical, spatial, body-kinesthetic, intrapersonal (e.g., insight, metacognition), and interpersonal (e.g., social skills). He later added naturalistic and existential intelligences to his list. Gardner also emphasized the cultural context of multiple intelligences. This theory supports the view that each culture tends to emphasize particular intelligences. For example, Gardner (1983) discussed the high spatial abilities of the Puluwat people of the Caroline Islands, who use these skills to navigate their canoes in the ocean. A great deal of educational research has been built on MI. In fact, Project Zero is an educational research group at the Graduate School of Education at Harvard University dedicated to MI research.

Social scientists use behavioral theories such as conflict theories, biological theories, social learning theories, etc. that offer varying perspectives on how members of societies interact and function. Psychology bases much research on theories and perspectives on classical conditioning, operant conditioning, cognitive development theories, and personality and trait theories. Biological scientists base their research on evolution theories and physical scientists rely on Newton's laws of motion or Einstein's famous energy theory $E = mc^2$. Whatever the discipline, theory is the foundation of all research and the method used to develop research should be based on sound principles and logic. According to Popper (1935), theory is "the net which we throw out in order to catch the world—to rationalize, explain, and dominate it" (p. 26).

In studies on leadership, there is extensive research on what makes leaders effective. There is a great deal of focus relating leadership to organizational change, vision building, and empowering others. Some of the theoretical constructs upon which these studies are built include the following:

1. <u>Systems theory</u>, which suggests the interrelations of the parts of an organization, for example, the coordination of central administration with its programs, engineering with manufacturing, supervisors with workers, etc. In the past, managers typically took one part and focused on that. Then they moved all attention to another part. The problem was that an organization could have a wonderful central administration and wonderful core of employees, but the departments might not function well together.
2. <u>Contingency theory</u>, which suggest that effective leadership styles vary according to the context. For example, Blake and Mouton's managerial grid has been very influential in organization development practice.

3. Herzberg's motivation-hygiene theory, which suggests that for employees to be motivated, hygiene factors must be present, which ensures employees are not dissatisfied. These hygiene factors include pay and security, company policies, and interpersonal relationships.

4. Path-goal theory, which suggests that a leader can change a subordinate's expectancy by clarifying the paths between the subordinate's action and the outcome, which is the goal the employee wants to achieve. Whether leader behavior can do so effectively also depends on situational factors. Path-goal theory draws on the expectancy theory of motivation and suggests there are four distinct leadership styles that effect change: supportive, directive, participative, and achievement oriented.

5. Chaos theory, which suggests that systems naturally move toward more complexity and as they do they become more volatile (or susceptible to cataclysmic events) and must expend more energy to maintain that complexity. As they expend more energy, they seek more structure to maintain stability. This trend continues until the system splits (bifurcates), combines with another complex system, or falls apart entirely. It also suggests that a small perturbation or change in the initial conditions of a system can drastically change the long-term behavior of the system. This sensitive dependence on initial conditions is known as the butterfly effect.

Keep in mind that most of these theories are North American or Western European centered and do not necessarily take into account differences found in other cultures. For more information on these and other theories of leadership, check out http://tinyurl.com/23pjpa.

FOR YOUR INFORMATION AND EDUCATION

Occam's Razor (Ockham's Razor) is a principle attributed to the 14th-century Englishman who believed that one should make no more assumptions than needed. When multiple explanations are available, the simplest version is preferred. For example, the reasons a charred tree was found on the ground could be attributed to a meteoroid or a lightning strike. According to Occam's Razor, the lightning strike is the preferred explanation as it requires the fewest assumptions.

1 cup Conceptual Framework

A conceptual framework helps elucidate why you are planning to do a study in a particular way. It enables you to *stand on the shoulders of others* who have addressed this, or a similar, problem. A conceptual framework is similar to a road map. You can read a map, because others have come up with common symbols to mark streets, highways, bodies of water, open spaces, points of interests, etc. The scale on a map tells you how far apart different places are, so you will get an idea of how long it might take to get from where you are now to where you would like to be. A map offers alternative routes to get to where you wish to go.

Your conceptual framework helps you decide and explain the route you are taking: why you plan to use certain methods and tools and not others, how you plan to get to a certain point, or achieve a certain outcome. Other researchers might have traveled a similar path and come across road blocks that you can now avoid. There could also be paths that have not been taken and that you can create on the way to your destination. Thus, a conceptual framework enables you to explain to others why you are choosing a particular path, is based on the experiences of those who have come before you, and explains what you expect to experience on the course you set. The conceptual framework will "link abstract concepts to empirical data" (Rudestam & Newton, 2007, p. 6).

---

1 cup Research Questions/Hypotheses

Your research should be guided by a central research question (or a series of closely connected questions) that serves as a funnel and frame for the investigation and includes the variables, concepts, or theories inherent in the study. Research questions are interrogative and narrow the purpose of the study to specific questions the researcher seeks to answer (Creswell, 2002, p. 648). Most dissertations and scholarly research projects contain one to three research questions. Clear and well-defined research questions help you to stay on target and avoid being distracted by interesting (but irrelevant) digressions. They should be in accord with the research paradigm and methodology guiding your study (Guba, 1990).

The wording of research questions in quantitative studies utilizes terms that directly relate to, or imply, a cause-and-effect relationship between the variables of the study. Some examples of research questions for quantitative studies include the following: What is the relationship between diet and health? What is the difference between Generation X and Generation Y regarding job retention? What is the effect of drug Alpha on reducing asthma in children? What is the relationship between the domains of learning and performance on standardized exams?

Note: Research questions that could yield a yes/no or numerical answer should be avoided. Thus, steer clear of starting a research question with words such as Do, Does, Is, Could, or How many, and eschew research questions that could be answered by going to one published source.

The wording of qualitative research questions utilize terms that are interpretive, exploratory, descriptive, understanding, defining, etc. These are terms that leave the judgment to the researcher to expand, expound, and add emerging questions, leaving the study with a potential open end, rather than a closed end as in quantitative studies. The following are some examples of research questions for qualitative studies: What are the lived experiences of survivors of the tsunami (phenomenological study)? Why do some women leave corporate America to form their own companies (case study)? What emergent theory or theories explain why some victims of tragic events become grassroots leaders and others do not (grounded theory)?

There is no set number of research questions, though typical dissertations have between one and three profound research questions. Qualitative research questions tend to be open and probative in nature and reflect the intent of the study. Research questions need to be manageable and contain appropriate restriction, qualification, and delineation. The formulation of research questions guides the selection of the research method and design. Keep your questions close to the topic you are researching. Questions that are too abstract or obtuse make it difficult for the reader to determine your question's relevance and intent. However, you need to link your question to a larger context and make sure the questions are consistent with the problem, purpose, and methodology.

Many qualitative research questions ask how or why events occur. Qualitative research questions are often exploratory in nature and are designed to generate hypotheses to be tested later in quantitative studies. The questions are reflective of the design. For example, in a phenomenological study the research questions should look to determine the lived experiences regarding a specific phenomenon. In a grounded theory study, the research questions should seek to develop a theory grounded in data. In a Delphi study, the questions are usually future oriented.

In quantitative studies, the research questions need to test a theory or claim. A correlational study will contain research questions such as: What is the relationship between the (independent variable) and the (dependent variable); an experimental study: What is the difference between (Group A) and (Group B) on (dependent variable)? A descriptive study establishes associations between variables. These can include the relationship or association between variables, as well as the differences between variables or groups.

After forming a research question, ask yourself: *What possible answers could be given to this question?*

Research Question criteria
1. The research questions are precise and concise, there are no unnecessary words. The research questions are manageable and contain appropriate restriction, qualification, and delineation
2. The research questions arise logically from the problem statement. The research questions reflect the type of study that will be conducted.
3. The research questions are of sufficient depth to warrant doctoral level research.
4. The research questions do not require a binary or numerical response.
5. The research questions are broad enough to guide the entire study.

Once you write your research questions, step aside for a while. Let the questions *aerate,* and then come back and think about possible responses to the research questions. Make certain that a profound answer is required.

*A research hypothesis is a conjectural declarative statement of the results the researcher expects to find among the variables a researcher intends to study. For quantitative studies, hypotheses are testable and variables are measurable. If confirmed, a hypothesis will support a theory. A research question might include several variables (constructs) and thus several research hypotheses might be needed to indicate all the anticipated relationships (Cooper & Schindler, 2003). Accordingly, the number of hypotheses is determined in an explanation of relationships among variables (constructs) or comparisons to be studied. A research hypothesis is essential to quantitative studies, but might or might not appear in qualitative studies. The rationale for making predictions (hypotheses) usually comes from hypothesized relationships suggested by prior research or from personal experiences and anecdotal data.

Example: If a social psychologist theorized that racial prejudice is due to ignorance, then the more highly educated a person, the less their prejudice should be. A hypothesis to test this theory:

> *There is an inverse relationship between the education of a person and the degree of racial prejudice.*

The following should be clear from the hypothesis and research questions:

1. What variable is the researcher manipulating or is the presumed *cause*, or *predictor,* in a study? **(This is the independent variable, or IV.)** In the example, the IV is education level.
2. What results are expected or what is the presumed effect of the study or the predicted result? **(This is the dependent variable, or DV).** In the example, the DV is the level of racial prejudice.

To test this hypothesis, the researcher could survey people with varying degrees of education. The survey would consist of a way to measure education level and a way to measure the degree of racial prejudice. A Pearson test could be used to test the hypothesis.

When formulating your hypotheses, the rationale for these expectations should be made explicit in light of your review of the research and statement of theory. If a survey is used to measure the IV and DV, there should be consistency among the answers and a way to grade each participant on each variable. Check out the discussion of survey research in **PHASE 2**. When you construct your data collection instrument, make certain that you are aware of how you will measure each variable. For further assistance, check out http://www.socialresearchmethods.net/.

Research hypotheses are sometimes referred to as working or substantive hypotheses. They are usually directional; that is, a researcher might believe there is a positive or inverse relationship, or something is more or less than a certain accepted notion or condition. For example, There is a positive relationship between the amount of homework and test scores, or This new program will require less hours of time to train technicians. However, they can also be nondirectional, such as, There is a relationship between homework and test scores, or There is a difference in training time between the two programs. The nondirectional hypotheses show less bias and are appropriate when conflicting information exists.

There is a difference between a substantive hypotheses and a statistical hypothesis. The former speculates, somewhat informally, on what you assume your study will reveal. The latter is a formal, testable conjecture that can be translated into mathematical symbols.

Example of a substantive hypothesis: Teachers who have integrated calculators into their personal lives are more likely to use calculators in their classrooms than teachers who rarely use calculators in their personal lives.

Example of statistical hypotheses:

H0: There is a relationship between teachers using calculators in the classroom and using calculators every day.

$r = 0$

and the alternative hypothesis:

H1: There is no relationship between teachers using calculators in the classroom and using calculators every day.

$r \neq 0$

Note: Statistical hypotheses (as discussed in **PHASE 2**) usually come in pairs (the null or no change hypothesis, which contains =, and the alternative or opposite hypothesis) and are expressed symbolically. In chapter 1, only the substantive hypotheses or your expectations need to be expressed. (Statistical hypotheses belong in chapter 3.)

Check the phrase(s) below that best complete(s) the following sentence: I believe that my study will disclose

___ 1. The extent to which a problem affects society or one of its institutions

___ 2. A relationship between an independent and dependent variable(s)

___ 3. A new theory to an old or new problem or condition

___ 4. That a program (or treatment) evaluated is effective (or ineffective)

___ 5. A significant relationship between factors scrutinized and a problem under investigation

___ 6. A need to make a change in an attitude/condition

___ 7. Conditions that exist that contribute to a problem studied

___ 8. Specific conditions that contribute to solutions of a problem studied

___ 9. One program is more effective than another program

___ 10. A need for a particular study or program

 Cutting Board

State as clearly and succinctly as possible what you expected the results of your study to show:

_____

½ cup Limitations, Scope, and Delimitations

Limitations are potential weaknesses in your study and are out of your control. If you are using a conventional *oven*, *food* in the middle racks often are *undercooked* while the *food* closest to the burner and the top can be well done. If you are using a sample of convenience, as opposed to a random sample, then the results of your study cannot be generally applied to a larger population, only suggested. If you are looking at one aspect, say achievement tests, the information is only as good as the test itself. Another limitation is time. A study conducted over a certain interval of time is a snapshot dependent on conditions occurring during that time. You must explain how you intend to deal with the limitations so as not to affect the outcome of the study.

The delimitations and scope of your study are in your control and address how the study will be narrowed or the boundaries of the study. For example, a study about education in California would not necessarily be applicable to other geographic regions. You can also give a philosophical framework to limit your study. When you prepare a *meal*, you get to determine how many *vegetables* you will serve. You will delineate special characteristics of your sample and the population that it comes from. The selected methodology and variables in your study will also set a boundary on what your findings can ascertain.

It can be humbling and empowering at the same time to realize you are critically limited in so many ways, including the availability of resources and even your own reasoning processes and human failings. The empowerment comes from recognizing your shortcomings and somehow adjusting the best way possible.

Note: When you are elaborating on the nature of your study or on the scope and limitations of your study, you might wish to discuss the following:

Ontology - How you, the researcher, views reality: Objectively? Subjectively? A combination of the two?

Epistemology - The methods you use to derive, elicit, and analyze data.

Theory -What interrelated constructs, definitions, and propositions you use to present a systematic view of the phenomenon under investigation. You need to specify relations among variables with the purpose of describing, explaining, and predicting the phenomenon you are studying.

---

2 Teaspoons Definitions

If you are using words in an unusual way, or you are employing words that have more than one definition, it is important that you set aside a section of your first chapter to define these terms. By understanding how you are using a term, the reader will be able to understand your research and *digest* it properly. Formal definitions consist of three parts: the term being defined, the general class to which the concept being defined belongs, and the specific characteristics that distinguish the term from other members of the class. For example, a study on nontraditional learning might include: for the purpose of this study, "distance education refers to imparting knowledge where the learner and the facilitator are at different locations" (Author, date, page number). Make sure the definitions provided in chapter 1 are for unique connotations or terms in the study. Those definitions that do not carry any unique connotation should not be included. To support the use of a term, a scholarly reference is usually used. Define acronyms and highlight terms only the first time they are used. Highlight the first use of keywords and terms in italics. If you think your reader might not recall a definition or the special use of a term later in the text, define the term again.

You should differentiate between conceptual and operational definitions. Conceptual (i.e., constitutive) definitions use words or concepts to define a construct. For example, attitude could be defined conceptually as a predisposition to respond favorably or unfavorably toward a person, object, or event. Critical thinking is the application of facts, concepts, and principles to solve problems and make decisions and the evaluation of these solutions for effectiveness (Hummel & Huitt, 1994).

Operational definitions indicate the meaning of variables through the specification of the manner by which they are measured, categorized, or controlled. When you operationalize a variable, you answer the following questions: How will I know it when I see it? How will I record or measure it? When possible, quote an author or source that uses the term in this manner. Operational definitions make intersubjective agreement (objectivity) possible, but they are almost always imperfect. For example, the operational definition of an obese person could be one who weighs more than 120% of his or her ideal weight as defined by an insurance company chart. However, this definition does not take into account muscle mass. A cubic inch of muscle weighs more than a cubic inch of fat. This is why fitness is not solely measured on the bathroom scale! Many fit athletes would be considered obese by this operational definition.

½ cup Assumptions

Assumptions in your study are things that are somewhat out of your control, but if they disappear your study would become irrelevant. For example, if you are doing a study on the middle school music curriculum, there is an underlying assumption that music will continue to be important in the middle school program. If you are conducting a survey, you need to assume that people will answer truthfully. If you are choosing a sample, you need to assume that this sample is representative of the population to which you wish to make inferences. Leedy and Ormrod (2001) noted, "Assumptions are so basic that, without them, the research problem itself could not exist" (p. 62).

You must justify that each assumption is "probably" true, otherwise the study cannot progress. To assume, for example, that participants will answer honestly, you can explain how anonymity and confidentiality will be preserved and that the participants are volunteers who may withdraw from the study at any time and with no ramifications. To assure the reader that a survey will get to the heart of the research problem and enable the researcher to answer the research questions, a pilot study is often performed.

CHAPTER 2
SOUP/SALAD
(Research Review)

Sit down before fact as a little child; be prepared to give up every conceived notion, follow humbly wherever and whatever abysses nature leads, or you will learn nothing.
—Thomas Huxley

A literature review is an integrated critical essay that analyzes and synthesizes the most relevant and current published knowledge on the topic under investigation. The review is organized around major ideas and themes. It consists of about 40 pages in the proposal and usually more than that in the dissertation. Most dissertations contain between 150 and 250 references. You need to keep track of all the sources that you reference in your literature review. You need to review critically other studies that have tried to answer the questions that you are asking and solve problems similar to the one you framed. You need to summarize these studies, compare them, contrast them, organize them, comment on their validity, and *stir* similar ones together. You need to make certain that you properly cite each quote, paraphrase, or idea that you get from a source. When analyzing a research study, report on the samples that were used and how they were selected, what instruments were used to obtain data, and the conclusions made. A substantive, thorough, and scholarly literature review is a prerequisite for doing substantive, thorough, and scholarly research. To be useful, scholarly research must be cumulative; it must build on and learn from prior research on the same or related problem under investigation. It must also clarify and resolve inconsistencies and tensions in the literature and thereby make a genuine contribution to the state of knowledge in the field (Boote & Beile, 2005).

Primary sources are preferred over secondary sources. Primary sources enable the researcher to get as close as possible to what actually happened and reflect the individual viewpoint of a participant or observer. A secondary source is a work that interprets or analyzes a historical event or phenomenon. It is generally at least one step removed from the event. Many people consider secondary references hearsay. If you find a quote in a secondary source, verify. Locating original sources helps ensure the information presented is accurate in the context of the original intent of the study.

Hernandez and White (1989) revealed a 43.7% inaccuracy rate for direct quotes used in secondary sources. Previous studies concerning paraphrasing cited in the Hernandez and White research revealed a 30% error rate, both minor and major. At issue is original intent. "Many changes do not adversely affect meaning, but as we have tried to illustrate, changes do occur which alter meaning but which often cannot be recognized by the reader as a deviation from the original" (Hernandez & White, 1989, p. 510).

It is important to locate original sources in your literature review to ensure that you are representing the full and correct content of the source. Choosing not to use the source document puts you at strong risk of using the bias or paraphrasing of an intermediate that might not have accurately represented the original source. By reviewing the original source, you will ensure that meaning is not *lost in translation*. According to Wright and Armstrong (2007), there is a high prevalence of faulty citations in scholarly papers. These infractions impede the growth of scientific knowledge. Faulty citations include omissions of relevant papers, incorrect references, and quotation errors that misreport findings. Please check out: http://tinyurl.com/2cvtg3b.

Note: Make sure you perform a *180 degree search*; that is, conduct searches using words that support and refute your beliefs. For example, if you believe that preschool is important to a healthy start in education, you should conduct searches on the advantages and disadvantages of preschool education.

Note: Encyclopedias or dictionaries, of any kind, including the very popular Wikipedia, dictionary.com, and Merriam Webster, are *not* primary sources and should not be cited or used as evidence in doctoral research. They can, however, be useful to help gather some background information and to point the way to more reliable sources.

An acronym and explanation for what the research/literature review chapter does is **LEADS**. That is, it leads the reader to the understanding of how your study fits into a larger picture of things, how others have dealt with and been affected by the problem, and why you chose to study the problem the way you did:

LEADS

1 cup	**L ays the foundation for your study**
2 cup	**E lucidates the problem**
1 cup	**A nalyzes why your study is appropriate**
1 cup	**D escribes why your study is capable of solving the problem**
1 cup	**S ynthesizes studies similar to yours.**

The literature/research review chapter is one of the most important parts of your dissertation or research project. It puts your research into a set with other studies and documents that have dealt with comparable issues. It gives you the knowledge to become an expert in the area that you are investigating and points out what your study will do that others have not done. A thorough review of the literature also safeguards against undertaking a study that might have already been conducted, might not be feasible, or might not be of much value when set against what needs to be researched in a particular field. A good review of the literature that critically synthesizes ideas and methods related to your topic is an indication of an accomplished scholar.

It is your responsibility to present a fair and balanced discussion of alternative viewpoints. For example, if you are researching the ill effects of the glass ceiling for woman executives, you need to look at studies that claim that there is no such thing as a glass ceiling. You are expected to scrutinize each study you present and challenge dubious beliefs based on sound logic and empirical evidence. It is imperative that you explain how you searched the literature and how you judged the suitability and quality of the literature reviewed.

The review will also include the most important aspects of the theory that you will examine or test and substantiate the rationale or conceptual framework for your study. You will also present relevant studies to justify each variable that is part of your study. The literature review should articulate what research needs to be conducted and provide a basis to compare your research to prior studies.

If there is a limited amount of literature on your topic, then place your topic in a larger set or sets and describe the literature in these areas. For example, a researcher investigating the effectiveness of employee leasing could look at leasing machinery and new ideas in business. In the past, a literature review was expected to be exhaustive, but this is no longer possible. Instead the review should be extensive and place your study among existing literature. Your job is to tie this literature into a cogent whole. Your approach should be analytical as well as descriptive.

Conducting a thorough and extensive literature review is one of the most important early steps in a research project. This is also one of the most humbling experiences you're likely to have because you're likely to find out that just about any worthwhile idea you will have has been thought of before, at least to some degree. Do not despair, you will also find holes in prior studies that your study can plug.

A personal note: Every time I teach a research methods course, I have at least one student complain that he or she could not find *anything* in the literature related to his or her topic. And virtually every time, I am able to determine that the student was only looking for articles that were exactly the same as the research topic posed. A literature review is designed to identify *related* research and to set the current research project within a conceptual and theoretical context. When looked at that way, there is almost no topic that is so new or unique that we cannot locate relevant and informative related research. One good search engine you should check out is www.scholar.google.com. Another is found at http://www.highbeam.com/library/index.asp and Copernic professional at http://www.copernic.com/en/products/agent/professional.html

Check back to **PHASE 1** in your *Recipes for Success's* PROCEED section and review the information on how to read efficiently to make sure that you are efficacious in your probing for information. Although there is no set rule on how many sources you need to consult for your dissertation, most *chefs* tend to review between 100 and 200 *dishes* or studies related to their topic, and most literature/research reviews constitute about ¼ to ½ of the written research paper. These numbers will vary depending on

1. How unique your study is
2. How far back in time you choose to go
3. How you define the related topics

Just as there are restaurants that only serve soup and salad as a meal, the research/ literature review itself could be a study. However in a dissertation, this would be extremely rare. Sometimes a key word search does not yield a sufficient amount of references. Do not despair… there is a software program that can help with finding key words. This program can also search the key words and provides you with a list of search engines that can assist. The cost of the program is about $40 and can be found at www.brainstormsw.com/

In the research/literature review chapter, you will slowly illuminate how careful you were in preparing your exemplary *meal* and how familiar you are with the previous *meals* that have been prepared in this area. As your readers *nibble* on the information you adeptly *dish out,* you can unveil in this chapter why you chose your *main course*, why you decided to serve the *meal* the way you did, and why the *utensils* you chose were appropriate for this type of *feast*. Keep in mind that every reference should relate back to your study. Every reference cited in chapter 1 should be elaborated on in chapter 2. Most universities (and research journals) require that the overwhelming majority of the citations come from peer-reviewed journals that publish refereed articles. A refereed article is an article that has been carefully reviewed and scrutinized by scholars or experts in the research topic of the article who are not members of the editorial staff or board. In many cases, one or more external readers have subjected the article to a blind review process. Walden University has prepared a guide to assist in finding acceptable scholarly material at http://library.waldenu.edu/HowDoI_23037.htm

Evaluating a source can begin even before you have the source in hand. You can initially appraise a source by first examining the bibliographic citation—a written description of a book, journal article, essay, or some other published material. Bibliographic citations characteristically have three main components: author, title, and publication information. These components can help you determine the usefulness of this source for your paper.

Make certain that you explain all of the following in your research report: title searches, keyword searches, the number of articles you reviewed, and the journals you researched.

Recipe for Appraising an Author

1. What are the author's credentials—educational background, past writings, or experience—in this area? Is the book or article written on a topic in the author's area of expertise?

2. Is the author associated with an institution or organization? What are the basic values or goals of the organization or institution?

3. Have you seen the author's name cited in other sources or bibliographies? Other scholars cite respected authors frequently. For this reason, always note those names that appear in many different sources.

4. What is the author's worldview (What presuppositions or assumptions are held consciously or subconsciously about the basic makeup of the world)?

As Merriam (1997) pointed out, "How the investigator views the world affects the entire process—from conceptualizing a problem, to collecting and analyzing data, to interpreting the findings" (p. 53). To know how a researcher construes the shape of the social world, and aims to give us a credible account of it, is to know our *conversational dinner* partner.

If a critical realist, a critical theorist, and a social phenomenologist are competing for our attention, we need to know where each is coming from. Each will have diverse views of what is real, what can be known, and how these social facts can be faithfully rendered (Creswell, 2002). In a quantitative study, theories are usually employed deductively and need to be placed in the beginning of the study. The researcher will generally present a theory (for example, why calculators are not being used in a classroom), gather data to test the theory, and then return to the theory at the end of the study to confirm or disconfirm.

In a qualitative study, an inductive mode of development tends to be used. Usually the qualitative researcher is more concerned with building a theory than testing it. A theoretical framework can be introduced in the beginning but will generally be modified and adjusted as the study proceeds. The theory or theories presented should be consistent with the type of qualitative design. It is generally something to develop, rather than to test, that shapes the research process and creates a visual model of the theory as it emerges. It can also be compared and contrasted with existing theories at the completion of the research (Simon & Francis, 2001). The theoretical framework serves as a *sieve* from which information flows.

A worldview should pass certain tests. First, it should be rational. It should not ask us to believe contradictory things. Second, it should be supported by evidence and consistent with what we observe. Third, it should give a satisfying comprehensive explanation of reality and enable us to explain why things are the way they are. Fourth, it should provide a satisfactory basis for living. It should not leave us feeling compelled to borrow elements of another worldview in order to live in this world. How you determine right from wrong helps determine your worldview. Some people believe that ethics are relative or situational, while others assert that ethical behavior is a universal fixed idea. Some people believe they have no free choice since all acts are entirely determined, while others believe the opposite.

In determining your worldview regarding the meaning of history, you might find you believe that history is determined as part of a mechanistic universe. Or you might believe that history is a linear stream of events linked by cause and effect but without purpose. Some people believe that history is meaningless because life is absurd.

One who adapts a postmodern worldview believes that everything is predominantly contextual. A realist's worldview, in contrast, is that there are predominantly absolutes—good versus bad; you are either with us or against us. History has shown the tragic results of a "might makes right" worldview held by despots and anarchists. Frequently the worldview within expository writing is not overtly written. It is written between the lines. (That is why most school curricula have hidden curricula within them.)

When you are researching articles and books, you should be trying to discern the worldview of the authors. If the worldview is not overtly stated, it might be because of the following reasons:

1. The writing is sloppy.

2. The writer knows her or his audience and knows that those particular readers already are aware of the unstated worldview.

3. The writer just *expects* the audience to know the unstated worldview as part of the general background information and through silence tells the reader that the reader is expected to know the unstated worldview. (This position contains the hidden message that tells the reader, "If you haven't done the requisite background studies, then do so if you want to fully comprehend what I've written.")

4. The writer assumes and presumes that the readers already know what the underpinning worldview is within the writing. This kind of assuming and presuming might be irresponsible on the part of the writer, but not necessarily. (That is part of the writer's worldview: he or she assumes and presumes that the readers within a given discipline will have already done their homework and assumes and presumes that the readers will happily accept that responsibility.)

5. The writer might tacitly hold the worldviews that underpin the writing and not know that he or she doesn't know that he or she holds those worldviews.

Any worldview model is an abstraction derived from certain observed phenomena, but is not a picture of those phenomena. Most would grant that in ethnically diverse classrooms a prima facie case can be made for worldview variations as a factor in the education process. The principal assumptions in this author's worldview theory in education are that the students in most, if not all, classrooms have subtle, worldview variations and that these variations constitute an important factor in achievement and attitude development.

Check the Date of Publication

1. When was the source published? This date is often located on the face of the title page below the name of the publisher. If it is not there, look for the copyright date on the reverse of the title page. On Web pages, the date of the last revision is usually at the bottom of the home page and sometimes on every page.

2. Is the source current or out of date for your topic? Topic areas of continuing and rapid development, such as technology, demand more current information. On the other hand, topics in the arts often require material written many years ago.

Check the Edition or Revision

Is this a first edition of this publication or not? Further editions indicate a source has been revised and updated to reflect changes in knowledge, include omissions, and harmonize with its intended readers' needs. Also, many printings or editions may indicate that the work has become a standard source in the area and is reliable.

Check the Publisher

If a university press publishes the source, it is likely to be scholarly. However, the fact that the publisher is reputable does not necessarily guarantee quality. It does show that the publisher has a high regard for the source being published.

Check the Title of Journal

Is this a scholarly or a popular journal? This distinction is important because it indicates different levels of complexity in conveying ideas. If you need help in determining the type of journal, you may wish to check your journal title in the latest edition of Katz's *Magazines for Libraries* (Uri's Ref Z 6941 .K21 1995) or Ulrich's *Serials Analysis System*: http://tinyurl.com/dk2wdk.

Ulrich's Publication Directory provides information on over 300, 000 serial publications. By consulting *Ulrich's Publication's Directory*, you can evaluate publications to determine their credibility as a doctoral source. By typing the name of a source in the search field, Ulrich's will indicate type of source such as trade publication, scholarly/academic journal, consumer magazine. It is likely that your university will provide free access to this site.

Keyword searching is a powerful and flexible way to find books, periodicals, and other materials. A keyword search looks for any word or combination of words in the author, title, and subject fields of databases. Keyword searches use connectors to search for two or more words in specific ways. The three most useful connectors are AND, OR, and ADJ. AND specifies both words must appear somewhere in the document, narrowing your search. OR specifies that either word may appear in the record. ADJ specifies that the words must be adjacent and in the same order, thus guaranteeing that the words are searched as a phrase. This can also be accomplished using quotation marks: "child psychology" works the same as child adj psychology.

In addition, most databases allow you to use a *truncation* symbol. Although the symbol used for truncation varies, the most common symbol is *. A truncation symbol placed at the end or middle of a term will retrieve variations of that word. For example, "child*" will return hits on child, child's, childhood, children, etc. Keyword searching allows you to enter any word or string of words. The database will search for all occurrences of the word(s) in citations, abstracts, and depending on the availability, full-text.

The questions below can be used to describe and assess the merits of previous studies and could be included when writing the literature/research review in your research paper. It is unlikely that any one study will provide the answers to all these questions, but the questions can serve as a guideline for critical reviews.

1. What was done? Was it effective?
2. When did the study take place? What was the accepted belief at this time?
3. Where did this study or event take place?
4. Who was involved?
5. What methodologies were used? How does the methodological choice affect the research findings?
6. What were the limitations? How were these limitations addressed?
7. What type of instruments were used?
8. What was the sample and population studied?
9. What did this add to the knowledge or solution of the problem?
10. What recommendations were made?
11. What contributions were made at the practical and scholarly level?
12. Who was affected by this study or program?

13. What are the similarities between this study and your study?

14. Was this an appropriate means of dealing with the problem?

According to Simpson (1989), a literature review functions as a means of conceptualizing, justifying, implementing, and interpreting a research investigation. Without a literature review, it is difficult for others to ascertain the significance of your study and how it will contribute to the knowledge base of a field.

Check the Logic in the Arguments Presented

The following is a list of common fallacies, when arguments are made, adapted from http://www.nobeliefs.com/fallacies.htm

Ad hominem or ATTACKING THE PERSON. Attacking the arguer rather than his or her argument. Saying a negative about Marx is insufficient to negate arguments that Marx made.

Ad ignorantium or APPEAL TO IGNORANCE. Arguing on the basis of what is known and can be proven. If you can't prove that something is true then it must be false (and vice versa). Example: You can't prove the No Child Left Behind (NCLB) Act has lead to a teacher exodus, therefore it cannot have had that effect.

AFFIRMING THE CONSEQUENT. An invalid form of the conditional argument in which the second premise affirms the consequent of the first premise and the conclusion affirms the antecedent. Example: If she wants to keep her job, she will join the union. She joined the union, therefore she wants to keep the job.

APPEAL TO EMOTION. In this fallacy, the arguer uses emotional appeals rather than logical reasons to persuade the listener. The fallacy can appeal to various emotions including pride, pity, fear, hate, vanity, or sympathy. Example: The abduction and death of a young girl by a sex offender means that the laws regarding sex offenders must be changed.

BLACK AND WHITE FALLACY or SLIPPERY SLOPE. A line of reasoning in which there is no gray area or middle ground. It states that x, y, z are implicit in Step a. The primary characteristic is that it fails to distinguish between (or among) degrees of difference. It argues for (or against) the first step because if you take the first step, you will inevitably follow through to the last. Example: We can't allow students to use calculators; if we do, they will never learn mathematics.

COMMON BELIEF. This fallacy is committed when we assert a statement to be true on the evidence that many other people allegedly believe it. Being widely believed is not proof or evidence of the truth. Example: Of course Deep Throat was a hero during the Watergate era. Everybody knows that.

CONTRARY TO FACT HYPOTHESIS. This fallacy is committed when we state with an unreasonable degree of certainty the results of an event that might have occurred but did not. Example: If President George W. Bush had not gone into Iraq with military force when he did, Saddam Hussein would have performed terrorist attacks on Israel.

DIVISION. This fallacy is committed when we conclude that any part of a particular whole must have a characteristic because the whole has that characteristic. Example: I am sure that Karine is good with money since her family owns several banks.

FALSE DILEMMA (often called the either/or fallacy because the argument nearly always includes the words "either... or..."). This fallacy assumes that we must choose between two opposite extremes instead of allowing for other possibilities, especially for the possibility of choosing an alternative between the extremes. Example: Women need to dedicate themselves to either their families or their jobs.

POST HOC ERGO PROPTER HOC. A form of hasty generalization in which it is inferred that because one event followed another it is necessarily caused by that event. Example: George W. Bush took office in 2000 and the next year we were attacked by terrorists. It was his fault.

INCONSISTENCY. A discourse is inconsistent or self-contradicting if it contains, explicitly or implicitly, two assertions that are logically incompatible. Inconsistency can also occur between words and actions. Example: A woman who demands equal rights and represents herself as a feminist, yet is upset when a date expects her to pay half the bill.

RED HERRING. This fallacy introduces an irrelevant issue into a discussion as a diversionary tactic. It takes people off the issue at hand; it is beside the point. Example: Many people say that teachers need money, but I would like to remind them how difficult it is to be an engineer.

STRAW MAN. This fallacy occurs when we misrepresent an opponent's position to make it easier to attack, usually by distorting his or her views to ridiculous extremes. This can also take the form of attacking only the weak premises in an opposing argument while ignoring the strong ones. Example: Those who favor gun-control legislation just want to take all guns away from responsible citizens and put them into the hands of the criminals.

TWO WRONGS MAKE A RIGHT. This fallacy is committed when we try to justify an apparently wrong action by charges of a similar wrong. The underlying assumption is that if they do it, then we can do it too and are somehow justified. Example: Supporters of apartheid often pointed to U.S. practices of slavery to justify their system.

 Cutting Board

As you examine articles, textbooks, speeches, video presentations, Web pages, documentaries, etc. that are related to your topic and the problem you are investigating, determine how logically the arguments were presented. If you find flaws in logic, make certain they are noted. Elaborate on how the materials dealt with the problem you are investigating and what you are doing differently.

In the space below, write down key words that are closely related to your research.

Remember to write down the following information, if applicable, after you have examined a source: Author, publisher, city of publisher, copyright date, title, page number, name of periodical, date, volume number, quotes you plan to use, and page number of quotes. An excellent source to help you evaluate a reference can be found at http://tinyurl.com/327scqq.

CHAPTER 3
½ MAIN COURSE
(Methodology: What Did You Do?)

Good job! Now that you have reached this point in your *Recipes for Success*, you are ready to put together many of the *ingredients* that you have carefully amassed in **PHASES 1** and **2** and create a splendid *main course*.

In chapter 3 you will *spoon-feed* your guests as you elaborate, in great detail, the research design that you selected and how it applies to your study. A research design is the "procedures for collecting, analyzing, and reporting research" (Creswell, 2002, p. 58) in a quantitative, qualitative, or mixed paradigm approach. Creswell suggested a litmus test to understand or decide between these paradigms. The test of a quantitative approach is whether explaining or predicting relationships among the variables is important, along with measuring, assessing the impacts of the variables, testing theories or broad explanations, and applying the results to a wider group than the population being studied. A qualitative study generally uses a naturalistic approach that seeks to understand phenomena in context-specific settings. Where quantitative researchers seek causal determination, prediction, and generalization of findings, qualitative researchers seek, instead, illumination, understanding, and extrapolation to similar situations. For further elaboration, check out http://tinyurl.com/2c6b9ck.

Chapter 3 is where you elaborate on why the paradigm and method you chose are appropriate to solve the problem you posed. If a qualitative design was chosen, an argument about how a quantitative method would not solve the problem should be included, with sources. Make certain to use a germinal book on the method to help justify your selection. Also let your work *marinate* so all parts come together and *tenderize* as needed to make your *feast palatable* to your *guests*.

The Cutting Board activity that follows can be used to prepare a *delicious and nutritious* chapter 3. For your proposal in a quantitative study, this is usually 10-15 pages; in your dissertation, it is usually 15-20 pages. In qualitative studies this is usually doubled. Make certain you have obtained a *cookbook*, that is, a classical or germinal text to help guide you through this section.

For example, if you are doing a case study design, you should consult with Yin or Stake, for grounded theory Glaser or Strauss are your "men," and for appreciative inquiry you will likely turn to Cooperrider and Srivastava for guidance.

 ## *Cutting Board*

From **PHASE 2,** obtain the following information:

1. What population did (will) you study and why?

2. How did you choose your sample? (What criteria did you use?)

3. How did you contact your participants or obtain the documentation you needed?

4. How large was your *n*? (How large was your sample size?) Justify this number.

5. What did you do to ensure the ethical protection of your participants?

6. Classify your study. (Look at the *What's Cooking* section and inform the reader about the type of research methodology you used.)

7. Explain why you chose this type of methodology.

8. What methodological book(s) are you using to guide your study?

9. If you used an experimental design, explain the treatment that was (will be) used.

10. What type of instrument(s) did (will) you use?

11. Why did you choose these types of instruments? Explain any means you had of knowing the instruments had validity (internal and external) and reliability.

12. Describe (in great detail) the procedure you used to administer your instruments and obtain your data. Explicate the process of gathering the data, i.e., how data were collected—electronic survey, a conference, f2f, postal mail.

13. If the design is qualitative, and you are using interviews to gather data, explain how the interview questions were created and authenticated. Include a copy of the interview questions in the text or in the appendix.

14. Who else is involved in this aspect of the study?

15. Explain any special things you needed to do to see that the information you sought after was obtained and reliable.

16. If you conducted a pilot study, what information did you obtain from that inquiry?

17. What were your statistical hypotheses?

18. What type of test did you use to test your hypotheses?

19. What assumptions were needed to employ this test?

20. Describe how you tested your hypotheses and the conclusions that were drawn. Make certain you include your test values and your p values.

21. If you used a statistical package on a computer what program was it? Why did you choose it?

22. If you used a qualitative data analyses program, explain why you chose it and how it was applied.

23. Describe any problems or snags that you encountered while obtaining your data.

Begin chapter 3 with a restatement of your purpose statement and describe how the selected research design derives logically from the problem statement. Give a brief overview of the *dishes you are serving* or what the reader can look forward to in this chapter. Next, elaborate on the rationale of the paradigm you chose (qualitative, quantitative, or mixed methods) and the appropriateness, including a discussion of why the proposed design (experimental, Delphi, phenomenology, correlational, etc.) will accomplish the study goals, why the design is the optimal choice for this specific study, and why other likely choices would be less effective.

Continue with a discussion of the population and the sample. Justify the sample size and explain the geographical region where the study takes place. Explain how the participants in the study are protected from any harm or ill effects. Then discuss the type and appropriateness of the data collected. Elaborate on the instruments chosen and their reliability and validity. Identify and justify the type of data analyses that will be done.

Each section of chapter 3 should be highlighted in some way. You want to convince the reader that you have (had) a well thought out plan to collect, organize, analyze, and interpret data. You must convince the reader that you can (did) achieve the purpose of your study.

It is usually easier to use an instrument that has an established *cooking* record rather than to create your own. This means that it has probably already been shown to be both valid and reliable. An excellent place to check for an appropriate instrument is at http://www.unl.edu/buros/. However, if you have created your own instrument for data collection, then you must describe what you have done to see that it is valid (does what it purports to do) and how you know it is reliable (consistent). Panels of experts, pilot studies, and content analysis can help in this respect.

Note to Qualitative Researchers: According to Guba (1978), qualitative researchers have few strict guidelines for when to stop the data collection process. Criteria include (a) exhaustion of resources, (b) emergence of regularities, and (c) overextension or going too far beyond the boundaries of the research. The decision to stop sampling must take into account the research goals, the need to achieve depth through triangulation of data sources, and the possibility of greater breadth through an examination of a variety of sampling sites.

Bogdan and Biklen (1982) defined qualitative data analysis as "working with data, organizing it, breaking it into manageable units, synthesizing it, searching for patterns, discovering what is important and what is to be learned, and deciding what you will tell others" (p. 145). Qualitative researchers tend to use inductive analysis of data, meaning that the critical themes emerge out of the data (Patton, 1990). Qualitative analysis requires some creativity, for the challenge is to place the raw data into logical, meaningful categories; to examine them in a holistic fashion; and to find a way to communicate this interpretation to others. The role of the researcher in the data collection procedure should be described.

Stir and *fry* all the *ingredients* together and arrange them in a pleasing and *delectable* manner and you will have ½ of your main course and chapter 3 of your dissertation complete! *Savor* the *taste.*

CHAPTER 4
OTHER ½ OF MAIN COURSE
(Presentation and Analysis of Data)

Here is where you provide the *punch* line, or tell the reader what you discovered from your study. You have already made the preliminary preparation for this chapter in **PHASE 2** of your *Recipes for Success*. You can use that information to guide you through the writing of chapter 4 of your dissertation. Chapter 4 presents, in sufficient detail, the research findings and data analyses and describes the systematic and careful application of the research methods. There is no single way to analyze the data; therefore, the organization of chapter 4 and analysis procedures will relate to the research design and research methods you selected. However, there are general guidelines to follow and components to include. The presentation and analysis chapter of your dissertation usually contains many of the *garnish*es listed below and provides an *affriander* (addition to a dish to give it a more appetizing appearance).

Check each *ingredient* that you plan to include. (Once you have successfully incorporated a particular component into the body of your paper, acknowledge that accomplishment by highlighting that task with a colorful pen or form an electronic list and use the highlighting feature in Word.)

_____ 1. A detailed description of the data uncovered and the data that were analyzed (include means, percentages, standard deviations, *t* or *z* values, rho values, chi-square values, *p* values, alpha values, ANOVA, etc.)

_____ 2. Tables and graphs depicting your data

_____ 3. The results of your hypothesis testing, include the assumptions

_____ 4. The statistical significance of your findings

_____ 5. The answer to every research question you posed

_____ 6. A summary of any interviews conducted, with direct quotes to support your analyses

_____ 7. Any observations that you, or a research assistant, made in relationship to the problem

_____8. If you used surveys or tests, explain how each item was weighted and how it was used to help you arrive at your conclusions

According to Bogdan and Biklen (1982), qualitative data analysis entails "working with data, organizing it, breaking it into manageable units, synthesizing it, searching for patterns, discovering what is important and what is to be learned, and deciding what you will tell others" (p. 145). The more conventional your analysis, the less detail you may need to provide, because the meaning of what you are doing will be more apparent to your readers. However, if you are doing something unusual, you should build the case for its legitimacy here.

Excellent software tools are available to help with both quantitative and qualitative data analyses. One of the most popular software packages to summarize and analyze quantitative data, and generate tables and graphs, is SPSS. Statistical analyses range from basic descriptive statistics, such as determining means and standard deviations, to advanced inferential statistics, such as regression models, ANOVA, and factor analysis. SPSS also contains several tools for manipulating data (in a good and ethical way☺), including functions for recoding data and computing new variables as well as merging and aggregating datasets. A good introduction to SPSS is found at http://www.microbiologybytes.com/maths/spss1.html.

For qualitative data collected by text, images, or sound, an excellent software program is NVivo, created by QSR International (Richards, 2002). NVivo software tools require sensitivity to detail, content, and accurate access to information (Richards, 2002). The program allows the data to be examined at increasing levels of understanding and generate an informed range of alternative solutions to complex issues and problems facing the qualitative researcher.

The only drawback is that most qualitative software programs are quite challenging to the novice user and have a fairly steep learning curve to master. Data Sense http://www.datasense.org offers excellent face-to-face and online training and project consultation to individuals and groups utilizing the most current version of QSR software. Data Sense can work with neophytes as well as professionals and have successfully guided hundreds of scholarly researchers through the myriad of documents obtained through interview transcripts, field notes, brochures, e-mails, and memos.

The following should be included in chapter 4:

1. A transition from chapter 3 as part of the introductory paragraph.

2. An explanation of what chapter 4 will cover as part of the introductory paragraph.

3. Research questions and/or hypotheses in separate sections.

4. An explanation of the data analysis procedure in a separate section.

5. For experimental designs, a careful and thorough explanation of the treatment and the type of design is explicated.

6. An explanation of how data were triangulated.

7. The raw data displayed in an organized manner.

8.   Each table should be explained in the text. Tables and figures should be as self-descriptive as possible, informative, and conform to standard dissertation format. They should be directly related to and referred to within the narrative text included in the chapter, have immediately adjacent comments, and be properly identified (titled or captioned). For qualitative studies you will need to explain the content analysis, themes, or patterns shown in a table format with columns for each pattern. If the tables are huge, they can be moved to an appendix. For quantitative studies, the tables should be summarized and appear in the text. Raw data can be placed in the appendix.

9. Section titles regarding each of the patterns for quantitative analyses and showing the results of each statistical test.

10. Discrepant cases and nonconfirming data are included in the findings.

11. Results are compared with major theories in literature and similarities or differences described (but not analyzed, save this for chapter 5).

12. A discussion on evidence of quality shows how the study followed procedures to ensure accuracy of the data (e.g., trustworthiness, member checks, triangulation, etc.). Appropriate evidence occurs in the appendixes (sample transcripts, researcher logs, field notes, etc.).

13. For qualitative studies, a discussion on data reduction techniques is essential. Some techniques are quantitative such as structuring your data into central tendencies and

ranges or frequency guided shapes, limiting the number of examples presented per category, or employing *summarizing talk* in which you talk about some of your data instead of presenting all the data in a juxtaposed style.

14.   Summary section including what was presented and leading into chapter 5

FOR YOUR INFORMATION AND EDUCATION

For qualitative studies, data can be organized around the unit of analysis, themes, constructs, patterns, models, meanings, systems, codes, and time frames. Organization begins with analysis (breaking down into component parts) by categorizing, coding, and then synthesizing (building back) relative constructs and then interpretation. Programs such as NVivo help! The quality in a qualitative research project is based upon how well you have collected quality data and how well you discern it. Make every effort to feature the data in your presentations. The review continues until theoretical saturation is achieved, that is, when no new themes or issues arise regarding a category of data and when the categories are well established and validated. Consult the gurus for the type of research you chose: Yin, Merriam, Stake, Glaser, Strauss, Moustakas, Cooperrider, Geertz, etc.

Note: Any of the following could be a unit of analysis: individuals, groups, archival documents (newspapers, memos, photographs, individual pieces of correspondence, diaries), geographical units (town, census tract, state; bodies of water), or social interactions (dating, divorces, arrests, parenting, doctor visits). It is the analysis you conduct in your study that determines what the unit is. In education, we could analyze individual student data or aggregate data to determine achievement.

Oftentimes when conducting research there are gray areas that do not fit well into categories or neat patterns. In quantitative studies these are called outliers; they distort the data analyses. It is your responsibility to let readers know how such instances were treated and why they were treated that way. In qualitative studies these are observations that oppose the trend. It is important to detect and identify these exceptions and ensure that they are reported for further consideration. A good look at the exceptions, or the ends of a distribution, can test and strengthen your basic finding. It not only tests the generality of the finding, but also protects against self-selecting biases. "You need to find the outliers and then verify whether what is present in them is absent or different in other, more mainstream examples" (Miles & Huberman, 1984, p. 237).

CHAPTER 5
DESSERT
(Conclusions, Implications and Recommandations)

Kudos, cheers, and compliments to the *chef*. It is now time to relax and *savor* the final moments of your eloquent *banquet*. Here is the time where you can editorialize about your study and advise future *cooks* on how to create *similar feasts*. Chapter 5 discusses the findings and expounds on their importance, meaning, and significance. Confirming and contradicting data are thoroughly discussed.

Conclusions made in chapter 5 should relate directly to your study. Here is your chance to tell what you found and unravel the power and importance of your research. What does it all mean? What's it all about, Alfie?☺

Put a check next to each item that you plan to serve for *dessert*:

____1. An introduction with a brief overview of why and how the study was done, reviewing the questions or issues addressed, and a brief summary of the findings.

____2. The interpretation of the findings including conclusions that address all of the research questions and that contains references to outcomes in chapter 4 and direct references to your study.

____3. A discourse on how your findings will affect your profession and society in general.

____4. Suggestions to others on how to serve a similar feast at a future banquet.

____5. Advice on what can be done to solve the problem in light of your findings and how this supports or contradicts other findings.

____6. A list of things that need closer examination in light of your findings.

____7. An opinion on how effective the program, product, or treatment you studied was in meeting its goals and how you would like to see change made in the future.

____8. An editorial on what your findings mean to the population you studied.

____9. Suggestions on how the program, theory, treatment, or model that you developed will, or could, be implemented while speculating on the anticipated results.

____10. For qualitative studies, there is a reflection on the researcher's experience with the research process in which the researcher discusses possible personal biases or preconceived ideas and values, the possible effects of the researcher on the participants or the situation, and any change in perception as a result of the study.

____11. What might you have done differently with the benefit of hindsight?

____12. What further study will most likely need to be done now that yours is complete?

____13. Who needs to pay attention to the results of your study and how will that information be given to them? Who could benefit from the revelations in your study?

____14. How will the information you obtained affect your sample? population? society?

____15. What surprises (if any) did you find in your research? What does this tell you about the assumptions, limitations, or conceptual or theoretical framework? If you were surprised about finding X, explain why. E.g. Regulation NMO would indicate a contrary finding, therefore….

____16. What has your study done to add to the understanding of the larger problem?

____17. What studies were most in accord with yours? What studies were most in opposition with yours?

____18. What questions did your study raise?

____19. What final conclusions, if any, can be drawn from your study?

____20. What is the broader social significance of your study?

____21. The solution you found must be explicated, genuine, authentic, real, and responsibly presented in your study.

____22. A strong concluding statement making the take-home message clear to the reader.

Chapter 5 should begin with a brief overview of why and how the study was don, a review of the questions or issues addressed and a brief summary of the findings. be followed with a section on Interpretation of Findings. The Interpretation of Find, includes conclusions that address all of the research questions, contains references to ....es in chapter 4, covers all the data, is bounded by the evidence collected, and relates the findings to a larger body of literature on the topic, including the conceptual/theoretical framework.

The Recommendation for Action section should flow logically from the conclusions, contain steps to useful action, explain who needs to pay attention to the results, and indicate how the results might be best disseminated.

A Recommendation for Further Study section should suggest topics that need closer examination and may generate new studies or new problems that need to be addressed. Ground each recommendation to the study's central problem, data collected, and specific findings and point to topics that need closer examination and might generate a new round of questions. Recommendations can and should be made for practitioners, managers, executives, and policy makers.

Chapter 5 should cover all the data collected and be bound by the analyses made and the body of literature related to the problem. If a clear picture did not emerge, try to determine why. Perhaps the results indicate that the problem could have been better worded or conceived? Perhaps the limitations of the study impacted the findings?

For qualitative studies, include a reflection on the researcher's experience with the research process and discuss possible personal biases or preconceived ideas and values, the possible effects of the researcher on the participants or the situation, and the researcher's change in thinking as a result of the study.

Your work should close with a strong concluding statement making the take-home message clear to the reader. Your *guests* should leave the *banquet* feeling *nourished* and provided with missives they could put into action.

In the words of Alvin Toffler, "The illiterate of the 21st century is not those who cannot read and write, but those who cannot learn, unlearn, and relearn."

FOR YOUR INFORMATION AND EDUCATION

This is a suggested *recipe* regarding the order of how to *serve* your *meal* at the *banquet*:

Abstract Title Page
Abstract
Title Page
Dedication
Acknowledgments
Table of Contents
List of Tables
List of Figures
Dissertation Report
References
Appendix

Note: Front matter is usually paginated with lowercase roman numerals; the page number is not printed on the following pages: title, copyright, or abstract.

Some Red Flags

As you put your proposal and research study together, keep in mind some things you do not want to include.

Do not use hyperbole—"everyone knows," "it is obvious," "this must be the case," "clearly." What is clear and obvious to one reader is not to another.

Do not use clichés—"in this ever changing world," "in this postmodern world."

Do not use gender-specific terms—"For a person to be successful, he must...."

Do not use a pronoun unless it is crystal clear whom the pronoun is referring to—"in their study they found."

Do not assume what you are trying to resolve. If you are trying to determine whether technology can help learning, do not start by assuming that technology helps learning.

Do not present only one view. There are many sides to an issue. Present as many views as you can and critically analyze all points of view, including your own.

Do not have headings that do not match the content.

Do not use articles that are not in peer-reviewed journals unless you have obtained permission from your committee.

Do not use someone else's survey (in part or in total) without obtaining permission.

Do not forget the rules of good writing—a paragraph should contain one thesis statement and sufficient supporting evidence. Every sentence needs a verb and a subject. You should stick to the point and make every word count. Paragraphs should not be too short or too long, they should be just right!

Do not pose a rhetorical question to the reader in a scholarly publication. Example: "Why do you suppose so many educators dislike NCLB?

Do not present unfounded and unsupportable generalizations (e.g., all large multinational corporations' abuse labor in developing countries).

Do not use absolute phrases such as "This study will contribute or will show"; instead use phrases such as "might contribute."

Do not use statements with "I," "me," "we," or "our." Most dissertations and formal research papers require the use of the third-person voice.

With the hope that the dissertation will be read for many years to come, do not use vague references for time, such as today, recent, currently.

Do not write in an informal voice. This is a scholarly paper.

Do not overuse the phrase "this researcher" when it may be more scholarly to simply state what occurred in the study.

Do not claim that your findings are "significant" if your study is qualitative; instead, you can claim they are "suggestive."

Do not be inconsistent! If you use a statistic more than once, make sure it is the same statistic.

Do not use faulty logic.

Oral Presentation or Defense of Your Dissertation

Dinner Entertainment

Most universities require an oral defense of your dissertation before the final version of your dissertation is submitted to the university. This is usually *icing on the cake* and a way to celebrate your great accomplishment. Most doctoral candidates are allowed 20–30 minutes for their initial presentation.

Prior to the oral defense, talk to your committee chair regarding areas of concern based on comments received from committee members. Be well prepared for your presentation—academically, mentally, and physically. Make certain you begin your presentation by introducing yourself and thanking your audience for attending. Your chair cannot tell you the specific questions the examiners will ask, but she or he can direct your attention to issues or areas that require some thinking or additional research. Discuss with your chair the possibility of having a PowerPoint presentation available for your defense. If you do prepare a PowerPoint presentation, make sure the slides are numbered, and if you put in links to add value to the presentation, explain how the links are to be used. If you are doing a teleconference, send the PowerPoint presentation to the participants via e-mail. If you are presenting your presentation in front of an audience, have copies of the slides so your audience can follow along and take notes as needed.

Occasionally, an examiner might ask a question that appears to be unfair or seems unrelated to your study. It is acceptable for you to ask for clarification and explain that this seems to be beyond the scope of your study. However, it would be a good idea to try your best to provide a response if you have one, with that caveat. If you find yourself in a situation where you do not know the answer to a legitimate question, acknowledge the value of the question and be honest about not knowing the answer. People can usually tell when you are trying to *serve* an inferior product.

Some general questions that are often asked at a defense include the following:

1. If you were to do it all over again, what changes would you make?
2. What surprises did you find in your study?

3. What specific aspects of your findings can be taken to practice?

4. How generalizable is your study?

5. What is the most important contribution of your study?

6. Is there an alternative interpretation of your findings?

7. How would a policy maker be able to utilize your findings?

8. Will your research change current thinking in the field? If so how?

9. How will you communicate your work to other scholars in your field?

10. What will you do, personally, with the findings to make a difference?

Make sure you are well rested and focused before your oral defense. In your preparation, don't try to memorize all the studies cited in your dissertation, but do know the details of a few key studies that form the basis of your conceptual framework and thus your investigation. You need to be ready to discuss why and how you selected the problem to investigate, the basic assumptions of your study, the theoretical framework, the methodology you chose, and how you solved your problem, reached your conclusions, answered your research questions, and obtained your purpose.

Some other helpful hints include treating your presentation as a public address. There could be people outside your profession at your presentation, so avoid using jargon from your field or presenting too much detail. You need to explain in simple, concise language (a) what you did, (b) why you did it, (c) how you did it, (d) what you found, and (e) what the results mean. Don't speak too fast and don't read from your notes. Try to keep friendly chit-chat to a minimum. Make sure that you practice your presentation and pace yourself well. Don't spend too much time on any one issue. Don't rush to answer each question. It is perfectly acceptable to think for a couple of seconds, or ask the questioner if you are on the right track. If you are not clear about the question ask for clarification. Try to be concise and to the point, but at the same time demonstrate that you have a good grasp of the complex issues involved in your study. In other words, do not give superficial answers, but at the same time, stay focused and speak with authority. Balance is important. Spend proportionately larger amounts of time with very important matters and less time with matters of medium importance. Quickly mention, or leave silent, matters of small importance.

The best defense is a good offense—anticipate what will be asked and be confident without being smug. A good defense means that you can provide strong logical arguments as well as empirical support to defend your position or conclusion. When an examiner criticizes your study and points out some flaws or weaknesses in your study, and the criticism is sound and well grounded, accept his or her criticism with humility, grace, and gratitude. Do not allow unfounded criticism to go unchallenged (using professional courtesy), since that will undermine the integrity of your work.

Remember, this dissertation will be part of your scholarly portfolio. Any improvement offered should be seen as a gift. After the oral defense, meet with your chair for debriefing and determine how best to revise your final dissertation. Putting together a change chart, where you acknowledge concerns that arose during the defense, who raised the concern, and how you dealt with the concern, is most useful. Don't lose momentum. Even if the requested revisions are extensive, it is advantageous to make them right away while they are still fresh in your mind.

FOR YOUR INFORMATION AND EDUCATION

Most nontraditional universities require that the oral defense be conducted via telephone. Once you have been authorized by your chair to conduct your presentation, contact all committee members to determine their availability to attend your presentation. Some things to keep in mind when arranging for a teleconference:

1. Be aware of different time zones when proposing times for the call. It is unreasonable to ask a person to participate before 8 AM or after 8 PM.

2. Respect the availability of your committee members. Committee members understand the time constraints you may be facing and will likely make accommodation to help you meet your goals, but you should be prepared to be as flexible as possible.

3. E-mail communication is an efficient way to determine committee members' availability. Make sure that everyone who needs to attend the presentation is copied on all e-mails regarding time availability.

4. After you have made arrangements with your committee members, contact a teleconferencing company to schedule the call. You can find a listing of many teleconference providers at this link: http://tinyurl.com/25cez.

5. Usually participants will be given a phone number and code for the conference call. It is a good idea to send a friendly e-mail reminder a day before the defense. It is also good to have a phone number to reach the participants, just in case. Bad connections, disconnections, and such may (and do) happen. Be prepared. Allow for mishaps. Keep the agenda flexible. Your chair will likely have alternative scenarios if a committee member loses connection, but just in case, be sure to have some alternatives of your own, especially if it is your chair that loses his or her connection.

6. It is a good idea to record the teleconference.

7. Review the tape of the oral presentation while revising your dissertation.

8. Try to remove all distracting noise from your environment. A barking dog or a radio in the background can divert your audience's attention from your presentation.

9. Follow up with a thank-you note. These are always appreciated.

ABSTRACT

Menu

Most research papers are preceded by an abstract, which is a brief summary of the research. This serves as a *menu* for your *feast*. When putting together your abstract gather together the following *ingredients:*

1. A statement of the problem you have investigated

2. A brief description of the research method and design

3. A brief statement of the research questions (do not write the questions)

4. A brief description of the theoretical framework

5. Major findings and their significance (if you have conducted a test of hypotheses, include the critical value and the p value)

6. Conclusions and recommendations

A reader should be able to decide from the abstract whether or not to read the entire dissertation. Since it is not part of the dissertation, it should neither be numbered nor counted as a page. To ensure the abstract title does *not* appear in the table of contents, use the "Normal Indent" formatting (APA Formatting toolbar or heading 5a on the headings toolbar). Note it is preformatted.

The abstract should be completed after you have written the research paper. The abstract provides a clear summary of the paper, indicating both content and tone of the paper. First-person narrative should not be used in the abstract. If learners want to publish the abstract of their research project to *Dissertation Abstracts International* (DAI), a clearinghouse of abstracts, the abstract should be no longer than 350 words. APA-publishable abstracts must be no longer than 120 words. The abstract paragraph should not be indented.

Nine items usually need to be present in the abstract for a proposal and 10 items for a dissertation:

1. State problem in one sentence

2. The paradigm: qualitative/quantitative/mixed method)

3. The method

4. A statement of the purpose

5. Rephrase the research question as a statement

6. The theoretical framework

7. The participants

8. The data collection techniques

9. An explanation of how data were or will be analyzed and managed

10. In the dissertation – the results and recommendations

In addition, you might need to explain how your study is aligned with the university's mission and goals.

Abstracts do not have paragraphs; the text is 1 long paragraph with no indentation. Check with the university on the number of words permitted. Rarely can an abstract be more than one page.

Form and style:

(2.5 cm)

Abstract [or ABSTRACT]

(double space)

Title

(double space)

by

(double space)

Author

(double space)

Text (double spaced and about 1.5 pages)

Acknowledgments

You can now celebrate the birth of an excellent contribution to society and a remarkable *repast*. You probably want to write *thank-you cards* by adding an acknowledgments page after the table of contents to show your appreciation to everyone who helped you create this *feast*.

Thank you for using your *Recipes for Success* to assist you in the preparation of this *culinary delight*. If you know a person who is ABD (All But Dissertation) or someone in need of a guide to successfully complete a research paper, please complete contact us at **dissertationrecipes.com** or fill out the form below and we will see that they receive their own copy of the *Dissertation and Scholarly Research Recipes for Success*.

BON APPETIT!

SUGGESTED READINGS

Fundamentals of Educational Research, by Gilbert Sax, Prentice Hall, New Jersey, 1979

This work is a practical guide to graduate-level research in education. It shows how to select a research project, how to conduct the research, and how to interpret the research. It carries the reader from analysis to presentation of research.

How We Know What Isn't So: The Fallibility of Human Reason in Everyday Life, by Thomas Gilovich, Free Press, New York, 1991

Gilovich explains in detail the truth to Artemus Ward's famous expression, "It ain't so much the things we don't know that get us in trouble. It's the things we know that just ain't so." He examines how questionable and erroneous beliefs are formed and how they are maintained. Despite popular opinion, people do not hold questionable beliefs simply because they have not been exposed to the relevant evidence or because they are unintelligent or gullible. Many questionable and erroneous beliefs have purely cognitive origins and can be traced to imperfections in our capacities to process information and draw conclusions. They are not the products of irrationality, but of flawed rationality.

Research Methods in Education: A Practical Guide, by Robert Slavin, Prentice Hall, New Jersey, 1984

This text is primarily designed to serve as a basic resource for a course on research methods of education but it can also be used by anyone who expects to conduct social science research. Its intent was to show how to use research designs and procedures to get the best possible answers to the best possible questions. It discusses research design issues in the light of the limitations and realities of institutional settings.

How to Conduct Surveys: A Step-by-Step Guide, by Arlene Fink and Jacqueline Kosekoff, Sage Publications, Beverly Hills, CA, 1985

The purpose of this guide is to help the reader organize a rigorous survey and evaluate the credibility of existing surveys. Its aim is for simplicity rather than embellishment.

Research in Education: An Introduction, by Bill Turney and George Robb, Dryden Press, Hinsdale, Illinois, 1971

This book deals with issues such as What constitutes research? What is the scientific approach to research? How do you select and evaluate a research problem? It offers advice on using the library in educational research and discusses in detail techniques and tools of the educational researcher.

Tests, Measurement and Evaluation: A Developmental Approach, by Arthur Bertrand and Joseph P. Cebula, Addison Wesley, Menlo Park, CA, 1980.

The testing movement in America has come under severe criticism in recent years by those who claim that there is too much emphasis on standardized instruments to measure intelligence and achievement. Some have even referred to such tests as dehumanizing and do not provide accurate assessment of individual differences.

The author takes the view that tests in and of themselves are not dangerous, but feels that when used properly they can provide the classroom teacher with a helpful set of assessment tools. It takes a developmental approach to learning and growth, emphasizing the need to understand each developmental stage of physical, cognitive, and personal growth and how each stage dramatically affects the others throughout a child's life.

Survey Research Methods, by Floyd J. Fowler, Jr., Sage Publications, Newbury Park, CA, 1988

The main purpose of this text is to produce a comprehensive summary of current knowledge about sources of error in surveys, in particular, the emphasis on minimizing nonsampling errors through question design. It also includes a chapter coding and filing preparation to reflect the current importance of computer-assisted telephone interviewing (CATI) and the direct data entry systems.

Improving Interview Methods and Questionnaire Design, by Norman Bradburn, Seymour Sudman, and Associates, Jossey-Bass, San Francisco, 1979

This book presents the results of a research program on "response affects" in surveys conducted by the National Opinion Research Center (NORC) and concentrates on research areas most in need of empirical work. The three major variables that affect response rate as delineated by the authors are: the task itself, the characteristics of the interviewer, and the characteristics of the respondents. The text not only attempts to describe and measure the response affects that are occurring but also attempts to suggest the procedures that yield the most accurate reporting.

Applying Educational Research, by Walter R. Borg, Longman, New York, 1987

The main goal of this book is to make the reader an intelligent consumer of educational research. This involves the ability to locate research relevant to a given problem, evaluate such research reports, and interpret the research findings.

The author feels that the useful information that has emerged from educational research is difficult to locate and even more difficult to interpret and to relate to the practical problems that teachers and school administrators must address. They quote a study by Reys and Yeager (1974) that reports 87.5% of in-service teachers never read research articles. He believes this trend must be reversed if teaching is to become a true profession.

Human Inquiry: A Sourcebook of New Paradigm Research, by Peter Reason and John Rowan, Wiley, New York, 1987

According to the authors, there has been much criticism of orthodox research but few have suggested alternatives. This book covers the philosophy, methodology, and practice of research, which is collaborative and experiential. They believe that social science research should be with people instead of on people.

Elementary Statistics, 7th edition, by Mario Triola, Benjamin Cummings, Menlo Park, California, 1999

A user-friendly text that does not require a strong mathematics background to be understood. It is an interesting and readable source to familiarize the reader with statistics and statistical methods, and it is even written with a sense of humor.

Educational Research, 6th edition, by Meredith Gall, Walter Borg, and Joyce Gall, Longman, New York, 1996

This is one of the most comprehensive introductions to educational research. There is an excellent balance between both quantitative and qualitative research methods.

YES!! I would like a copy of the *Recipes for Success* sent to:

Name_____

Address_____

City _____ State_____ Zip _____

Telephone (   ) _____

Enclosed, please find a check for_____ copies of *Recipes for Success* at $49.95 each for a total of $_____, which includes shipping, handling and any applicable tax. (For first-class shipping add $5.00/order)

    Make your check or money order payable to:

Dissertation Success, LLC
P.O. Box 100
Cottage Grove, Oregon 97424

Alternatively, you may purchase a print or electronic copy (PDF) of *Recipes for Success* for yourself or a colleague online using your credit card or PayPal at our website: www.dissertationrecipes.com, where you will also find online resources, tools, and discussions to help in crafting your recipe for dissertation success.

We appreciate your order and are pleased to offer you this service. We would also appreciate your comments about your *Recipes for Success*.

Did your *Recipes for Success* meet your expectations? _____

Please Explain: _____

What part(s) did you find the most useful? _____

How could your *Recipes for Success* be amended to better suit your needs?

_____

I would like a list of other books by Dr. Simon (Please fill out the information below if it is different from the address above):

Your Name _____ School _____

Mailing Address_____

ABOUT THE AUTHOR

MARILYN K. SIMON, PhD, has been actively involved in Mathematics and Computer Education since 1969 and has taught all levels of mathematics and study skill development from pre-school through graduate school with extraordinary results. She has published numerous books on mathematics education, scholarly research, high stakes test-preparation, and online learning.

Dr. Simon is a faculty member at Walden University and the University of Phoenix, School of Advanced Studies, where she supervises doctoral students. She is also one of the nation's authorities on Overcoming Mathanxiety and online learning, and conducts workshops and seminars for the University of California, Webster University; Upper Iowa University Online, and for school districts and businesses across the nation, and is an international lecturer on online learning and women and mathematics.

Dr. Simon is the president of MathPower, and co-founder of Best-Prep, educational consulting firms. She has conducted post doctorate research at the Institute of Advanced Studies in Princeton, NJ, and was selected as an Outstanding Young Woman of America, and as a mathematics education delegate to South Africa.

ACKNOWLEDGMENTS

I want to take the opportunity to thank many individuals. First and foremost, I thank my husband, Dr. Ronald Simon, and my sons Matthew and Jonathon, for their continuous emotional support of my efforts. The simultaneous hard work and delight of writing this book was always wonderfully encircled by the context of their love.

I wish to thank my wonderful Kendall Hunt editor, Janice Samuels, and the incomparable Toni Williams, who, as a great editor, demonstrates a strong empathy and bond with the reader and the author and an uncanny sense of what will be interesting and important to him or her. They are wonderful examples of how editors can work positively and responsively with others to get a book to print and ensure the book is of high quality.

A special thank you goes to my excellent colleagues: Jim Goes, Phillip Goldfeder, Frank Morelli, Carolyn Salerno, Kimberly Blum, Sybil Delevan, Rita Edwards, Karen Conger, Jeff Zuckerman, Freda Turner, and, of course, Bruce Francis, my co-author for the *Dissertation and Research Cookbook*, the precursor to *Recipes for Success*. These exemplary educators are completely familiar with, and sympathetic to scholarly research. Because of all the terrific assistance they have provided, I feel compelled to note that any imperfections in the book are mine.

In addition, I want to express my deepest gratitude to Raghu B. Korrapati and Meghan Siddall, who painfully went through each URL in the text and prepared the annotated bibliography and syllabi that will be of great assistance to the consumers of this book.

This book was simmering in my mind for many years and, for that reason, I thank all of the students who have sat through my statistics classes and all the wonderful doctoral students that I have had the honor to mentor. Each of you has added to the book in your own special way and has a special place in my heart.

- *Marilyn K. Simon, Ph.D.*

REFERENCES

Agar, M. (1996). *Professional stranger: An informal introduction to ethnography* (2nd ed.). New York: Academic Press.

American Psychological Association. (1994). *Publication manual of the American Psychological Association* (4th ed.). Washington, DC: Author.

American Psychological Association. (2001). *Publication manual of the American Psychological Association* (5th ed.). Washington, DC: Author.

American Psychological Association. (2009). *Publication manual of the American Psychological Association* (6th ed.). Washington, DC: Author.

Atkinson, J. R. (1992). *Q-Method* (Version 1.0) [Computer software]. Kent, OH: Computer Center, Kent State University.

Babbie, E. (1998). *The practice of social research* (8th ed.). Belmont, CA: Wadsworth.

Babbie, E. (2001). *The practice of social research*. Australia: Wadsworth Thomson Learning.

Baker, T. L. (1994). *Doing social research* (2nd ed.). New York: McGraw-Hill.

Barrett, F. J., Thomas, G. F., & Hocevar, S. P. (1995). The central role of discourse in large-scale change: A social construction perspective. *Journal of Applied Behavioral Science, 31*, 352-372.

Beane, A. L. (1999). *Bully free classroom*. Minneapolis: Free Press.

Bertrand, A., & Cebula. J. P. (1980). *Tests, measurement and evaluation*. Menlo Park, CA: Addison Wesley.

Blair, J. (2003, February 5). Cyber bullying. *Education Week*, pp. 3-4.

Bloland, P. A. (1992). *Qualitative research in student affairs*. Los Angeles, CA: University of California at Los Angeles. (ERIC Document Reproduction Service No. ED 347 487)

Bogdan, R. C., & Biklen, S. K. (1982). *Qualitative research for education: An introduction to theory and methods*. Boston: Allyn & Bacon.

Bogdan , R. C., & Biklen, S. K. (1992). *Introduction to qualitative research for education: An introduction to theory and methods*. Boston: Allyn & Bacon.

Boote, D. N., & Beile, P. (2005). Scholars before researchers: On the centrality of the dissertation literature review in research preparation. *Educational Research, 34*(6), 3-15.

Borg, W. R. (1987). *Applying educational research*. New York: Longman.

Borgatti, S. B., Everett, M. G., & Freeman, L. C. (1999). Ucinet 5 for Windows: Software for social network analysis. Boston: Analytic Technologies.

Bradburn, N., Sudman, S., and Associates. (1979). *Improving interview methods and questionnaire design*. San Francisco: Jossey-Bass.

Brooks, A. J., & Penn, P. E. (1999). Final report to National Institute on Drug Abuse. Five years, twelve steps, and REBT in the treatment of dual diagnosis. *Journal of Rational Emotive and Cognitive-Behavior Therapy, 18*, 197-208.

Burns, J. M. (1989). *The American experiment.* New York: Knopf.

Burns, N., & Grove, K. (1993). *The practice of nursing research: Conduct, critique and utilization* (2nd ed.). Philadelphia: Saunders.

Bushe, G. (1995). Advances in appreciative inquiry as an organization development intervention. *Organization Development Journal, 13*(3), 14-22.

Charles, J. (2003). Diversity management: An exploratory assessment of minority group representation in state government. *Public Personnel Management, 32*, 561-567. Retrieved July 6, 2005, from EBSCOhost: Business Source Premier database.

Charmaz, K. (2000). Grounded theory: Objectivist and constructivist methods. In N. K. Denzin & Y. S. Lincoln (Eds.), *Handbook of qualitative research* (2nd ed., pp. 509-535). Thousand Oaks, CA: Sage.

Clements, D. (1990). *Mathematical modeling: A case study approach.* Cambridge, MA: Cambridge University Press.

COEHS. (2005, January). *Guidelines for MS Plan: A thesis and doctoral dissertation research proposal.* Retrieved May 16, 2005, from http://www.coe.usu.edu/brs/PLANA.htm

Cook, T. D., & Campbell, D. T. (1979). *Quasi-experimentation: Design & analysis for field settings.* Chicago: Rand McNally.

Cooper, D. R., & Schindler, P. S. (2002). *Business research methods* (8th ed.). Boston: Irwin.

Cooperrider, D. (1990) Positive image, positive action: The affirmative basis of organizing. In S. Srivastava & D. Cooperrider (Eds.), *Appreciative management and leadership: The power of positive thought and action in organizations.* San Francisco: Jossey-Bass.

Cormack, D. (1991). *Team spirit motivation and commitment team leadership and membership. team evaluation.* Grand Rapids, MI: Pyranee Books.

Council of Graduate Schools. (2005). *Distinguishing characteristics of the dissertation research and dissertations.* Retrieved May 11, 2005, from http://www.cgsnet.org/PublicationsPolicyRes/appendixa.htm

Crane, B. (2004). Retrieved August 1, 2004, from http://web.isp.cz/jcrane/IB/triangulation.html

Creswell, J. W. (1994). *Research design: Qualitative & quantitative approaches.* Thousand Oaks, CA: Sage.

Creswell, J. (1997). *Research design: Qualitative and quantitative approaches.* Thousand Oaks, CA: Sage.

Creswell, J. (2002). *Research design: Qualitative and quantitative approaches.* Thousand Oaks, CA: Sage.

Creswell, J. W. (2003). *Research design: Qualitative, quantitative, and mixed methods approaches* (2nd ed.). Thousand Oaks, CA: Sage.

Creswell, J. W. (2005). *Educational research: Planning, conducting, and evaluating quantitative and qualitative research* (2nd ed.) [electronic version]. Upper Saddle River, NJ: Pearson Education.

Crossen, C. (1995). *The tainted truth: The manipulation of fact in America.* New York: Simon & Schuster.

Crowl, T. K. (1993). *Fundamentals of educational research.* Madison, WI: Brown and Benchmark.

Custer, R. L., Scarcella, J. A., & Stewart, B. R. (1999). The modified Delphi technique: A rotational modification. *Journal of Vocational and Technical Education, 15*(2), 1–11. Retrieved August 31, 2004, from http://scholar.lib.vt.edu/ejournals/JVTE/v15n2/custer.html

Dalkey, N. (1984). *The Delphi method: An experimental study of group opinion.* Thousand Oaks, CA: Sage.

Dennis, K. E., & Goldberg, A. P. (1996). Weight control self-efficacy types and transitions affect weight-loss outcomes in obese women. *Addictive Behaviors, 21,* 103–116.

Denzin, N. K., & Lincoln, Y. S. (Eds.). (2000). *Handbook of qualitative research* (2nd ed.). Thousand Oaks, CA: Sage.

De Vaus, D. A. (1993). Surveys in social research (3rd ed.), London: UCL Press.

Discenza, R., Howard, C., & Schenk, K. (Eds.). (2002). *The design and management of effective distance learning programs.* Hershey, PA: Idea.

Durkheim, E. (1951). *Suicide* (J. A. Spaulding, Trans., & G. Simpson, Ed.). New York: Free Press.

Dzurec, L. C. (1989). The necessity for and evolution of multiple paradigms for nursing research: A poststructuralist perspective. *Advances in Nursing Science, 11*(4), 69-77.

Eisenhart, M. (2001). Changing the conceptions of culture and ethnographic methodology: Recent thematic shifts and their implications for research on teaching. In V. Richardson (Ed.), *The handbook of research on teaching* (4th ed.). Washington, DC: American Educational Research Association.

Eisner, E. W. (1997). The new frontier in qualitative research methodology. *Qualitative Inquiry, 3,* 259–273.

Erlandson, D., Harris, E., Skipper, B., & Allen, S. (1993). *Doing naturalistic inquiry. A guide to methods.* Newbury Park, CA: Sage.

Fink, A., & Kosekoff, J. (1985). *How to conduct surveys: A step-by-step guide.* Beverly Hills, CA: Sage.

Fowler, F. J., Jr. (1988). Survey research methods. Newbury Park, CA: Sage.

Gall, M., Borg, W., & Gall, J. (1996). *Educational research* (6th ed.). New York: Longman.

Gardner, H. (1983). *Frames of mind.* New York: Basic Books.

Gay, L. R. (1996). *Educational research: Competencies for analysis and application* (4th ed.). Beverly Hills, CA: Sage.

Gay, L. R., & Airasian, P. (2000). *Educational research: Competencies for analysis and application* (6th ed.). Upper Saddle River, NJ: Prentice Hall.

Gergen, K. J. (1990). Beyond life narratives in the therapeutic encounter. In J. E. Birren et al. (Eds.), *Aging and biography* (pp. 205-223). New York: Springer.

Gilovich, T. (1991). *How what we know isn't so*. New York: Free Press.

Glaser, B. (1992). *Basics of grounded theory analysis*. Mill Valley, CA: Sociology Press.

Glaser, B., & Strauss, A. (1967). *The discovery of grounded theory*. Chicago: Aldine.

Glaser, B. G. (1998). *Doing grounded theory: Issues and discussions*. Mill Valley, CA: Sociology Press.

Goetz, J. P., & LeCompte, M. D. (1984). *Ethnography and qualitative design in educational research*. San Diego, CA: Academic Press.

Goldstein, M., & Goldstein, N. (1985). *How we know: The experience of science: An interdisciplinary approach*. New York: Plenum Press.

Greene, J. C., Caracelli, V. J., & Graham, W. F. (1989). Toward a conceptual framework for mixed-method evaluation design. *Educational Evaluation and Policy Analysis, 11,* 255-274.

Guba, E. (1978). *Toward a methodology of naturalistic inquiry in educational evaluation. Monograph 8*. Los Angeles: UCLA Center for the Study of Evaluation

Guba, E. (1990). *The paradigm dialogue*. Newbury, CA: Sage.

Guba, E., & Lincoln, Y. S. (1986). *Effective evaluation*. San Francisco: Jossey-Bass.

Guba, E., & Lincoln, Y. S. (1989). *Fourth generation evaluation*. San Francisco: Jossey-Bass.

Hanau, L. (1975). *The study game: How to play and win with "statement-pie."* New York: Barnes & Noble Books.

Harris, R. (2001). *The plagiarism handbook: Strategies for preventing, detecting, and dealing with plagiarism.* Los Angeles, CA: Pyrczak.

Heppner, P. P., Kivlighan, D. M., & Wampold, B. E. (1992). *Research design in counseling.* Pacific Grove, CA: Brooks/Cole.

Hernandez, N., & White, A. (1989). Pass it on: Errors in direct quotes in a sample of scholarly journal articles. *Journal of Counseling and Development, 67,* 509.

Hitchcock, G., & Hughes, D. (1995). *Research and the teacher: A qualitative introduction to school based research.* London: Routledge.

Huck, S. W., & Cormier, W. H. (1996). Principles of research design. In C. Jennison (Ed.), *Reading statistics and research* (2nd ed., pp. 578-622). New York: Harper Collins.

Hummel, J., & Huitt, W. (1994). What you measure is what you get. *GaASCD Newsletter: The Reporter,* pp. 10–11.

Jaccard, J., & Wan, C. K. (1996). *LISREL approaches to interaction effects in multiple regression.* Thousand Oaks, CA: Sage.

Kerlinger, F. N. (1986). *Foundations of behavioral research* (3rd ed.). Fort Worth, TX: Holt, Rinehart, and Winston.

Kivlighan, D. M., & Jauquet, C. A. (1990). Quality of group member agendas and group session climate. *Small Group Research, 21,* 205-219.

Koehler, K. J., & Larntz, K. (1980). An empirical investigation of goodness-of-fit statistics for sparse multinomials. *Journal of the American Statistical Association, 75,* 336–344.

Kuhn, T. (1962). *The structure of scientific revolutions.* Chicago: University of Chicago Press.

Leedy, P., & Ormrod, J. E. (2001). *Practical research planning and design* (8th ed.). New York: Macmillan.

Legewie, H., & Schervier-Legewie, B. (2004). Forschung ist harte Arbeit, es ist immer ein Stück Leiden damit verbunden. Deshalb muss es auf der anderen Seite Spaß machen. Anselm Strauss interviewed by Heiner Legewie and Barbara Schervier-Legewie. *Forum: Qualitative Social Research On-line Journal, 5*(3), Art. 22.

Lewin, K. (1946). Group decision and social change. In S. B. Merriam & E. L. Simpson (Eds.), *A guide to research for educators and trainers of adults.* Malabar, FL: Krieger.

Lewin, K. (1952). *Field theory in social science.* London: Tavistock.

Lichtman, M., & Taylor, S. I. (1993). *The first book of Lotus 1-2-3* (3rd ed.). Indianapolis, IN: Sams.

Lierr, P., & Smith, M. J. (n.d). *Frameworks for research.* Retrieved June 7, 2005, from http://64.233.167.104/search?q=cache:u5koEnvEKNEJ:homepage.psy.utexas.edu/HomePage/Class/Psy394/

Likert, R. (1932, June). A technique for the measurement of attitudes. *Archives of Psychology, 140.*

Lindstone, J., & Turoff, M. (1975). *The Delphi method, techniques and applications.* London: Addison-Wesley.

Marrow, A. F. (1969). *The practical theorist: The life and work of Kurt Lewin.* New York: Basic Books.

Maslow, A. (1970). *Motivation and personality.* New York: Harper & Row.

Mason, R., & McKenney, J. (1997). *An historical method for MIS research: Steps and assumptions.* Retrieved September 17, 2004, from GALILEO.

McPhillip, J. (1997). *Needs analysis: Tools for the human services of education.* Beverly Hills, CA: Sage.

Mead, G. H. (1934). *Mind, self, and society.* Englewood Cliffs, NJ: Prentice-Hall.

Merriam, S. B. (1988). Finding your way through the maze: A guide to the literature on adult learning. *Lifelong Learning, 11*(6), 4–7.

Merriam, S. B. (1997). *Qualitative research and case study applications in education*. San Francisco: Jossey-Bass.

Miles, M., & Huberman, M. (1984). *Qualitative data analysis: A sourcebook of methods*. Newbury Park, CA: Sage.

Mills-Novoa, B. (1997). The use of qualitative methods in the evaluation of grant-funded projects. In J. Ferguson (Ed.), *The grantseeker's guide to project evaluation* (2nd ed., pp. 63-69). Alexandria, VA: Capitol.

Mitroff, I., & Kilman, R. H. (1978). *Methodological approaches to social science*. San Francisco: Jossey-Bass.

Mitroff, I., & Kilman, R. H. (1983). Intellectual resistance to useful knowledge: An archetypal social analysis. In R. H. Kilman, K. W. Thomas, D. P. Slevin, R. Nath, & S. L .Jerrell (Eds.), *Producing useful knowledge for organizations* (pp. 266–280). New York: Praeger.

Morris, M., & Muzychka, M. (2002). *Participatory research and action. A guide to becoming a researcher for social change*. Ottawa, ON: Canadian Research Institute for the Advancement of Women.

Morse, J. (1989). Qualitative nursing research: A free-for-all? In J. M. Morse (Ed.), *Qualitative nursing research: A contemporary dialogue* (pp. 14-22). Rockville, MD: Aspen.

Moustakas, C. (1961). Heuristic research. In J. Bugental (Ed.), *Challenges of humanistic psychology*. New York: McGraw-Hill.

Munhall, K. G., & Stetson, R. H. (1989). R. H. Stetson's motor phonetics (2nd ed.). New York: Little, Brown.

Parker, P., & Parker, J. (2003). *Alcohol abuse a medical dictionary, bibliography, and annotated research guide to Internet references*. San Diego, CA: Icon Health.

Patton, M. Q. (1990). *Qualitative evaluation and research methods* (2nd ed.). Newbury Park, CA: Sage.

Philips, G., & Brown, W. (1989). *Making sense of your world*. Salem, WA: Sheffield.

Polit, D., Beck, C., & Hungler, B. (2001). *Essentials of nursing research: Methods, appraisal and utilization* (5th ed.). Philadelphia: Lippincott Williams & Wilkins.

Polit, D., & Hungler, B. (1991). *Nursing research: Principals and methods* (4th ed.). Philadelphia: Lippincott.

Popper, K. (1935). *Logik der Forschung*. Berlin: Springer Verlag.

Reason, P., & Rowan, J. (1987). *A sourcebook of new paradigm research*. New York: Longman.

Remenyi, D. (1998). Central ethical considerations for masters and doctoral research in business and management studies. *South African Journal of Business Management, 29*(3), 109–118. Retrieved May 6, 2005, from EBSCOhost database.

Richards, L. (2002). *NVivo: Using NVivo in qualitative research*. Melbourne, Australia: QSR International.

Rosnow, R. L. (1991). Inside rumor: A personal journey. *American Psychologist, 46,* 484-496.

Rubin, A. (2007). *Practitioner's guide to using research for evidence-based practice.* New York: Wiley.

Rudestam, K. E., & Newton, R. R. (2007). *Surviving your dissertation: A comprehensive guide to content and process* (3rd ed.). Los Angeles: Sage.

Salkind, N. J. (1985). *Theories of human development* (2nd ed.). New York: Wiley.

Sandelowski, M. (1986). The problem of rigor in qualitative research. *Advances in Nursing Science, 8*(3), 27-37.

Sax, G. (1979). *Fundamentals of educational research.* Englewood Cliffs, NJ: Prentice Hall.

Seidman, I. (2006). *Interviewing as qualitative research: A guide for researchers in education and the social sciences* (3rd ed.). New York: Teachers College Press.

Sell, D. K., & Brown, S. R. (1984). Q methodology as a bridge between qualitative and quantitative research: Application to the analysis of attitude change in foreign study program participants. In J. L. Vacca & H. A. Johnson (Eds.), *Qualitative research in education* (Graduate School of Education Monograph Series) (pp. 79–87). Kent, OH: Kent State University, Bureau of Educational Research and Service.

Siegel, L. (1992). *Criminology.* St. Paul, MN: West.

Simon, M., & Francis, B. (2001). *The dissertation and research cookbook* (3rd ed.). Dubuque, IA: Kendall- Hunt.

Simpson, M. (1989). *A guide to research for educators and trainers of adults.* Malabar, FL: Krieger.

Sire, J. (1997). *The universe next door: A basic worldview catalog.* New York: Prentice Hall.

Slavin, R. (1984). *Research methods in education: A practical guide.* Englewood Cliffs, NJ: Prentice Hall.

Sproull, N. (1995). *Handbook of research methods: A guide for practitioners in the social sciences.* Metchen, NJ: Scarecrow Press.

Stake, R. E. (1978, February). The case study method in social inquiry. *Educational Researcher, 7*(2), 5–8.

Stake, R. E. (1995). *The art of case study research.* Thousand Oaks, CA: Sage.

Stephenson, W. (1953). *The study of behavior: Q-technique and its methodology.* Chicago: University of Chicago Press.

Strauss, A. L., & Corbin, J. M. (1998). *Basics of qualitative research: Techniques and procedures for developing grounded theory.* Thousand Oaks, CA: Sage.

Stringer, E .T. (1996). *Action research: A handbook for practitioners.* Thousand Oaks, CA: Sage.

Sudzina, M., & Kilbane, C. (1992). Applications of a case study text to undergraduate teacher preparation. In H. E. Klein (Ed.), *Forging new partnerships with cases, simulations, games and other interactive methods.* Needham, MA: WACRA.

Suskie, L. (1996). *Questionnaire survey research: What works* (2nd ed.). Washington, DC: Association for International Research.

Taylor R., & Meinhardt, R. (1985). Defining computer information needs for small business, a Delphi Method. *Journal of Small Business Management, 23*, 3.

Thomeé, R., Grimby, G., Wright, B. D., & Linacre, J. M. (1995). Rasch analysis of Visual Analog Scale measurements before and after treatment of patellofemoral pain syndrome in women. *Scandinavian Journal of Rehabilitation Medicine 27,* 145–151.

Thompson, J. (1990). Hermeneutic inquiry. In L. E. Moody (Ed.), *Advancing nursing science through research.* Newbury Park, CA: Sage.

Tower, J. G., Brown, J., & Cheek, W. K. (1992). *Verification: The key to arms control in the 1990s.* Dulles, VA: Brassey's.

Triola, M. (1999). *Elementary statistics* (7th ed.). Chicago: Addison-Wesley.

Trochim, W. M. (2004). *The research methods knowledge base.* Retrieved from http://www.socialresearchmethods.net/

Turney, B., & Robb, G. (1971). *Research in education: An introduction.* Hinsdale, IL: Dryden Press.

Van Slyke, C., Bostrom, R., Courtney, J., McLean, E., Snyder, C., & Watson, T. (2003). Experts' advice to information systems doctoral students. *Communications of AIS, 12*, 469–480.

Vygotsky, L. S. (1978). Mind in society: The development of higher psychological processes (M. Cole, V. John-Steiner, S. Scribner, & E. Souberman, Eds.). Cambridge, MA: Harvard University Press.

Weber, R. P. (1990). Basic content analysis (2nd ed.). Newbury Park, CA: Sage.

Wood & Brink. (1989). *Principles of string theory.* New York: Plenum Press.

Yager, J. (1991). *Business protocol: How to survive and succeed in business.* New York: Wiley.

Yin, R. (2005). *Introducing the world of education: A case study reader.* Thousand Oaks, CA: Sage.

Yin, R. (2004). *The case study anthology.* London: Sage.

Yin, R. K. (2003). *Case study research* (5th ed.). Thousand Oaks, CA: Sage.

Zuber-Skerritt, O. (1996). *New directions in action research.* London: Falmer Press.

INDEX

African American race possesses a pattern of behavior later called "racial temperment" that is virtually fixed, innate and non responsive to environmental forces & education